"Dynamics of Muslim Worlds develops a ⌐ _   o⌐ ────g───────────l
engagement with anthropological and sociological perspectives. The missiological
assessments offered are from multiple perspectives that are helpful, constructive,
and thoroughly biblical. New analytical frameworks are proposed for understanding
and defining the diversity of ever-changing Islamic societies. The reader will be
enabled to reflect upon the implications for gospel proclamation among Muslims in
the twenty-first century. An excellent resource for practitioners and scholars."

Paul Martindale, ranked adjunct assistant professor of Islamic studies and cross-cultural
ministry, Gordon-Conwell Theological Seminary

DYNAMICS OF MUSLIM WORLDS

Regional, Theological, and Missiological Perspectives

Edited by
EVELYNE A. REISACHER

IVP Academic

An imprint of InterVarsity Press
Downers Grove, Illinois

InterVarsity Press
P.O. Box 1400, Downers Grove, IL 60515-1426
ivpress.com
email@ivpress.com

InterVarsity Press® is the book-publishing division of InterVarsity Christian Fellowship/USA®, a movement of students and faculty active on campus at hundreds of universities, colleges, and schools of nursing in the United States of America, and a member movement of the International Fellowship of Evangelical Students. For information about local and regional activities, visit intervarsity.org.

Scripture quotations, unless otherwise noted, are The Holy Bible, New International Version®, NIV®. Copyright © 1973, 1978, 1984, 2011 by Biblica, Inc.™ Used by permission of Zondervan. All rights reserved worldwide. www.zondervan.com. The "NIV" and "New International Version" are trademarks registered in the United States Patent and Trademark Office by Biblica, Inc.™

While any stories in this book are true, some names and identifying information may have been changed to protect the privacy of individuals.

Cover design: David Fassett
Interior design: Beth McGill
Images: ©baxsyl / Getty Images

ISBN 978-0-8308-5101-0 (print)
ISBN 978-0-8308-8915-0 (digital)

Printed in the United States of America ♾

InterVarsity Press is committed to ecological stewardship and to the conservation of natural resources in all our operations. This book was printed using sustainably sourced paper.

Library of Congress Cataloging-in-Publication Data
A catalog record for this book is available from the Library of Congress.

P	23	22	21	20	19	18	17	16	15	14	13	12	11	10	9	8	7	6	5	4	3	2	1
Y	36	35	34	33	32	31	30	29	28	27	26	25	24	23	22	21	20	19	18	17			

Contents

Preface   vii

Introduction   1
   Evelyne A. Reisacher

PART I: REGIONAL PERSPECTIVES

1 Mission in a World Gone Wild and Violent:
  Challenging the Monochromatic View of
  Islam from a "Silent Majority" Position   11
  Martin Accad

2 The Western Frontier: Euro-Islam
  and the Remaking of Global Faith   37
  Philip Jenkins

3 Christian-Muslim Relations and the Ethos
  of State Formation in West Africa   57
  Nimi Wariboko

4 Islam in South Asia: Dynamics of Contemporary
  Muslim Societies in Hyderabad Deccan   82
  David Emmanuel Singh

PART II: THEMATIC ANALYSES

5 Negotiating from the Margins: Women's
  Voices (Re)Imagining Islam   113
  Cathy Hine

6 The Islamic Punishment for Blasphemy:
  Diversity in Sources and Societies   135
  Gordon Nickel

7 Shari'a in a Globalized World: Historical
  Overview, Regional Contrasts, and the
  Challenge of Pluralism   156
  David L. Johnston

PART III: MISSIOLOGICAL ASSESSMENTS

8 Diversity and Change in Contemporary
Muslim Societies: Missional Emphases
and Implications   183
John Jay Travis

9 Peacemaking Initiatives Among Muslims   203
Rick Love

10 Defining Islam and Muslim Societies
in Missiological Discourse   219
Evelyne A. Reisacher

List of Contributors   243

Author Index   247

Subject Index   251

Preface

This volume is a collection of the papers presented initially at the Missiology Lectures of Fuller Theological Seminary's School of Intercultural Studies (SIS) held on the Pasadena, California, campus on November 3 and 4, 2016, under the title "Dynamics of Contemporary Muslim Societies: Christian Theological and Missiological Implications." Three additional chapters in this volume were written by SIS professors of Islamic studies and by Fuller Theological Seminary alumni who took an active part in the conference.

The lectures brought together a wide cross-section of local and international theologians, missiologists, and mission practitioners. They engaged in fruitful discussions and networking, the results of which, as this volume reveals, are already shaping new theories and practices in Christian engagement in the Muslim world.

Here I want to thank all those who made the 2016 Missiology Lectures and this volume possible. I am particularly thankful to my colleague Amos Yong, who is professor of theology and mission at Fuller Seminary. As director of the Center for Missiological Research, he is the key organizer of the yearly Missiology Lectures at Fuller Theological Seminary. I found it delightful to co-organize the 2016 lectures with him and cannot thank him enough for his faithful support. He also helped me review this volume by giving many insightful comments.

I am also deeply thankful to Scott W. Sunquist, dean of the School of Intercultural Studies, for his cheerful support of the Islamic studies program at Fuller Theological Seminary and for his decision to choose a theme related to Islam for the 2016 Missiology Lectures. I value his ongoing encouragement and commitment to helping the church become better equipped to engage with Muslims.

I want to thank Irene Neller, vice president for communications, marketing, and admissions, and her "events" staff. I also wish to particularly thank Sarah Bucek, assistant director of events, communications, and marketing, for her vital role and outstanding job in assisting with the planning and organizing of the conference on a daily basis and for her attention to every detail. The SIS staff, including Wendy Walker, Silvia Gutierrez, and Colton Curry, also gave much help.

I want to express appreciation to my Fuller Seminary colleagues Diane Obenchain, Enoch Jinsik Kim, J. Dudley Woodberry, Cynthia B. Eriksson, Richard J. Mouw, and Veli-Matti Kärkkäinen, who were respondents to the presentations, as well as Bulus Galadima, dean of the Cook School of Intercultural Studies at Biola University.

I also wish to thank Mark Labberton, president of Fuller Theological Seminary, Juan Martínez, professor of Hispanic studies and pastoral leadership, and Roberta R. King, associate professor of communication and ethnomusicology, for their active participation in the program.

Many other events of the Missiology Lectures are not reproduced in this volume: a panel titled "Current Issues in Christian Witness Among Contemporary Muslim Societies," moderated by Scott W. Sunquist; a panel with all the plenary speakers titled "Exploding Stereotypes About Islam: On the Diversification of Islamic Worlds in the Next Generation," moderated by Evelyne A. Reisacher; and a panel with Atilla Kahveci, Edina Lekovic, Jamaal Diwan, and Maria Khani, members of the Los Angeles Muslim community, moderated by Michal Meulenberg. The audio recordings of these panels and plenary sessions can be accessed at soundcloud.com/fullerstudio/sets/missiology-lectures-2016.

I want to express my gratitude to the Global Arts Worship Team, which organized and led worship during both days of the conference. The worship segments were extremely important in achieving a seamless approach to the spirituality-academics interface. Special thanks goes to Roberta R. King, who assembled the worship team, and to Sunita Puleo, Eric Sarwar, and Michael Jadrich, who helped facilitate.

The lectures also included lunch-table discussions where burning issues in mission were explored, and these were led by mission practitioners and Fuller students. I want to thank the following moderators of those discussions: John Becker, Farida Saïdi, Rick Love, Michal Meulenberg, Eric Sarwar,

Kevin Higgins, Wanjiru Gitau, Alex Massad, Uchenna Anyanwu, L. David Waterman, and Paul Dzubinski. I also wish to thank Gail Schlosser and Andres Prins, who participated with mission practitioners on the panel "Current Issues in Christian Witness."

During the Missiology Lectures participants had the opportunity to visit a photography exhibition featuring Maya-Inès Touam, a French artist from Paris. The exhibit was titled *Révéler l'étoffe* ("Unveiling the Cloth"). It showed a series of pictures of Algerian women from all ages and spheres of society, demonstrating the numerous opinions that Algerian women have regarding the veil. This exhibition reflected beautifully the theme of diversity in Muslim societies. I am thankful to Maria Fee and Andrea Kraybill from the Fuller Brehm Center for helping organize and set up the exhibit.

I am grateful also to St. Andrew's Presbyterian Church in Costa Mesa for their support of the conference. And finally I want to express my deep appreciation to Dan Reid, Ethan McCarthy, and the rest of the InterVarsity Press staff for their astute editorial guidance and for making the publication of this volume possible.

Introduction

Evelyne A. Reisacher

Christians today seem increasingly puzzled about the identity of Islam and of Muslim societies, especially in view of violent conflicts involving Muslim communities in various parts of the world. The perplexity of Christians increases when they hear about beheadings in the name of Islam or watch the flow of refugees fleeing the Middle East. The challenge of understanding Islam is further complicated by the fact that an already very diverse Islam across the world stage is also fluid and dynamic, with changes motivated as much by Islamic agency from within as by forces impinging "from without." Consequently, missiologists and mission practitioners often find themselves entangled in unending debates about the nature of Islam. Some describe it as a complex and heterogeneous phenomenon, while others see it as monolithic. Such disagreements often lead to fierce mission controversies and seemingly irreconcilable approaches in witness and ministry.

Furthermore, after a season of significant church growth in the Muslim world, the latest conflicts involving Muslim and Christian populations potentially have dramatic implications for witness. Given that a recent Pew Research study predicted that the number of Muslims may nearly equal the number of Christians around the world by the year 2050,[1] it is crucial to help the Christian community become increasingly conversant with the current religious and social climate in Muslim-majority contexts as they engage in witness among Muslims. To address these needs and enhance the effectiveness

---

[1]Conrad Hackett, Alan Cooperman, and Katherine Ritchey, "The Future of World Religions: Population Growth Projections, 2010–2050," Pew Research Center, April 2, 2015, www.pewforum .org/2015/04/02/religious-projections-2010-2050.

of Christian witness in Muslim contexts, the School of Intercultural Studies at Fuller Theological Seminary chose to focus its 2016 Missiology Lectures on Islam, selecting the theme "Dynamics of Contemporary Muslim Societies: Christian Theological and Missiological Implications." The goal was twofold: to unfold as accurately and as broadly as possible the dynamics of Islamic societies and to formulate Christian theological and missiological assessments in response.

At first glance, this theme appears to ignore the two hottest issues currently debated in churches, namely, the refugee crisis in the Middle East and the ongoing violence by ISIS and other related groups. But these issues are precisely why the lectures focused on the dynamics of Muslim societies: to help Christians make sense of the cacophony of ideas, voices, and rumors about Islam that they are presented with every day. In order to develop a robust understanding of Muslim people, it is essential to grapple with the concept of unity and diversity within Muslim societies. The study of the Qur'an, the hadith (Muslim tradition), and the *sīra* (the biography of Muhammad) reveals a plethora of interpretations that makes it almost impossible to summarize Islam in a nutshell (though some people in search of a quick fix to Islam-related issues inevitably try!). When engaging with Muslims on a personal level, one quickly discovers layers of diversity generated by various cultural and social factors shaping Muslim societies. The worldwide Muslim community differs widely in matters of belief, behavior, and religious belonging.

For that reason, without abandoning the exploration of theological textbooks on Islam, we must look at the "living" Islam (as anthropologists like to call their object of study). At Fuller Theological Seminary, students are required to take two foundational classes within the Islamic studies emphasis. The first is titled "Introduction to Islam," and it deals with theology and history. Students learn, for example, how Islamic schools of law and thought have disputed for centuries the exact meaning of qur'anic passages on peace and violence. The second course, "Muslim Societies," explores Islam by studying people and their social networks through the lenses of anthropology and sociology. Given that mission is about loving and caring for people, one cannot properly study Islam without looking at how Muslim individuals, families, and communities live, think, feel, and relate to others.

These lenses help us better understand why there are so many different manifestations of Islam. My hope is that readers of this volume will grasp the great complexity of Muslim societies and not feel threatened by it, instead learning to think missiologically within this complexity and develop new models of witness that are relevant to contemporary Islamic contexts.

This volume is a collection of papers presented initially at the 2016 Missiology Lectures of Fuller Theological Seminary with an additional three chapters by scholars who teach at the seminary and who took an active part in the lectures. The essays cover a great diversity of topics, all related to the general theme of the lectures. Presenters offered insightful analysis of Muslim societies in various regions of the world, challenging some existing theological and missiological approaches and suggesting innovative and promising new paradigms that will help Christians better understand Muslim societies and engage with Muslims in meaningful ways. Their discussions focused on specific parts of the Muslim world, undertook thematic and theological analyses, and provided explicit missiological assessments and proposals—the three parts of this book. All of the chapters in their own way also include at least implicitly (although in almost all cases explicitly) exploratory implications for mission in Islamic contexts.

The first part of the book is focused on regional developments. Given that the Middle East is at the center of many political and social concerns worldwide, this volume opens with a chapter by Martin Accad. He shows that in much of the popular mind today the world is divided between Muslims and "the rest," believing that Christians of the East are an oppressed "minority" that needs rescuing by the West and that Muslims are largely on a grand mission to conquer the world. Accad then asks whether a group like ISIS confirms such a vision of the world or challenges it and considers whether the very existence of ISIS forecasts new developments within Islam during the twenty-first century. Accad challenges brash generalizations about Islam. He argues that the world is mostly populated with a "silent majority" of people of faith that the "clash theory" tends to brush off as insignificant to world tensions and conflicts. Can the global church reclaim a missional vision that adopts the perspective of the "silent majority"? Accad concludes by suggesting a kerygmatic, "suprareligious" approach to contemporary mission and missiological thinking.

In the second chapter Philip Jenkins looks at Europe, which, with the Syrian refugee crisis and recent terrorist attacks carried out by people who claim to be Muslims, is another region of the world making daily headlines related to Islam. Although Europe is home only to a tiny proportion of the world's Muslims, Jenkins contends that these communities carry a significance far beyond their numbers. He believes that, quite apart from any discussion of terrorist threats, Europe's Islamic communities are the setting for far-reaching social and cultural experiments that are already transforming the practice of faith in majority-Muslim nations. He sees the demographic aspect as especially important in igniting an extensive transformation. Intellectually speaking, Europe represents something unprecedented in the historical Muslim experience: namely, a free space in which believers from all nations can meet and interact. While these exchanges have at times produced baneful extremism and militancy, Jenkins reports other aspects that are far more encouraging. Paradoxically, the chief obstacle to progress in Europe is European governments themselves, specifically their policies of engagement with conservative Muslim nations and religious authorities. At every point, according to Jenkins, these developments are of critical interest to European Christian churches.

In the third chapter of this volume, Nimi Wariboko encourages us to look at Islam and at Muslim societies from historical and sociopolitical perspectives. Focusing essentially on West Africa, he offers a new paradigm for Muslim-Christian relations and conflicts, believing that current models are overused. His chapter examines the impact of Christian-Muslim relations on state formation, particularly the creation and sustenance of rapacious state institutions in postcolonial West Africa. How did the forces of Christianity and Islam interact in one common field of state/society formation over a long period of time? Wariboko contends that the state in West Africa is not only a strategic site for conflict and collaboration between Christianity and Islam, but that it also co-opts them to steadily attack its citizens. His chapter highlights the significant roles of Christianity and Islam in the functioning and dysfunctioning of a state that is antagonistic to its citizenry, providing a veritable lens to ethically examine the political theology of state and society that conditions Christian-Muslim relations in postcolonial West Africa. He then unpacks the missiological implications of the logic of both religions, which have historically intersected and intertwined in African statecraft. His approach has many implications not only for West Africa but also for many other regions of the world experiencing similar interplay of state formation and mission.

In the final chapter of part one, David Singh focuses on a cross-section of living Islam in South Asia as a window into broader Muslim culture before attempting to offer reflections for a theological and missiological discussion. He shares findings from research on the African Cavalry Guards (ACG) in Hyderabad Deccan as an illustration not only of diversity but also of proactive interschool/community interactions. In expounding this, he draws on two contrasting cases: first, the case of two major Muslim *maslaks* (schools of thought) developing a strategy for sustained contact (and possibly exchange), namely, the *munazara* (debate/discussion); second, the case of an Afro-Indian Muslim community seeking through performative means to bridge the existing local and non-local fault lines. He directs these South Asian considerations toward unpacking the missiological implications of Christian witness to Islam in the contemporary global context.

Part two of the book brings together analyses of three important issues and theological themes in the contemporary Islamic world that are also of importance for thinking about Christian-Muslim relations and missiological engagements. As a volume without discussion on the role of gender in Muslim societies would remain crucially incomplete, the fifth chapter discusses how women's roles in the formation of Islamic thought and practice have been undervalued and misunderstood both from within Islam and as a dynamic in missiological engagement. Cathy Hine contends that this has meant a denial of Muslim women's agency, a failure to reflect the multiple forces for change at work within Islam, and the marginalization of women in missiology and mission strategies. Hine shows how women's voices engage from the margin, where the margin is not a site of deprivation, but one of dynamic possibility for negotiating change. Her chapter explores three sets of voices from the margins engaging Islam for change today: the voices of women calling for a radical reinterpretation of Islam, the voices of women expressed in the piety movement, and the voices of women activists demanding social change.

She examines the dynamic of these women's agency in (re)shaping Islam and asks how understanding these forces for change may enable a re-imagining of our missiologies.

In chapter six, Gordon Nickel discusses the diversity in Islam by looking at the Islamic punishment for blasphemy, an issue with dire implications for Christians living in Muslim societies. Starting with two contemporary cases of punishment for blasphemy in Pakistan, Nickel delves deep into an academic study of the sourcebooks of Islam and examines Muslim societies in the majority world, especially South Asia, to better understand the nature and multiple interpretations of blasphemy in the context of Islam. Given that Muslims around the world agree on their twin sources of authority—the Qur'an and the Sunnah—Nickel explores what then accounts for the diversity observable among various Islamic groups today. An important part of this chapter is devoted to a discussion on the veneration of Muhammad and how it affects the interpretation of blasphemy laws. Nickel believes a better understanding of what shapes this diversity should encourage a multifaceted missiological response.

Shari'a (Islamic law) is a word now familiar to most non-Muslims. The way it is defined, however, plays an important role in how non-Muslims view and evaluate Islamic societies. To debunk certain myths and help Christians better understand the nature of shari'a and its diverse interpretations, in chapter seven David L. Johnston presents a brief primer of shari'a and looks at its various manifestations in the colonial and post-colonial period. Readers will gather much insight from his analysis of Muslim interpretations of Islamic law. He also discusses how shari'a is applied in various countries, including Turkey, Pakistan, and Tunisia, and explains how the concept of pluralism—and more specifically "legal pluralism"—works in contemporary societies as well as how it is perceived in mission. Finally, Johnston offers three possible missiological directions that will help Christians further reflect on this issue at the core of so many debates within mission.

The final three chapters of this book focus explicitly on missiological considerations. Given that this volume looks at how the dynamics of Muslim societies impact mission, it was important to include a chapter entirely devoted to how missionaries have traditionally perceived this diversity as they have engaged with Muslim contexts. In chapter eight John Travis identifies four types of diversity and changes encountered in mission: (1) ethnic, linguistic, and socioreligious; (2) political and national; (3) educational and socioeconomic; and (4) spiritual and individual. After highlighting a small but significant spiritual shift in the Muslim world, Travis offers five emphases and missional implications for contemporary missional engagement with Muslims: proximate witness, prayer and miracles, Jesus over religion, the testimony of Scripture, and new expressions of following Jesus.

Given the current conflicts among Muslims and Christians in many parts of the world, Christian scholars are developing new models of peaceful interfaith engagement. In chapter nine, Rick Love analyzes peacemaking initiatives among Muslims from three perspectives: the biblical mandate for peacemaking, the strategic urgency of peacemaking between Christians and Muslims, and the practical peacemaking initiatives taking place in the twenty-first century. An extensive biblical consideration invites readers to reflect on the importance of peacemaking in their engagement with Muslims. This chapter highlights the importance of advancing missional paradigms that are relevant for developing Muslim-Christian relations and addressing societal issues.

The volume concludes with Evelyne A. Reisacher's presentation "Defining Islam and Muslim Societies in Missiological Discourse." Traditionally, the study of Islam in Christian circles has focused on theological and historical research. More recently a growing body of missiological research has been exploring Muslim societies from anthropological and sociological perspectives. These newer approaches, which focus on the living expressions of Islam, highlight the diversity of Islam in local contexts as well as the multiple identities of Muslims and press Christian scholars to address the question of whether there are multiple islams. This chapter also briefly reviews contemporary academic debates regarding the issue of universal and local expressions of Islam and concludes with an examination of the works of missiologists and mission practitioners to observe how they deal with the question of unity and diversity in Islam and in Muslim societies.

Readers are summoned through the theories and concepts presented in this volume to adopt their own analytical frameworks for defining the dynamics observed in Muslim societies. It is hoped that the publication of the papers presented at the Missiological Lectures along with the additional chapters in this volume will further contribute to a better understanding and engagement with Muslim societies, enabling biblically based adaptations to the diversity of contemporary Islamic societies.

Note that the authors were each free to choose their own transliteration system.

PART I

Regional Perspectives

Mission in a World Gone Wild and Violent

Challenging the Monochromatic View of Islam from a "Silent Majority" Position

Martin Accad

In the summer of 2014, the group calling itself the Islamic State in Iraq and Syria (ISIS—or in Iraq and the Levant, ISIL) went on a rampage, conquering and massacring Christians, Yazidis, Shi'ites, and any Sunnis who disagreed with its program. Beginning at the border regions of Iraq and Syria, ISIS gradually pushed deeper into each country, occupying what came to represent about a third of Syria and a quarter of Iraq. At the time of writing this chapter, ISIS appears to be on its way out, with Western powers, together with their military coalition in the region, preparing for an invasion of Mosul. While it is hard to predict the fate of ISIS at this point, what is quite clear is that the root problems that allowed for the emergence of ISIS have not been addressed. ISIS may go extinct over the next few months, but there is little doubt that an equivalent, if not more horrendous, monster will eventually emerge in its place. Therefore, seeking to understand the nature and root causes of the emergence of ISIS remains imminently necessary, for until these are addressed the world will likely keep moving toward greater religious extremism and violence.

Strikingly, the first thing ISIS did after emerging onto the world stage in 2014 was the supremely symbolic act of tearing down the international border demarcation between Iraq and Syria. On May 16, 2016, the West commemorated the one hundredth anniversary of a secret deal between Britain and France known today as the Sykes-Picot Agreement. Following secret negotiations in 1916, Britain and France decided on new borders for the Middle East as they predicted the fall of the Ottoman Empire at the end of World War I (1914–1918). A third, minor party to the agreement was the Tsarist government of Russia. But following the Bolshevik Revolution and the end of the Tsarist era, Russia would fall out of the agreement, and the Bolsheviks would make the agreement public on November 23, 1917. With the elimination of the Sykes-Picot border by ISIS, the challenge to the post-colonial order imposed by Western nations on the Middle East region had been launched.

In a seminal 1992 lecture at the American Enterprise Institute, political scientist Samuel Huntington proposed the notion of a "clash of civilizations" as a key to understanding the nature of global conflict in the post–Cold War era. An article followed—the title ending in a question mark—in a 1993 edition of *Foreign Affairs*.[1] After he published a more assertive book with the same title in 1996,[2] it became popular to think of Islam as the single most significant divisive agent in today's world. In much of the popular mind, the world was now divided between the Muslims and "the rest." Christians of the East became an oppressed "minority" that needed rescuing by the rest in "the West." And Muslims were largely on a grand mission to conquer the world.

It has now been over three years since the rise of ISIS. Has the group's behavior confirmed Huntington's vision of the world or challenged it? How do we understand militant jihadism within the grander scheme of the Is-lamist and Salafi ideologies of the twentieth century? What does a twenty-first-century perspective on the Middle East and global developments tell us? A discussion of the main ideas of Huntington's hypothesis in the first section will lead us to dwell on the roots of Salafism, no doubt the most prominently featuring descriptor of Islam in popular discourse and the media today. In my second section, I will argue that twentieth-century post-colonial realities represented jihadi Salafism's raison d'être and attractiveness

---

[1]Samuel P. Huntington, "The Clash of Civilizations?," *Foreign Affairs* 72, no. 3 (Summer 1993): 22–49.
[2]Samuel P. Huntington, *The Clash of Civilizations and the Remaking of World Order* (New York: Simon & Schuster, 1996).

in the last century as well as at the turn of the twenty-first. Dwelling further on ISIS as a jihadi Salafi group, we will consider, third, that the biggest draw of ISIS on young people is its rebellious stance toward the dominant order imposed by world powers. For disillusioned young people living under post-colonial, paternalistic, corrupt, yet largely Western-supported regimes in the Arab and Muslim world, affiliating with a movement that dares to chal- *young ppls motiv.* lenge the dominant order under the victorious black banners of ISIS is an extremely defiant and invigorating act. As French sociologist Olivier Roy has demonstrated through comprehensive research into the recruitment draw of ISIS in Europe,[3] the thrill of affiliation with ISIS has more to do with the disaffection of young Europeans from second- or third-generation mi-grant communities living in ghettoized societies than commitment and loyalty to Islamic theology. Young millennial and iGeneration converts are also attracted to the service of revolutionary hordes with no apparent moral boundaries. In my final analysis, I will argue that instead of confirming the Huntington thesis, the very existence of ISIS forecasts new, deep, and com-prehensive developments within Islam in the near and long-term future.

Moving from analysis to implications for the church, the basic thrust of this chapter will be that the world is mostly populated with ordinary people who simply want to live their lives and provide a decent future for their children. This in itself challenges popular notions that draw brash general-izations about Islam. Most Christians, Muslims, Jews, Hindus, Buddhists, Baha'is, Yazidis, and others who do not identify with a particular faith ef-fectively represent the "silent majority," which the clash theory tends to brush off as of no significance to world tensions and conflicts. Yet the recent uprisings in the Arab world, to a large extent the result of globalization and social media, seem to have inaugurated a new role for this silent majority. Searching for the Islamic roots of ISIS in the Qur'an and in Islamic traditions may yield some interesting results for scholars of world religions. And their work may be useful in the long run, as scholars of different faiths engage in conversation about theology and its impact on politics. But the more im-portant question from the perspective of socioreligious studies is the reverse:

---

[3]Olivier Roy, "What Is the Driving Force Behind Jihadist Terrorism? A Scientific Perspective on the Causes/Circumstances of Joining the Scene," *Inside Story*, December 18, 2015, http://insidestory .org.au/what-is-the-driving-force-behind-jihadist-terrorism.

How are current events and manifestations of contemporary Islam, together with reactions to the religion among adherents of other faiths, particularly Christianity and Judaism, going to affect Islam and other religions in the long term? Scholars who study the phenomenon of religion are more interested in defining a religion based on the behavior of its adherents than on the basis of some grand theological themes that are supposed to be the driving force of its people of faith.

The world-religions approach has a tendency to view people of faith as prisoners of theological systems, where adherents' every move can be predicted by the sacred scriptures of their communities. But the sociology-of-religions approach offers a dynamic vision of mutually influential forces between theology and the practice of religion. As a foundation of my missiological section I will argue that the latter vision offers us a far richer field of inquiry, engagement, and action than the former. From a missional perspective, the sociological perspective is far more useful, empowering, and energizing, inviting us to consider new possibilities for the creative and constructive action required for the mission of God.

THE HUNTINGTON THESIS AND THE REMAKING OF WORLD ORDER

In his book *The Clash of Civilizations*, Samuel Huntington notes that since the end of the Cold War it has no longer been natural to think of the world as polarized between the two superpowers of America and the Soviet Union. But he warns that the emerging order will not be the utopian "one harmonious world" imagined by Fukuyama in his thesis on the end of history.[4] Huntington suggests that we are now living in a multipolar world, with each pole needing to be defined in terms of "civilization." He further defines civilization as "the highest cultural grouping of people and the broadest level of cultural identity people have short of that which distinguishes humans from other species."[5] One can now identify, he suggests, about eight distinct civilizations that embrace large swaths of territory, peoples, cultures, and societies: Sinic, Japanese, Hindu, Islamic, Orthodox, Western, Latin American, and

---

[4]Samuel P. Huntington, *The Clash of Civilizations and the Remaking of World Order* (New York: Simon & Schuster, 2007), 32. For Fukuyama's thesis, see Francis Fukuyama, *The End of History and the Last Man* (New York: Avon Books, 1992).
[5]Huntington, *Clash of Civilizations*, 43.

(possibly) African.[6] The most distinct feature of each of these civilizations is ethnic and cultural identity. "In this new world," he asserts, "local politics is the politics of ethnicity; global politics is the politics of civilizations. The rivalry of the superpowers is replaced by the clash of civilizations."[7]

Huntington's thesis seems to have some relevance in the current situation of world events. It helps explain various phenomena at both the macrolevel (nations) as well as the microlevel (individuals and communities within societies). Perhaps the strength of his argument is that it does not radically reimagine the world. The bipolarity of the Cold War divided the world and created alliances along "unnatural" lines. The colonial and postcolonial periods, though dividing the world largely between Western colonial powers and colonized peoples, did not erase cultural, ethnic, and religious distinctives of various colonized populations. But those differences were set aside for a time as a result of Western-induced subjugation. The post–Cold War reality seems largely to return us to the precolonial era, when Western Christendom was rarely at peace with Eastern "Muslimdom," when sub-Saharan African, Sinic, and Hindu cultures were always distinct from the Muslim empire that had extended from Andalusia to East Asia since the end of the seventh century.

The unique conditions in today's world are not caused so much by emerging distinctions between hitherto nonexistent civilizations and cultures, but rather by the unprecedented connectivity of, and therefore interaction between, the distinct cultures that have always been there. It seems to me that it is this unprecedented closeness rather than the emergence of anything radically new that has revealed the post–Cold War "fault lines" between those cultures that Huntington calls "civilizations." This closeness between peoples of different cultures has not only created a connectivity that cannot be avoided; it has also flattened the polarity of power between the West and "the rest" and created a world much more complex in terms of the power dynamics between its now seven or eight distinct poles.

As Huntington's thesis indicates, and as policymakers globally have been increasingly asserting, religion may no longer be viewed separately from politics. "The Westphalian separation of religion and international politics,

---

[6]Ibid., 45-47.
[7]Ibid., 28.

an idiosyncratic product of Western civilization," as Huntington calls it, "is coming to an end, and religion . . . is 'increasingly likely to intrude into international affairs.'"[8] There is little doubt that religion, a core component of the identities of each of the "civilizations" that Huntington identifies, will play an increasingly central role in shaping our societies. But whether religion will play a negative or positive role between nations remains the big question.

Despite his somewhat insightful thesis, the problem with Huntington is that he seems unable to extricate himself from the negative bias that his own "civilizational belonging" gives him toward Islam. "Islamic culture," he asserts, "explains in large part the failure of democracy to emerge in much of the Muslim world."[9] His descriptions of the spread of Islam as an inevitable outcome of its rapid reproductive growth end up unwittingly promoting fear of Muslims among non-Muslims. "In the long run," he forebodes, "Mohammed wins out. Christianity spreads primarily by conversion, Islam by conversion and reproduction."[10] His assertions and predictions are furthermore questionable in light of his own argument. Clearly, population growth has to do with culture and tradition, not religion. If Christianity is growing among non-Western cultures, particularly in Africa, Latin America, and some parts of Asia, as Huntington himself asserts, then the rate of population growth must also be growing with it. In the same way, as Islam is adopted increasingly within Western culture and as more Muslims from non-Western cultures settle in and adapt to Western societies, population growth among Muslims should be expected to decrease in the long run. Does this not skew the demographics on which his predictions are based?

Another dimension of the current world order that Huntington seems to partly disregard is the intense cross-pollination that the postcolonial world's demographics have been undergoing over the past century, largely as an outcome of the colonial era. As Huntington's world emerges with acute emphasis on distinct cultures and ethnicities, emerging generations everywhere are increasingly moving beyond race, beyond ethnicity, beyond culture, and to a certain extent even beyond institutional religion. If the seven or eight civilizations emerging from the post–Cold War era help us

---

[8]Ibid., 54.
[9]Ibid., 29.
[10]Ibid., 65.

understand our world today, how is this picture rapidly changing as a result of the unprecedented rapprochement and intermarriage between the civilizations of the world? And to what extent is it then correct to claim that Western demographics were due to drop from "slightly over 13 percent of humanity" in 1993 "to about 11 percent early in the next century and to 10 percent by 2025"? Why are Muslims in the West excluded from the count of "western populations"?[11] I would suggest that Huntington's distinction between Western territory and Western civilization is too strong.

Brilliant novelist, historian, and philosopher Amin Maalouf, who is both Lebanese and French (rather than half and half, as he himself vehemently protests), affirms that "every individual is a meeting ground for many different allegiances."[12] Can human beings today really be classified into the neat civilizational categories identified by Huntington? While the clash theory is considered useful by some for political analysis and prediction and for the forging of nations' foreign policies, it could be detrimental and destructive for the enterprise of shaping cohesive societies in the twenty-first century. In his book Maalouf asserts that, because most citizens in societies today are the locus of many different allegiances (due largely to the intertwined nature of the postcolonial world), "they have a special role to play in forging links, eliminating misunderstandings, making some parties more reasonable and others less belligerent, smoothing out difficulties, seeking compromise. Their role is to act as bridges, go-betweens, mediators between the various communities and cultures." He warns that "if they themselves cannot sustain their multiple allegiances, if they are continually being pressed to take sides or ordered to stay within their own tribe, then all of us have reason to be uneasy about the way the world is going."[13]

While not wanting to dismiss completely the lens provided by Huntington as unhelpful for a better understanding of current world events, I believe that as Christ's followers we ought to root the missional vision of the church in a more prophetic perspective, one that is helpfully informed by Maalouf's analysis of culture and its impact on identity. We ought to heed

---

[11]Ibid., 84.
[12]Amin Maalouf, *In the Name of Identity: Violence and the Need to Belong* (New York: Penguin Books, 2003), 4.
[13]Ibid., 5.

Maalouf's call to curb those "habits of thought and expression deeply rooted
in us all . . . because of a narrow, exclusive, bigoted, simplistic attitude that
reduces identity in all its many aspects to one single affiliation, and one that
is proclaimed in anger."[14]

SALAFISM, ISLAMISM, ISIS, AND OTHER REINVENTED
ISLAMS IN OUR POSTCOLONIAL WORLD

The notion of a clash of civilizations helps us understand the growing conflicts of the world today. But the concept of "multiple allegiances" provides
us with an understanding of current world events and offers us possibilities
in addressing conflict, both actual and potential, both now and future. We
cannot understand the twentieth century without understanding the ex-
cruciatingly influential phenomenon of conflicting allegiances at the front
end of the postcolonial world. It is at this intersection of allegiances—between East and West, Christianity and Islam, religion and secularism, Islamism and nationalism—that the Salafi method emerged at the turn of the
twentieth century.

Those in the West have become accustomed, largely as a result of the
overarching media discourse, to thinking of Salafism in terms of the ideology it shares with jihadi groups, which are often referred to as Salafis, to
the point that Salafism has almost become synonymous with terrorism and
violence. But before it became the trademark of narrow-minded religious
fanaticism, the Salafi method was a promising framework for renewal. One
of its founders, Egyptian reformer Muhammad Abduh (d. 1905), urged
Islam to adapt to modernity. Together with his teacher and colleague Jamal
ad-Din al-Afghani (d. 1897), and to a lesser extent his disciple Rashid Rida
(d. 1935), Abduh called for a greater synthesis between religions, and both
Abduh and al-Afghani preached and practiced friendship with Jews, Christians, Baha'is, and even Shi'ites.[15]

---

[14]Ibid.

[15]Many edited collections, primary-source readers, and monographs have been written on late
   nineteenth- to early twentieth-century Islamic reformism and provide good studies on the
   thought of Abduh, al-Afghani, Rida, and others. See for example John Esposito, Yvonne Haddad,
   and John Voll, *The Contemporary Islamic Revival: A Critical Survey and Bibliography* (Westport,
   CT: Greenwood, 1991); John Esposito and John Voll, *Makers of Contemporary Islam* (New York:
   Oxford University Press, 2001); John Donohue and John Esposito, eds., *Islam in Transition:
   Muslim Perspectives*, 2nd ed. (New York: Oxford University Press, 2006).

Salafism in this original form stood on the premise that Muslims were not to consider themselves bound to the official schools of Islamic law, which were blamed for Islam's regressive state at the end of the nineteenth and early twentieth century. Salafism's call to return to the first four generations of Islam—*as-salaf as-salih* ("the righteous ancestors")—as a means for Islamic renewal and reinvigoration could lead in two possible directions: liberalism or fundamentalism. Sayyid Qutb, the principal Egyptian ideologue of the Muslim Brotherhood who was hanged by the regime of Gamal Abdel Nasser in 1966 after much duress in prison, took the Salafi method to its most fundamentalist conclusion. As a clerically untrained scholar of the Qur'an, Qutb developed a revolutionary ideology of *takfir*, which called for the individual religious responsibility of every Muslim to reform self, society, and eventually the state. Besides his considerably influential multivolume commentary on the Qur'an, *In the Shadow of the Qur'an*, his book *Signposts on the Road* (also known in English as *Milestones*)[16] quickly became the handbook of emerging *takfiri* and jihadi Salafi movements of the latter half of the twentieth century, to which the 9/11 attackers and notorious ISIS members belong.

The paradox of Salafism is that, while capable of inspiring armed revolution and jihadism, it is also likely the most promising methodology for continued renewal and reformation in twenty-first-century Islam. Not unlike the Protestant Reformation, the Salafi method, by ridding itself of the burdens and boundaries of traditional scriptural interpretation, carries unlimited possibilities, including the transformation of Islam into the constructive and inspiring spiritual and moral ideology espoused by contemporary progressive Muslims in the West. A significant part of this transformation has already been occurring in what Asef Bayat has identified as a fundamental shift throughout the world from Islamism to post-Islamism.[17]

In his 2004 publication *Western Muslims and the Future of Islam*, Swiss-born scholar of Egyptian descent Tariq Ramadan attempts to classify the main manifestations of Islam in the West into what he calls "six major

---

[16]For a good edition of Qutb's work, see Sayyid Qutb, *Milestones* (New Delhi: Islamic Book Service, 2006).

[17]Asef Bayat, ed., *Post-Islamism: The Changing Faces of Political Islam* (New York: Oxford University Press, 2013).

tendencies,"[18] three of which fall under the classification of "Salafi." Policy-makers, analysts, and the media would do well to pay attention again to the distinction he makes between "Salafi Literalism," "Salafi Reformism," and "Political Literalist Salafism." Salafi Literalists are primarily interested in scholarly pursuits along the lines of the traditionalists. They share the same "space" as the "Scholastic Traditionalists," but their hermeneutical starting point is different in that they do not consider themselves bound to the scholarly opinions of their predecessors beyond the third generation of Muhammad's followers. Political Literalist Salafists are those Salafi Muslims who adopt a shallow reading of the early texts of Islam and take them as a literal guide for day-to-day behavior and practice. This tendency has developed into what many (including myself) call "Jihadi Salafism." The Salafi hermeneutic, married to political and militant pragmatism, manifests itself in terrorist practice.

It is Salafi Reformism, on the other hand, that should be considered the most faithful manifestation of the original intent of the Salafism of such early reformers as Abduh, al-Afghani, Rida, and others. This is probably also the tendency in which Ramadan would locate himself. This hermeneutic is faithful enough to the founding texts of Islam to remain within the fold of the Islamic mainstream, yet its agenda is progressive enough and its methodology flexible and rational enough to provide the dynamism needed for Islam to continue to adjust to a changing environment. In daily practice, Salafi Reformism is concerned primarily with the "purpose of the Law" (*maqāṣid ash-Sharīʿa*) rather than blind adherence to past applications. Salafi reformists are no doubt those scholars most likely to engage with Christians and secularists alike to work together in the shaping of societies globally.

FUTURE DIRECTIONS: FROM ISLAMISM TO POST-ISLAMISM

The grassroots movements that emerged in the 2011 Arab Spring revolution have raised concerns in many circles, including the West. Even though most of these movements, which occurred in places like Tunisia, Egypt, Morocco,

---

[18]The "tendencies" he identified were "Scholastic Traditionalism," "Salafi Literalism," "Salafi Reformism," "Political Literalist Salafism," "Liberal" or "Rationalist Reformism," and "Sufism," in Tariq Ramadan, *Western Muslims and the Future of Islam* (New York: Oxford University Press, 2004), 24-30.

and even Syria, did not emerge from Islamist breeding grounds, underground Islamist movements that had been repressed but that often reached a high level of organization in the Muslim world under totalitarian regimes were able to ride the wave of the revolutions. Many political analysts as well as Western governments became alarmed when religious groups such as Hizb an-Nahda in Tunisia, the Muslim Brotherhood and Salafi Hizb an-Nour in Egypt, and the Justice and Development Party in Morocco accomplished impressive gains and victories during the fall 2011 general elections.

Asef Bayat, in his introduction to the essays collected in *Post-Islamism: The Changing Faces of Political Islam*, defines Islamism as "those ideologies and movements that strive to establish some kind of an 'Islamic order'—a religious state, shari'a law, and moral codes in Muslim societies and communities."[19] Though the primary purpose of Islamist movements derives from the qur'anic principle of "commanding right and forbidding wrong" (*al-amr bi al-maʿrūf wa an-nahyʿan al-munkar*), Bayat argues that the ideology of Islamist groups "has been an ideology and a movement that rests on a blend of religiosity and obligation, with little commitment to a language of rights—something that distinguishes it from a post-Islamist worldview."[20]

Post-Islamism, on the other hand, "represents an endeavor to fuse religiosity and rights, faith and freedom, Islam and liberty," according to Bayat. "Whereas Islamism is defined by the fusion of religion and responsibility, post-Islamism emphasizes religiosity and rights. Yet, while it favors a civil and nonreligious state, it accords an active role for religion in the public sphere."[21] The shift that took place within movements, transforming them from Islamist to post-Islamist in countries like Iran, Turkey, Morocco, and Indonesia, has occurred primarily through internal pressures. Whether it was the ineptitude of Islamist governments (Iran, for example), the failure of Islamist movements using violence to achieve political ends within their societies (such as in Morocco and Indonesia), or an inability to overpower secularist forces in state and society (such as in Turkey), grassroots groups have gradually metamorphosed into movements seeking the establishment of justice, good governance, and human rights within a secular state rather

---

[19]Bayat, *Post-Islamism*, 4.
[20]Ibid., 7.
[21]Ibid., 8.

than through the establishment of an Islamic state.[22] In many ways, then, post-Islamism represents a reaction both to the failed outcomes of the Islamization of politics and to the debilitating effect of the politicization of Islam on religion.

In Pakistan and Saudi Arabia, on the other hand, as the focused studies of Bayat's book show, post-Islamist trends have been aborted primarily as a result of American military involvement in the Muslim world. The rising post–9/11 anti-Western voices have resulted in the rejection of "ideas of freedom, choice, and tolerance, because they are easily framed and rejected as imported values associated with the West, the United States, and imperialism."[23]

Finally, Bayat's collection of essays demonstrates the unique situation that has prevailed in Sudan and Syria. Both countries witnessed pioneering expressions of post-Islamism long before the movement's more pervasive emergence in other nations in the mid-1990s. In Sudan, the proto-Islamism of the Mahdi movement eventually gave rise, once the death of Mahdi revealed the failure of his revolutionary program and the lies of his prophecies, to post-Islamist expressions. The most radical and progressive post-Islamist expression in Sudan emerged in the fascinating personality and ideas of Mahmoud Mohamed Taha, who argued for the revival of "Meccan Islam" as the most authentic expression of the religion, expounding a strong message of freedom, equality, and human rights.[24]

The fact that the ideology of the Muslim Brotherhood spread primarily among the educated bourgeoisie of urban centers in Syria caused it, according to Thomas Pierret,[25] to be somewhat post-Islamist from the start. The movement, both before and after the Baathist revolution, sought integration into the political system of Syria. All but decimated after a crushing defeat by Hafez al-Assad's regime in 1982, at his death the Baath party "supported a peaceful democratic transition in Syria."[26] As we will see, any party or community not supportive of the Syrian regime's repressive policies has been "minoritized" and crushed. It is very difficult to know, at this point, which

---

[22]Ibid., 9-15.

[23]Ibid., 20.

[24]Ibid., 21-22.

[25]Thomas Pierret, "Syria's Unusual 'Islamic Trend': Political Reformists, the Ulema, and Democracy," in Bayat, *Post-Islamism*, 321-41.

[26]Asef Bayat, "Post-Islamism at Large," in Bayat, *Post-Islamism*, 23.

direction the country will take in the aftermath of its current war. Dozens of splinters of Islamist and jihadi Salafi groups are vying for one thing: the demise of the Assad regime. But once Syria transitions from a state of war to re-building state structures from total ruin, the post-Islamist agenda of estab-lishing a civil democratic state may become the only viable option, particularly if—and this seems likely from the heavy Russian involvement in the country— the Alawite community is able to maintain a notable role in the future of Syria.

Bayat concludes that

> post-Islamism may be understood as a critical departure from Islamist pol-itics. It describes transcending from the duty-centered and exclusive Islamist politics toward a more rights-centered and inclusive outlook that favors a civil/secular state operating within a pious society.[27]

But for the post-Islamist trend to arrive at fruition and full expression in the societies of the twenty-first century, it seems that Islam itself will need to go through a more fundamental reform, allowing it to accommodate Islamic morality in the public sphere with respect for liberal democratic values. It is difficult to imagine this happening outside a radical reinterpretation of au-thentic Islam such as Meccan Islam, as envisioned by Mahmoud Taha. In other words, we may very well expect that Islam in the twenty-first century, in its effort to adapt to new global realities, will revisit its rather static view of the Qur'an as an immutable text that literally "came down" on the Prophet Muhammad as expressed in the doctrine of *tanzīl*. Only through a more dynamic view of their scriptures will Muslims be able to bring the sort of religious reform that is needed for a full integration of Islam into the emerging world of this century.

The preceding analysis of the changes occurring in Islam offers some glimpses of hope amidst the dreadful situation we are currently witnessing in Syria and Iraq. It is my belief that imminent and radical change in Islam will occur over the next few decades. But in the meantime, Islamism in the form of jihadi Salafism is dying hard, its ISIS incarnation being possibly the most vicious political and militant expression of Islam ever seen in history. As we will see, mainstream Islam wants nothing to do with it. Yet ISIS has been successfully recruiting young men, and even women, who identify

---

[27]Ibid., 29.

themselves as Muslims. Before delving into the long-term global impact of ISIS, we need to analyze its recruitment strategy in an effort to better understand the movement.

JIHADI RECRUITMENT STRATEGIES IN A WORLD WITHOUT PURPOSE

Religious ideology, far from static dogma and stratified religious discourse, claims to offer an answer to personal, social, and global human problems and struggles. In an incisive study examining the personal stories of ISIS recruits, French sociologist of Islam Olivier Roy attempts to identify the "driving force behind jihadist terrorism." He sums up his article by stating that

> radicalisation is a youth revolt against society, articulated on an Islamic religious narrative of jihad. It is not the uprising of a Muslim community that is victim to poverty and racism: only young people join, including converts who did not share in the "suffering" of Muslims in Europe. These rebels without a cause find in jihad a noble and global cause, and are consequently instrumentalised by a radical organisation (al Qaeda, ISIS), that has a strategic agenda.[28]

Roy arrives at a number of interesting conclusions, some of them unexpected given the many stereotypes held about terrorism actors. A strong motivation of radical recruits is "frustration and resentment against society." Most of the recruits are second-generation Muslims or converts to Islam. Many of them have a history of petty crimes and drugs followed by a sudden experience of "conversion." Recruits were often previously connected with other radicals in the context of prison, the Internet, or a gym before they joined a radical group. Only a few had previous connections with militant groups, and even fewer of those were previously active members of established mosques or had a past history of piety. Roy identifies the principal motivation for joining jihad as a "fascination for a narrative we could call 'the small brotherhood of superheroes who avenge the Muslim ummah.'" What most of these recruits are seeking is what Roy calls "self-realisation (as an answer to frustration)," deriving from what he calls "generational nihilism."[29]

---

[28]Roy, "What Is the Driving Force Behind Jihadist Terrorism?"
[29]Ibid.

In other words, prime targets of jihadi recruitment are young people struggling with a deep sense of hopelessness and crisis for meaning. When they suddenly come across plausible narratives of heroism and success, they go through a sort of religious awakening that sparks in them a new sense of hope. Roy argues in conclusion that the aim of fighting jihadi recruitment should be "to accentuate the estrangement of radicals from the Muslim population and to dry up the narrative of Islam as the religion of the oppressed." This sense of nihilism, expressed in hopeless and largely incoherent religious fanaticism—observable in the behavior of ISIS, Boko Haram, and al-Shabab recruits—is vastly different from the constructive revolutionary system of, say, Sayyid Qutb.

The Islamist answer to modernity in the twentieth century, then, reflected the famous slogan of the Muslim Brotherhood: "Islam is the solution!" But while "purer" and "more authentic" Islam was viewed as the constructive communal solution for the Muslim ummah's sense of stagnancy at the twilight of the colonial era, the sort of ideology promoted by violent groups like ISIS has become much more reactive. The revolutionary Islamists of the first half of the twentieth century sought to construct, through the Salafist method, a positive alternative both to Islamic traditionalism and to Westernization. Jihadi Salafism, on the other hand, has increasingly developed, from the latter decades of the twentieth century to the present, a reactive revolutionary narrative of rejection, and often—it is felt—of rejection as an end in itself: "Rebels without a cause," as Roy calls them. The growing realities of the twenty-first-century call for the development of a new alternative narrative, one that can offer true hope in the face of this "generational nihilism."[30] We will turn to this question in the closing missiological section. Before proposing solutions from outside Islam, however, let us see what reactions to ISIS have emerged from within Islam.

Reactions to ISIS in the Muslim World and
the Deep Transformation of Islam

At a briefing delivered in Beirut in February 2016 during a consultation on "Religion, Failed States, and Violence,"[31] I argued that the reactions to ISIS in

---

[30]Ibid.

[31]The conference was organized by the Centre on Religion and Global Affairs (www.crga.org.uk),

the Muslim world since the notorious group's emergence during the summer
of 2014 carried the potential of transforming the nature of Islam more than
any preceding reform movement in the religion's history. Although conferences in defense of Islam's values of peace and tolerance are not a new phenomenon, the intense frequency of such conferences since summer 2014 has
been striking. At the time of the conference, merely eighteen months after
the rise of ISIS, the Institute of Middle East Studies in Lebanon had gathered
the proceedings of nearly thirty such conferences.[32]

Pervasive buzzwords in these conferences are "coexistence," "reform," "renewal of discourse," "moderacy," "tolerance," "median way," and "equal citizenship." Critical revision of school curricula in the Arab world is also a
major focus. The motivation of most of these conferences seems quite clearly
to be a deep sense of embarrassment with the behavior of ISIS in the name
of Islam, and thus the principal goal of these initiatives is to rescue the
"image" of Islam—not a surprising phenomenon in honor-shame societies.
A massive focus is on reforming Islam's "religious discourse," the development of new school curricula promoting the moderate way in religion,
and the centralization of the process of issuing legal decisions (fatwas) as
means to preventing the emergence of "deviant" forms of Islam. These conferences go so far as to state clearly that armed jihad is not a legitimate form
of Islamic political expression, that the concept of a caliphate has become
redundant in the contemporary world, and that most modern legal systems
are not at odds fundamentally with Islamic law (shari'a).

These ideas and positions have always existed in some sense, but the
novelty is in their current embrace and public declaration by mainstream
Muslim organizations and scholars from across the world. Individual
Muslim scholars here and there may state certain positions, and these
may be remembered to represent some stream in Muslim society. But
when a large enough and varied enough representative sample of Muslim
scholars throughout the Muslim world agree on a theological position,
on the interpretation of a particular verse of the Qur'an, or on a common

---

a think tank exploring the intersection of religion and politics that I cofounded with social
scientist and political analyst Ziya Meral and Islam scholar John Azumah in 2015.

[32]Martin Accad, "ISIS and the Future of Islam," The Institute of Middle East Studies, November
6, 2015, imes.blog/2015/11/06/isis-and-the-future-of-islam.

understanding of a specific legal issue, Muslims call this *ijmā'*—"consensus." *Ijmā'* in Islam is not taken lightly. It is one of the core principles of Islamic jurisprudence, setting a precedent in the fields of exegesis and law, and it may form the common ground and new starting point for the relationship between the Muslim ummah (community) and non-Muslims. What ISIS has been doing for the Muslim world over the past three years is what certain historical practices of the Catholic Church, such as selling indulgences or real estate in heaven, did for the Christian world. Of course, there are always at least two ways of interpreting historical events. For some in the Catholic Church, the Lutheran reaction is viewed historically as having led to a disastrous split within the church. But from another perspective, the Protestant Reformation and the Counter Reformation it provoked within the Catholic Church are seen in retrospect both as blessings and as events that had to happen for the church to be propelled into a new era of enlightenment.

I do not wish to overstate the parallel, and I would certainly refrain from either demonizing Catholicism or idealizing Protestantism. What I am trying to illustrate, however, is the fact that Islam, like every other religion— including Christianity—goes through stages of transformation and change throughout history that are deeply significant and in retrospect will be viewed as having been radically "reorienting" for Islamic theology. I believe that the reactions in the Muslim world that ISIS has been provoking are at that level of significance. The reinterpretations of qur'anic verses and renewed understandings of legal and theological concepts are not new. Just as Protestant Reformers rediscovered notions of salvation by grace from patristic writings (for example, from Augustine) and refocused them to become central in the Protestant theological system, Muslim scholars everywhere have been recovering more balanced and moderate meanings for qur'anic verses concerning jihad and armed combat and for theological, legal, and political concepts, such as the *khilāfa*, the Islamic state, or the instructions of shari'a with regard to the ordering of relationships with non-Muslims. Having observed reactions to ISIS within the Muslim world, we now move to the implications of ISIS's behavior on non-Muslim communities in the Muslim world.

RELIGIOUS "MINORITIES" AND THE
RISING TIDE OF THE "SILENT MAJORITY"

In many ways, the Huntington thesis does not bode well for religious groups that represent numeric minorities within any civilization. Just as Muslims currently living within countries belonging to "Western civilization" feel threatened or under scrutiny because of their religion, many Arab Christians have a long-standing and complex sense of a lack of belonging within the geographical areas that have been their home for nearly two thousand years. Is there a way, from this perspective, to reframe the conversation about the place and role of Arab Christians in the Middle East? Can we even consider the possibility of working toward a paradigm shift in our thinking about where we as Christians belong and who our allies are? Based on Huntington, it would appear that we are condemned to always consider Muslims as our enemies or at least as wholly other, as those among whom we will never really belong.

But could it be possible that the rise of a criminal and repulsive group like ISIS may actually provoke such a strong reaction in the Muslim world that new alliances may form between religiously moderate peoples who, although they do not share the same religion, nevertheless share the same culture? This may be happening even now, both in the Muslim world and outside of it, as I have argued above. The paradigm shift that may help Christians in the Middle East view themselves once more as active and significant contributors to the building and development of the societies in which they live needs to come from social anthropology.

In 2014, Najib George Awad, Syrian theologian and critic at Hartford Seminary, alarmed by the marginalization that Christians in Syria were beginning to feel, published an article in the mainstream Lebanese daily newspaper *Al-Mustaqbal* titled "On the 'Protection of Minorities' and Christians in the Syrian Question."[33] In this article, Awad reframes our understanding of term *minority* by expounding upon the definition used by French social anthropologists Gilles Deleuze and Félix Guattari. Along with these scholars, Awad rejects the definition of the term *minority* as a static ontological descriptor,

---

[33]Najib George Awad, "On the 'Protection of Minorities' and Christians in the Syrian Question," *Al-Mustaqbal*, accessed October 16, 2016, www.almustaqbal.com/v4/Article.aspx?Type =np&Articleid=604364.

arguing instead that it refers to the status that a group of people attain as a result of the process of "minoritization" imposed on them, either actively or passively, from the outside. The minoritization process is passive when a group chooses to define itself, often on ethical grounds, in opposition and contrast to a perceived social majority. An active process of minoritization takes place when a leading political force views anyone opposing its policies as traitors and unworthy of being part of the national fabric. Awad uses this lens to argue that in the Syrian context all those who have opposed the Assad regime over the past fifty years have been subjected to minoritization regardless of their sectarian affiliation as Christians (a numeric minority), Alawites (who belong to the same sect as the Assad family), or even Sunnis (a vast numeric majority, yet the most minoritized politically under Assad). In the same way, an oppressive political regime will apply the process of "majoritization" on any individual or group—with any religious or ethnic affiliation—that will support its policies. Such groups and individuals will receive disproportionate favors in that system irrespective of their identification with a numerically minor or major group within the social fabric.

Based on these definitions of *minority* and *majority*, I would argue that we must work toward a paradigm shift in self-perception as a new starting point for the Middle Eastern church's missional thinking in the context of Islam. If Arab Christians begin to reject this minoritization imposed on them both by those who mean well and wish to protect them from outside forces as well as by those who mean them harm and want to make them feel as outsiders in the region, then they may begin to reintegrate as an essential part of the social fabric once again.

The principal objector in this process may be the Christian community itself. But within the oppressive societies in which Christians live, I believe the church is called to work hand in hand in solidarity with others who refuse to be connected with those who use religious fanaticism, extremism, and violence as a means of minoritizing those different from them. Religious fanatics may claim to represent the majority and the only legitimate expression of Islam. But the strong reaction they are currently provoking within the mainstream Muslim world is an opportunity for the church to reframe the conversation and work toward the rise of a moral—though "silent"—majority within our societies, people who would see their faith as an inspiration for good and openness to others rather than for violent ascendency to power and the building of a religiously exclusivist social order.

I would argue, therefore, that both for the numerically minor Arab church and for the increasingly minor church in the West, the future of mission lies neither in a triumphalistic and increasingly militant self-affirmation against the current tides of religious ascent nor in the growing affirmation of their minority status. Rather, the future of vibrant and fruitful mission lies in the global church's ability to embrace its position as a shrinking numeric minority—increasingly becoming part of a silent majority throughout the world—made up of people who believe their faith should be a source of love, tolerance, and embrace of others rather than a source of violence, extremism, and exclusion. In the following missiological sections, I will consider how the church might maintain this vibrant witness to the scandalous message of Jesus while at the same time embracing its place within this silent majority.

MISSIOLOGICAL IMPLICATIONS

In the preceding sections we have observed the potential power that may visit the church when it ceases to align with monochromatic political visions of the world. When the focus is taken off stereotypes driven by fear and returned to God's hopeful mission to individual human beings in their diversity, the global church can then reclaim its missional vision.

In order to recover its vibrant missional vision, the church needs to go through a paradigm shift in self-perception. Instead of a triumphalistic militancy or a self-protective "minority complex," the church globally needs to rediscover its transformative role as Christ's body—confident in its Lord, yet comfortable in a post-Christendom world, which is closer than ever to the pre-Constantinian, pre-Christendom world. In the twenty-first century, this will consist in the church embracing its position as a shrinking numeric minority that is increasingly becoming part of a silent majority throughout the world. But is Jesus still of any significance when a more existential, low-boundaries approach to religion is taken? What does a kerygmatic, suprareligious approach to mission have to offer our contemporary missiological thinking? The latter two concepts—kerygmatic and suprareligious—are the two angles that I intend to use in this concluding section to develop a new framework for a missiological vision in the twenty-first century.

MISSION IN A MULTIDIRECTIONAL WORLD

In his civilizational interpretation of the world, Huntington suggests that in the twentieth century our world "moved from a phase dominated by the unidirectional impact of one civilization on all others to one of intense, sustained, and multidirectional interactions among all civilizations."[34] The evidence seems to suggest that we should think of mission in a similar way. In 2003, Peruvian missiologist Samuel Escobar expressed this idea when he spoke of mission as "the Gospel from everywhere to everyone."[35] Noting that two-thirds of the world's Christians are now located in Latin America, Africa, and Asia, Escobar noticed that global mission was moving in the same direction as Huntington's theory of civilizational influence.

The West is no longer the single source of the church's missionary efforts to the rest of the world. Instead, the growth of the missionary movement from Latin America, Africa, and Asia is now well established globally. With the effective ideological collapse of Western Christendom, in which Western missionaries took to the mission field a gospel clothed in Western culture, where does this leave the global church in terms of the nature of its gospel message, carried now through the multiple cultural identities of its messengers?

There is much evidence to suggest that a large proportion of global mission is in fact emulating the methods and characteristics of its Western parent. Missionaries from Latin America, Africa, and Asia, being themselves the descendants of those converted under Western missionaries, tend mostly to spread a form of the Christian faith inherited from the West. And even among missionaries less influenced by the West, the method of proclaiming a gospel clothed in the culture of its proclaimer is an entrapment hard to break away from. We should not be naive in believing that the gospel can exist in a vacuum, bereft of some sort of cultural clothing. But there is a significant difference between missionaries who are aware of the cultural

---

[34]Huntington, *Clash of Civilizations*, 53.
[35]Samuel Escobar, *The New Global Mission: The Gospel from Everywhere to Everyone* (Downers Grove, IL: InterVarsity Press, 2003).

trappings of their message and those who are blind to this fact, believing that there can be only one message and that theirs is identical to the gospel of Christ in all of its dimensions. What should be, then, the nature of the gospel proclamation in the twenty-first century?

A LOW-BOUNDARIES, SUPRARELIGIOUS
APPROACH TO THE *MISSIO DEI*

I have suggested[36] that Christ's proclamation of the gospel is best described as "suprareligious." In John 3, Jesus challenges Nicodemus's assumption regarding entrance into the kingdom of God (which Nicodemus sees as inherited through the seed of Abraham) by inviting him to be "born again," this time from above and by the Spirit, not from below or by the flesh. "Flesh gives birth to flesh, but the Spirit gives birth to spirit" (Jn 3:6). In the same way, in John 4 Jesus meets the Samaritan woman at the location representing the core of her religious identity: the well of her "father Jacob." Once more he affirms that the cultural spring of religion cannot quench human spiritual thirst. In response to her protests and attempts to maintain the sanctity of tradition, he replies, "Everyone who drinks this water will be thirsty again, but whoever drinks the water I give them will never thirst. Indeed, the water I give them will become in them a spring of water welling up to eternal life" (Jn 4:13-14).

Jesus did not reject the legitimacy of the cultures and traditions associated with religion. He simply affirmed that these dimensions of faith were not essential to being part of the kingdom of God. He did not negate the law of Moses, but in his rhetorical constructions—"You have heard that it was said. . . . But I tell you" (see the Sermon on the Mount in Matthew 5–7)—he brought his hearers back to the essence of the law and God's core intent for it. Likewise, he rattled the Jewish interpretation of the sanctity of the Sabbath by proclaiming that "the Sabbath was made for man, not man for the Sabbath" (Mk 2:27), reaffirming the absolute importance of regular rest for God's creation and dismantling the legalism attached to it, which sought to transform a religious practice into a doorway for salvation.

---

[36]See especially Martin Accad, "Christian Attitudes Toward Islam and Muslims: A Kerygmatic Approach," in *Toward Respectful Understanding and Witness Among Muslims: Essays in Honor of J. Dudley Woodberry*, ed. Evelyne A. Reisacher et al. (Pasadena, CA: William Carey Library, 2012).

Peter understood that Jesus shattered the ethnic and cultural boundaries of the gospel when he affirmed to the culturally and ethnically diverse readers of his first letter,

> But you are a chosen people, a royal priesthood, a holy nation, God's special possession, that you may declare the praises of him who called you out of darkness into his wonderful light. Once you were not a people, but now you are the people of God; once you had not received mercy, but now you have received mercy. (1 Pet 2:9-10)

With this incredible proclamation, Peter was not replacing Judaism with Christianity as an exclusivist alternative religion. Rather, he was reaffirming the essence of the gospel that Jesus had proclaimed: the grace and mercy of God are not encapsulated in any religious tradition or culture but rather centered on the values and culture of the kingdom of God as expressed in the teaching and life of Jesus, the manifestation of God's presence, a presence maintained permanently through the gift of the Holy Spirit across both historical epochs and geographical boundaries.

ADOPTING A KERYGMATIC MISSIOLOGY

I hope to have demonstrated through this analysis of the world and of Islam the radical new reality confronting the global church today. The world has moved far beyond the monodirectional focus of mission that pervaded the colonial era. The church has also learned that the classic dichotomy between a verbal and social gospel is no longer helpful. The sort of Christ-followers that the church needs today are those who live their lives in mission within churches that exist in mission to the world. As Islam continues to go through radical transformation, developing a post-Islamist vision of politics and society, the post-Christendom church likewise needs to embrace a suprareligious identity and message. In this suprareligious stance, the church expresses its mission in what I call "kerygmatic missiology." This missiology is best represented in the radical mandate of Jesus Christ expressed in Luke 4:18-19:

> The Spirit of the Lord is on me, because he has anointed me to proclaim good news to the poor. He has sent me to proclaim [*kēryxai*] freedom for the prisoners and recovery of sight for the blind, to set the oppressed free, to proclaim [*kēryxai*] the year of the Lord's favor.

At this critical juncture in the launch of his ministry, Jesus identified his kerygma (through the verbal form *kēryxai*) as both the powerful act of liberation for prisoners, the sick, and the oppressed as well as the radical proclamation of the good news to the poor, who have entered the year of the Lord's favor. What does this same kerygma look like in the expression of the suprareligious church?

Kerygmatic missiology is passionate about God's mission in the world. As we interact with members of a religion that holds a comprehensive view of the world, twenty-first-century followers of Jesus need to live life as mission in the world. The suprareligious church abandons the dichotomy between the secular and the sacred. As post-Islamist Islam establishes itself globally, there will be less and less space for classic secularism (*laïcité* in French). Yet at the same time, as religion gains prominence in the public space, it will not do for the church to be more "religious." Only a suprareligious gospel will be able to undertake an authentic transformation of society. A more religious church will simply blend into the mainstream, leaving little impact on the world.

Kerygmatic missiology is thoroughly Christ centered. As religion and religious pluralism increase in the world, the impact of the church's message will decrease when it concentrates on Christianity and will increase when it emphasizes Christ. But if religion is abandoned by the church, what will take its place? The post-Christendom church needs to return to its pre-Christendom state. Before Christianity became the religion of empire, being a *Christianos* meant being "of Christ"—in other words, belonging to Christ. Being a Christian in the New Testament sense had nothing to do with opting for one religious alternative over another.

As Christians engage with Muslims today, they should not approach these relationships as though entering a competition. Approaching conversation with Muslims from a Christ-centered rather than a Christianity-centered starting point is extremely liberating. We can relinquish any aggressive approach that causes us to deconstruct Islam in order to legitimize the reconstruction of Christianity. When our message is Christ, we can simply proclaim him as the one who transforms reality, delivers us from religion—any religion—and invites us to be reborn into the community of God's Spirit. The gospel message as Christianity will fatally and uncontrollably swerve into a conflict of religions, but the church will soar above warring faiths as it learns to catch the wave of the suprareligious message of Christ.

Kerygmatic missiology is prophetic. Following Walter Brueggemann's definition of *prophetic* as the dual project of "criticizing" and "energizing,"[37] kerygmatic missiology needs to be prophetic. Christ's followers in the twenty-first century need to deploy a sharp sense of criticism, both of self and of society, as they cast an alternative vision that dismantles the dominant religious consciousness (Brueggemann calls it the "royal consciousness").[38] When political leaders who represent our religious views and positions come to power, we can become quickly carried away with excitement at the thought of Christianity rising to a place of greater power in society. Likewise there are times when our political leaders betray Christian religious ideals, and this can make us fall into despair.

History teaches us, however, that more religion does not lead to more justice and equality in society. Religion-driven societies tend to be co-opted by leaders who blend politics and religion in order to keep themselves in power and hide their own corruption and lack of morality. A prophetic church that fights corruption and stands up for the poor and the oppressed will pay a high price for its critique of government. But only when it learns to stand with the marginalized and poor will the church be able to offer an alternative divine vision in a twenty-first-century world.

Kerygmatic missiology is intentional in its witness to the gospel. Dangers exist in religious societies co-opted by religiously inclined political leaders, but the gospel also risks being compromised in religiously pluralistic societies. This reality will only be overcome by followers of Christ who are intentional in their witness to the good news of the kingdom inaugurated by Jesus. Issues-driven Christianity politicizes the gospel. Only a church that understands the essence of the good news as an invitation for the world to fellowship with God through Christ will be able to shine as light and provide the right level of saltiness in twenty-first-century societies.

Kerygmatic missiology is above all about hope. I have argued above that one of the deepest needs of the world today is hope. Hopelessness has been clearly identified as the primary cause of religious extremism and as the

---

[37]Walter Brueggemann, *The Prophetic Imagination*, 2nd ed. (Minneapolis: Fortress Press, 2001), 4.
[38]Ibid., 39.

most powerful tool in the recruitment strategies of religiously violent, nihil-istic movements like ISIS. Considering this, what does the Bible have to offer as a remedy? Hopelessness often leads to passivity and a lack of appetite for life, and religious extremism provides an active program that makes false promises about meaning in the present life and in the life to come. But bib-lical hope is *active* hope; it is never passive. For disciples of Jesus, it is the basis of personal responsibility. The nature of Christ's call is both simple and overwhelming. It is simple inasmuch as it means following in the footsteps of Jesus. Yet it is overwhelming in that Jesus' life and teaching were and continue to be utterly countercultural.

TOWARD A BIBLICAL THEOLOGY OF HOPE

Jesus' mandate is a unique blend of practical and verbal comfort and liberation: to proclaim the dawning of a new age in which liberation from sin and the gift of life are offered to all those who will accept Christ's divine grace. This good news goes hand in hand with a radical lifestyle of solidarity with the poor, the sick, and the oppressed. As valuable as these externals are, if the discipleship mandate ends with externals, it would not differ much from the best of hu-manitarian or religious ideals. The uniqueness of the Christ mandate is therefore seen more in its extent than in its nature, as demonstrated in John 15:13: "Greater love has no one than this: to lay down one's life for one's friends." Paul, in Romans 5:7-8, further expands on this statement of Jesus when he says, "Very rarely will anyone die for a righteous person, though for a good person someone might possibly dare to die. But God demonstrates his own love for us in this: While we were still sinners, Christ died for us."

We must move away from theoretical conversations about the mere plau-sibility of Jesus' death on the cross. The message of the New Testament would snatch us away from abstract discussions about the cross as simply some event in the past. It invites us instead to embrace the cross as a way of being. We are called to live a life of self-givingness, not just for our friends or family members, nor even for members of our broader tribe, but also for enemies who would wish us dead. This is the foundation of a revolutionary project that alone can bring back hope in the wild and violent world in which we live.

2
....

The Western Frontier

Euro-Islam and the Remaking of Global Faith

Philip Jenkins

If there is a single point I would like to make about understanding Islam, it would be this: historically, Islam is as diverse as Christianity. It has a comparably broad range of manifestations, a like diversity of beliefs, practices, and speculations. And as in Christianity, our sense of this diversity is masked somewhat by the tendency to demarcate certain forms of the faith as "not truly Islamic." Like Christianity, Islam changes over time, and often does so in response to secular changes in the societies in which it operates, changes that might be social, political, cultural, or economic. Once those changes have become established, later generations assume that the recently transformed faith represents an original pristine reality, the way the faith was always meant to be.

I make this point because Islam presently faces a radically new setting that is certain to cause major changes in religious faith and practice, and by that I mean the growing presence of Muslim populations in Europe. Although Europe is home to only a tiny proportion of the world's Muslims, these communities have a significance far beyond their numbers. Quite apart from any discussion of terrorist threats, Europe's Islamic communities are the setting for far-reaching social and cultural experiments, which are already transforming the practice of faith in majority Muslim nations. The demographic aspect is especially important in igniting a far-reaching transformation. Intellectually, too, Europe represents something unprecedented in the historical Muslim experience—namely, a free space where believers from all nations can meet and interact. Sometimes those exchanges have produced baneful extremism and militancy, but other aspects have been far more encouraging. At every point, these developments are of critical interest to European Christian churches. If I may raise a sensitive point, I would be extremely cautious about any claims that are made about Christian expansion among Muslims, as I see little convincing evidence of any serious growth of this kind. The Christian expansion that can be reliably observed is overwhelmed by the figures for Muslim evangelism among former Christians. What we can hope for, though, is the expansion of forms of Islam with which Christian communities can relate easily and congenially, finding areas of commonality in practice and social outreach.

NUMBERS

The statistics for European Islam are highly controversial, and we should always beware of wild claims presented for political ends. Some of the best evidence we have presently comes from the Pew Research Center, which suggested a figure of 44 million European Muslims as of 2015. That initially struck me as very high, until I realized exactly what was the area under discussion; namely, the whole of Europe including the very substantial communities in Russia. Over a third of Europe's Muslim population represents old-established communities in the southeastern quadrant of the continent, in Albania, Bulgaria, and the nations that comprised the former Yugoslavia, together with the island of Cyprus. Within the EU, from Ireland to the Carpathians, we are probably speaking of some 20 million people. Europe's Muslim population has been rising at about a percentage point a decade, from 4 percent in 1990 to 6 percent in 2010, and a probable 8 percent in 2030.[1]

I should say that defining *Muslims* for these purposes is far from easy, and this is not merely statistical nitpicking, but rather gets to essential questions of cultural identity. Imagine two young men, both born in Europe and speaking only the language of their country of birth: call them Tony and Tariq. Tony, of white European stock, was baptized Catholic but very rarely sets foot inside the precincts of a church, except possibly for a wedding or

---

[1]Conrad Hackett, "5 Facts About the Muslim Population in Europe," Pew Research Center, July 19, 2016, www.pewresearch.org/fact-tank/2016/07/19/5-facts-about-the-muslim-population-in -europe.

funeral, and his knowledge of Christian doctrine or history is close to non-existent. Tariq is of ethnic Pakistani or Moroccan origin, but his connection to the faith of Islam is just as tenuous. He drinks, fails to observe Ramadan, is not careful about observing dietary laws, and is as sexually opportunistic as Tony. He has a vague idea that his father attends a mosque but is not sure where it is. Tariq is, in short, anything but a good Muslim.

In compiling religious statistics, however, agencies would almost certainly count an "ethnic" individual like Tariq as a Muslim, and part of Europe's Muslim population. This casual attitude toward religious classification would not matter if agencies applied the same standards across the board, but they do not. Tony, our hypothetical man of Catholic origins, might be counted as a Christian in some statistics but not others. When estimating religious communities, both agencies and scholars tend to accept the very broad definition of Islam offered by that religion itself, which defines as a Muslim anyone brought up in a Muslim community, or whose father is a Muslim. (Honest demographers speak more vaguely of counting "potential Muslims.") Christians, in contrast, are defined in terms of self-identification or religious practice—for instance, by regular church attendance. *Muslim* is an ethnic label loosely applied; *Christian* is a religious classification that demands some knowledge of the individual's personal belief system.

In many statistical analyses, the word *Muslim* is actually shorthand for any member of ethnic communities established in Europe quite recently, and drawn from African or Asian nations where Islam represents the default religion. For my present purposes, the existence of a great many "Tariqs" is critical in pointing to populations who might easily be drawn into various versions of Islam, from militant to accommodating.

FERTILITY AND FAITH

The other danger in assessing religious statistics is in projecting present trends, and assuming they will carry on indefinitely as they are at present. European Muslims demonstrate a very common pattern in the demographics of migration. People who migrate tend to be young and fertile, and their birth rates are higher than those of old-stock residents. After a generation or so, migrant rates fall to something like the existing norm, and that is true regardless of faith. A growth of individualism and feminism would

radically change demographic projections, since Muslim women dedicated
to professional and personal fulfillment are much less likely to want large
families, helping to bring ethnic birth rates in line with old-stock European
figures. Education and literacy—especially for girls and women—also contribute mightily to lowering birth rates.

There is no such thing as a "Muslim birth rate," since actual figures
depend wholly on social and economic settings. Moreover, some of the
lowest fertility rates in the Muslim world are found in its western regions,
those that have the closest relationships to Europe, whether through migration patterns or mass media. While Italians worry about being swamped
by Albanian Muslims, the Albanian fertility rate now stands at an extraor-
dinarily low 1.5 and is falling precipitously; Bosnia's is 1.27.[2]

Partly, migrants who travel to a new land rarely sever their ties to their
homelands and families, and that is especially true in an age of easy travel
by air and road. Muslims who come to Europe transmit attitudes, customs,
and tastes to their homelands, where they reshape old-established patterns
of culture and belief. That pattern is reinforced by the very widespread
power of Western media: just look at the satellite dishes that blanket the
skylines of so many Middle Eastern cities. And those trends certainly
affect family structures and fertility. We note the astonishing decline in
birth rates now in progress across much of North Africa, in the regions
most closely tied to Europe. Surely, here, we see the impact of new Western-
derived gender attitudes. The change is fascinating, because smaller family
size in a community often correlates to long-term secularization. If current
trends continue, it would be only a few years before all the nations of the
Maghreb—Algeria, Morocco, and Tunisia—reached the very low Spanish
or Italian birth rates, and this region would find it ever harder to serve as
a source of migrants.

Even if Islam presently threatens (or promises) to overwhelm Europe,
then Europe could well, in its turn, transform Islam. Instead of Europe
merging with the Arab Maghreb, we might equally imagine the Maghreb
itself joining the southern portions of Europe.

[2]"The Future of the Global Muslim Population: Region: Europe," Pew Research Center, January 27,
2011, www.pewforum.org/2011/01/27/future-of-the-global-muslim-population-regional-europe.

A New Islam

Our first impression of the impact of migration is therefore to stress Europeanization, however counterintuitive that might seem. Of course, that is only part of the story, as migration changes religion in other ways. To understand this, it is helpful to look at the characteristic forms of religion that prevailed in the countries from which many Muslim migrants came, in South Asia or North Africa. To use a term that might seem inappropriate, those forms may strike us as "Catholic" or even medieval, a point made by a fine scholar like Olivier Roy. In books like *Holy Ignorance*, Roy relates global religious change to such megatrends as mass migration, urbanization, and modernization.[3] He stresses how deeply integrated Islam was in traditional societies like Morocco or Pakistan, where faith was tied to particular communities and clan structures, to shrines, saints, and sacred landscapes, and to a sacred calendar. All were severed with the migration to the West, creating an Islam that was suddenly and painfully deterritorialized.

While early immigrants kept their personal memories alive, none of these traditions was available to younger generations born in Europe. Like their Christian counterparts, they lost their roots, all moorings of sacred time and place. As Roy remarks, "The religion of their parents is linked to a culture that is no longer theirs."[4] Yet while losing traditional culture and faith, they find little appeal in the materialist values offered by their new host countries. Muslims, like Christians, face an age-old dilemma: how can they sing the Lord's song in a strange country? The young respond by rejecting both the lost traditional culture and the new Western alternative. They turn instead to the apparent certainties of a universalized or globalized Islam, which in practice offers the sternest and most demanding standards of the Wahhabis or Salafists. But in return, believers receive a vision of themselves as the heroes of a glorious historical narrative, in which faith defeats the temporary and illusory triumph of disbelief and paganism.

We could, tragically, cite countless examples of this approach, but I just mention one recent case, namely that of Anjem Choudary, recently

---

[3]Olivier Roy, *Holy Ignorance: When Religion and Culture Part Ways* (New York: Columbia University Press, 2010).
[4]Olivier Roy, "Born Again to Kill," *Sign and Sight*, August 4, 2005, www.signandsight.com/features /296.html.

convicted in England for his loyalty to the Islamic State. Choudary—who is, incidentally, London-born—issued a series of hair-raising propaganda statements advocating violent jihad. Among other things, these proclaim that

> we don't have any borders, my dear Muslims. It is about time we resumed conquering for the sake of Allah. Next time when your child is at school and the teacher says "what do you want when you grow up, what is your ambition?" they should say to dominate the whole world by Islam, including Britain, that is my ambition.[5]

Although presented as pure and exclusive Islamic truth, these ideologies are in fact quite recent concoctions that would have made little sense to most Muslims only a century or so ago. This seemingly ancient version of faith is a quintessentially postmodern response to social dislocation and destabilization, and it is presented through strictly modern electronic media. The roots of Islamist terrorism in Europe are thus easy to comprehend.

THE NEW THINKERS

Extremism in European Islam owes much to globalization, in the sense of new media, wider access to news and information, and much greater opportunities to travel and communicate, and to explore alternative ideas. Yet exactly the same forces have inspired Muslim reformers, who see heady prospects in Europe's intellectual freedom and whose ideas are transmitted back to the Muslim nations. I offer a very mixed picture. We can find plenty of thinkers and activists who seem to foreshadow such changes—what Westerners misleadingly call an Islamic Reformation—but those figures would themselves be the first to admit that they face an uphill struggle. Tellingly, some of the most daring statements of liberalism and accommodation have been in furious and near-despairing response to grotesque terrorist atrocities.

Let me present the story in as balanced a way as I can. In an idealized future, Europe would play the same role for the Muslim world that the Netherlands did for Europe's Christian societies during the Enlightenment. In the century after 1660, the Netherlands represented liberated space where

---

[5]Jamie Grierson, Vikram Dodd, and Jason Rodrigues, "Anjem Choudary Convicted of Supporting Islamic State," *The Guardian*, August 16, 2016, www.theguardian.com/uk-news/2016/aug/16/anjem-choudary-convicted-of-supporting-islamic-state.

exiles could take refuge, truly radical ideas could be explored, and books of virtually any intellectual content could be safely published before being exported across the continent. It was the sort of society in which a radical skeptic like Baruch Spinoza could write without being executed.

Today, Europe provides territory in which scholars, Islamic and others, can perform on the Qur'an the same task of scholarly criticism and analysis that their predecessors did on Jewish and Christian scriptures. Many scholars recognize that the Qur'an, like the Christian Bible, is a text formed over a long historical period, drawing on diverse sources and influences: variant readings competed for authority until one final text achieved canonized form. Such an approach directly challenges the common view of a perfect Qur'an directly dictated to the prophet in the seventh century AD. One scholarly pioneer was Nasr Hamid Abu Zaid, whose innovative qur'anic studies led to his life being threatened in Egypt. He fled to the Netherlands, where he taught at Utrecht and Leiden until his death in 2010. France is the base for Syrian-born scholar Bassam Tahhan, who seeks a progressive and individualistic "Protestant Islam." He argues that

> to read the Koran rationally is to accept that the Koran is open [to interpretation] and has many meanings. The tradition regards the Koran as one-dimensional and fixed. This approach is not rationalist. To be a rationalist is to accept that each era, with its [particular] methods and discoveries, presents its own reading of the Koran, and this is the way it will be until the end of days.[6]

Another example would be the Iranian-born exile Kader Abdolah, who based himself in the Netherlands. Not only did he offer a bold translation of the Qur'an, but he took the extraordinary step of adding his own 115th sura to the collection, in order to portray the Prophet's death.[7] He also popularized his very human story of Muhammad in his novelistic *The Messenger*.[8]

---

[6]Bassam Tahhan, "Muslim Intellectual Calls for 'Protestant Islam,'" MEMRI (The Middle East Media Research Institute), Special Dispatch No. 1198, July 6, 2006, www.memri.org/report/en /print1734.htm.

[7]Claire Kodah Hazelton, "Rewriting the Qur'an: Kader Abdolah and His Controversial Interpretation of Islam's Holy Book," *The Guardian*, July 4, 2016, www.theguardian.com/books/2016/jul/04/ rewriting-the-quran-kader-abdolah-and-his-controversial-interpretation-of-islams-holy-book.

[8]Kader Abdolah, *The Messenger: A Tale Retold*, trans. Niusha and Nouri Nighting (Breda, Netherlands: World Editions, 2016).

Radical scholarly findings about the early history of Islam are popularized in books such as *The Rock*, a 2001 novel written by Iraqi Kanan Makiya in his London exile.[9] The book reconstructs a time in the seventh century when Islam, Judaism, and Christianity were virtually branches of one common faith. In this view, "Islam" as known by scholars through the centuries was invented long after Muhammad's time, and Muhammad's life and work were constructed retroactively. In the words of a British observer, the book is

> an attempt to smuggle the latest research on the Prophet Mohammed to an Arab audience. Censorship and the appeasing of Islamic fundamentalism means that historians tend to hide their work in obscure academic journals for fear of receiving the Rushdie treatment. Makiya believes their conclusions deserve a wider readership.[10]

And that goal can best be achieved from a European base. Though it might take decades for the results of such scholarship to have its full impact on ordinary believers, work of this kind should in the long run have an enormous impact on Muslim belief, and particularly the nature of scriptural authority.

ISLAMIC REFORMERS

Another central question is that of citizenship and national loyalty. Since earliest times, Muslim thinkers have assumed that the normal state of affairs for Muslims involves living in a society dominated by Islamic government and law, and radicals dream of returning to such conditions. Egyptian Sheikh Yusuf al-Qaradawi, an important if controversial thinker, wrote a book with the loaded title *On Law and the Jurisprudence of Muslim Minorities: The Life of Muslims in Other Societies*.[11] By implication, one either lives as a Muslim in a Muslim society or as a transient resident in an Other, presumably hostile community. From their experience in Europe, though, other thinkers ask what it means to live in a pluralist, multifaith society in which the government shows preference to no religion, treating all equally. In that

[9]Kanan Makiya, *The Rock: A Tale of Seventh-Century Jerusalem* (New York: Pantheon, 2001).
[10]Nick Cohen, "A Question of Faith," *The Guardian*, May 11, 2002, www.theguardian.com/politics/2002/may/12/politicalcolumnists.comment.
[11]Yusuf al-Qaradawi, *Fi Fiqh al-Aqalliyyat al-Muslimah: Hayat al-Muslimin wasat al-Mujtamaʿat al-ʾUkhra (On Law and the Jurisprudence of Muslim Minorities: The Life of Muslims in Other Societies)* (Cairo, Egypt: Dar El-Shuruk, 2001).

case, Muslims must accept a secular notion of citizenship, and in fact must learn to separate religious and secular loyalties and to recognize a firm distinction between mosque and state.

Europe now provides a base for several leading reformers who are exploring the implications for Islam of living in an advanced Western society. In practical terms, one of the most important for many years was Mustafa Cerić, the Islamic *Ra'īs al-ʿulamāʾ* (Grand Mufti) of Bosnia. He has worked diligently to promote understanding between Europe's Muslim, Jewish, and Christian leaders. Cerić also speaks forcefully to European Muslims, who face the twin seductions of secularism and Islamist extremism. Muslims, he says, must reject any view that "the only hope is in the Muslim past as a way of life and a goal of history."[12] In words that apply across religions, "he urges Muslim migrants to Western Europe to follow three fundamental laws: learn the language of your host country; obey its laws; and try and do something good for that country."[13]

And there are many others, chiefly academics. One of the pioneers was Bassam Tibi, who in 1992 actually coined the phrase Euro-Islam, on the analogy of the Euro-Communism that had been so much discussed in previous decades. Prior to his retirement in 2009, Tibi urged Muslims to accept what he terms the *Leitkultur* (the leading or guiding culture), which in the European context means the Enlightenment-derived idea of the dignity and freedom of the individual.[14] For Tibi, this idea is

> based on the foundation of a democratic community whose members are bound together through a collective identity as citizens of that community. Such a collective identity—in the sense of the French *citoyenité* (citizenship)— stands above religious identity. Religion may, of course, be practiced privately, but in public only citizenship counts. Such a concept would unite Muslims with non-Muslims.[15]

Once European Muslims accept this core value, he suggests, other conflicts—for instance over free speech issues—can be resolved through debate

---

[12]Mustafa Cerić, "A Declaration of European Muslims," *Radio Free Europe Radio Liberty*, March 16, 2006, www.rferl.org/a/1066751.html.

[13]Philip Jenkins, "Revival in the Balkans," *Christian Century* 131, no. 14 (July 9, 2014): 45.

[14]Philip Jenkins, *God's Continent: Christianity, Islam, and Europe's Religious Crisis* (Oxford: Oxford University Press, 2007), 141.

[15]Quoted in Jenkins, *God's Continent*, 141.

and compromise. Recently, though, Tibi has become far more pessimistic about the hopes for progress in religious matters. Following the mass sexual assaults in Cologne this past New Year, Tibi wrote despairingly:

> As a Syrian from Damascus, I have been living in Germany since 1962, and I know: Patriarchally minded men from a misogynistic culture cannot be integrated. A European, civil Islam that the Islamic functionaries in these parts have rejected as Euro-Islam, would be the alternative. At the present time, it doesn't have a chance. My teacher Max Horkheimer called Europe "an island of freedom in an ocean of dictatorships." Today I see this freedom endangered.[16]

THE CASE OF TARIQ RAMADAN

Reformist ideas find a prominent face in Tariq Ramadan, who in recent years has been widely seen as the prophet of a new Euro-Islam. *Time* magazine has named him one of the "hundred most important intellectuals of the 21st century," while the *Washington Post* calls him a "Muslim Martin Luther."[17] Ramadan is a very controversial figure and presently finds it all but impossible to find public platforms to speak in France. His critics portray him as a sinister ally of the hard-line extremists who has nevertheless succeeded in winning the favor of gullible Westerners. The hard-line connections can in fact be traced quite easily, though it is an open question whether they detract from the content of his message.

Tariq Ramadan's family origins give him immense prestige among traditional and conservative Muslims. His grandfather, Hassan al-Banna, actually founded the Muslim Brotherhood, and his father, Said Ramadan, carried the organization's activities into Europe, establishing the Munich mosque that would become a center of Islamist radicalism in Germany. (Much has been written about the circumstances surrounding the creation of this mosque in the early 1960s.)[18] Tariq himself was born in Switzerland

---

[16]Bassam Tibi, "Junge Männer, die die Kultur der Gewalt mitbringen," *Welt* 4, May 8, 2016, www.welt .de/debatte/kommentare/article155134929/Junge-Maenner-die-die-Kultur-der-Gewalt-mitbringen .html. English translation in "Bassam Tibi: Euro-Islam Doesn't Have a Chance," *Gates of Vienna*, May 13, 2016, gatesofvienna.net/2016/05/bassam-tibi-euro-islam-doesnt-have-a-chance/.

[17]Paul Donnelly, "The Ban on a Muslim Scholar," *Washington Post*, August 27, 2004, www .washingtonpost.com/wp-dyn/articles/A40222-2004Aug27.html.

[18]Jenkins, *God's Continent*, 142.

in 1962, and he came to prominence in the mid-1990s. According to his critics, he personified the Muslim Brotherhood strategy to gain influence in Europe. For those foes, Tariq Ramadan's writings and public pronouncements almost have to be decoded, since he uses such different approaches for different audiences. To Westerners, he sounds like a breath of liberalizing fresh air; to Muslim audiences, though, he presents a more familiar Brotherhood message. Critics accuse him of adopting the strategy of *taqiyya*, dissembling, or double-talk for infidels. Ramadan remains close to the extreme and confrontational Yusuf al-Qaradawi and has written favorable introductions for his books.

Having said this, Ramadan has in recent years called explicitly for fundamental revisions of Muslim political and social assumptions, putting forth ideas that will find a large audience precisely because of his traditionalist credentials, and he describes his own ideological stance as Salafist reformism. This initially sounds as if he is aligning himself with the most committed extremists and fundamentalists, but rather implies a stripping away of the doctrines that have surrounded Islamic teaching since the time of Muhammad. A Christian equivalent might be the social progressive who claims to be a fundamentalist in the sense of returning to the pure words of Jesus, minus later accretions.

Whatever the label, Ramadan, like Tibi, explores questions of identity and loyalty in a quite innovative way, arguing that Western Muslims "are at home, and should not only say so but feel so."[19] Muslims should feel comfortable being citizens of their particular nations: "Muslim identity is a response to the question: 'Why?', while national identity is a response to the question: 'How?', and it would be absurd and stupid to expect geographical attachment to resolve the question of being."[20] Ramadan himself has written that "in my memories, I'm Egyptian; in my citizenship, I'm Swiss; in my belief, I'm Muslim."[21] Critically, he feels that Muslims must abandon the ancient division between *dar al-Islam* and *dar al-harb*, the world of Islam and the world of war. Instead, the non-Muslim world should be seen as the *dar al-da'wa*, the

---

[19] Tariq Ramadan, *Western Muslims and the Future of Islam* (Oxford: Oxford University Press, 2004), 53.

[20] Ibid., 93.

[21] Martin Beglinger, "Under Suspicion," August 2, 2006, www.signandsight.com/features/586.html; quoted in Jenkins, *God's Continent*, 143.

world of proclamation or of calling to God, in which Muslims should seek to spread their teachings by example. And once they do spread their views, the results would by no means involve a denial of Europe's Enlightenment tradition. After all, "In medieval Europe, Islam contributed significantly to the formation of rationalist, secular and modern thought."[22] Taken together, this looks like a recipe for a new pluralistic European Islam that fully acknowledges the realities of living in the contemporary multifaith West.

Ramadan argues further that this quest for a reconstructed identity represents a powerful new movement in the Muslim world:

> More and more young people and intellectuals are actively looking for a way to live in harmony with their faith while participating in the societies that are their societies, whether they like it or not. . . . Far from media attention, going through the risks of a process of maturation that is necessarily slow, they are drawing the shape of European and American Islam: faithful to the principles of Islam, dressed in European and American cultures, and definitively rooted in Western societies. This grassroots movement will soon exert considerable influence over worldwide Islam: in view of globalization and the Westernization of the world, these are the same questions as those already being raised from Morocco to Indonesia.[23]

Even if we hold the darkest views of Ramadan's secret intentions, the mass circulation of his ideas cannot fail to generate debate about how the children of immigrants can live authentically Muslim lives in a secular West.

GERMAN VOICES

To understand the breadth of attitudes toward Islam today, I will take the case of one pivotal country, namely Germany. The virtue of doing this is that the range of voices here is truly diverse, and moreover the names are not well-known in North America.

We might look, for instance, at Mouhanad Khorchide, the Palestinian-born professor of Islamic Education at the University of Münster. He is the author of a series of books with titles that demand our attention, including *Islam Is Compassion: The Foundations of a Modern Religion* (2012); *Sharia—The Misunderstood God: The Way to a Modern Islamic Ethic* (2013); and *God*

---

[22]Quoted in Jenkins, *God's Continent*, 143.
[23]Ramadan, *Western Muslims*, 4.

Believes in Humanity: Towards a New Humanism With Islam (2015).[24] Khorchide argues that the Qur'an has been fundamentally misunderstood as a work of fear and judgment, whereas it is no such thing. Rather, it is God's love letter to humanity. As he says,

> God is not an archaic tribal leader, he's not a dictator. Of the book's 114 suras, why do 113 of them begin with the phrase "In the name of God, Most Gracious, Most Merciful"? There has to be a reason for this. The Koranic God presents himself as a loving God. That's why the relationship between God and man is a bond of love similar to the one between a mother and child. I would like Muslims to emancipate themselves from the image of an archaic God that's being connoted in many mosques, in religious education or during courses of theological instruction.[25]

Khorchide argues that the dictatorial view of God runs flat contrary to a proper Islamic understanding of human nature:

> From the theological perspective and from my perspective as a believer, it would be: God didn't create man in order to be worshipped by him. God—considered as absolute—is not dependent on man; God gives unconditionally, He doesn't want to infantilize man, he has given him the capacity to take the wheel himself and act independently. . . . Islam suffers terribly from the way we as Muslims reduce it to a legal, normative level. The main thing a believer wants to know is: "What am I allowed to do and what am I not?"; "What is permitted and what is forbidden?" But the Koran wants to bring up mature human beings who develop their own religious nature. Religion aims to touch people's hearts. But how can I love and have faith in God if my relationship to Him is solely defined by legal categories?[26]

Nor is it difficult to determine where such misinterpretations come from. They are presented because they serve the purposes of repression, obscurantism, and elitism:

---

[24]Mouhanad Khorchide, *Islam ist Barmherzigkeit. Grundzüge einer modernen Religion* (Freiburg im Breisgau: Herder, 2012); *Scharia—der missverstandene Gott: Der Weg zu einer modernen islamischen Ethik* (Freiburg im Breisgau: Herder, 2013); *Gott glaubt an den Menschen: Mit dem Islam zu einem neuen Humanismus* (Freiburg im Breisgau: Herder, 2015).

[25]Interview by Arnfrid Schenk and Martin Spiewak with Mouhanad Khorchide, "God Is Not a Dictator," *Qantara.de*, 2012, en.qantara.de/content/interview-with-mouhanad-khorchide-god-is-not-a-dictator.

[26]Interview by Canan Topcu with Mouhanad Khorchide, "Religion Seeks to Touch People's Hearts," trans. Ruth Martin, *Qantara.de*, 2015, en.qantara.de/content/interview-with-mouhanad-khorchide-religion-seeks-to-touch-peoples-hearts.

Many rulers of Islamic kingdoms describe themselves as "shadows of God on earth." This sends out an unequivocal message: anyone contradicting the ruler is also contradicting God. In order to make sure that the populace remains compliant, they construct the image of a God for whom obedience is paramount. To this very day, this plays an important role in a dictatorial state such as Saudi Arabia, where any opposition is not only held up as a secular opposition, but also as a movement against God.[27]

That repressive aspect has been a potent and often dominant force within Islam since the ninth century.

Another intellectual figure is the Afghanistan-born Ahmad Milad Karimi, who has written on Islamic issues and published a new translation of the Qur'an, and who has published several books jointly authored or edited with Mouhanad Khorchide. He has also authored the wonderfully titled *Osama Bin Laden Sleeps with the Fishes*.[28] Through all his work, Karimi claims the right to work with the original texts, unpolluted by later traditions, and is unafraid of borrowing from other cultures:

> The Koran is about humankind and a human being is always a question. I don't allow myself to be blinded by names, nationalities or religious affiliations. For me, it's all about the subject matter. In this, I follow the example of the Islamic tradition of the Middle Ages. Al-Kindi und [sic] Ibn-Rushd didn't read Aristotle because he was a good Muslim—they read him because they relished his incredibly challenging insights. Al-Maturidi, Islam's great influential theologian, posed the same question as Leibniz would subsequently— of why there is creation and not nothing.[29]

That demand to get beyond clericalism runs through much of the new reformist writing in today's Germany. Inevitably in the European context, the role of women in Islam occupies many thinkers, a good number of whom define themselves as Islamic feminists. One prominent activist in Germany is Turkish-born Emel Zeynelabidin, who stresses that much of what ordinary people believe to be normative Islam in fact derives from later clerical interpretations:

[27]Interview with Khorchide, "God Is Not a Dictator."
[28]Ahmad Milad Karimi, *Osama bin Laden schläft bei den Fischen* (Freiburg im Breisgau: Herder, 2013).
[29]Interview by Ruth Renée Reif with Ahmad Milad Karimi, "Accessing the Koran," trans. Ruth Martin, *Qantara.de*, 2016, en.qantara.de/content/interview-with-the-islam-scholar-ahmad-milad-karimi-accessing-the-koran.

For generations, Islamic teaching has been dominated by the *taqlid* tradition, the imitation of what clerics determined as fixed duties in religious practice many centuries ago. This principle was then supplemented by patriarchal traditions. To this day, these traditions' hierarchic distinctions between old and young, women and men continue to plant thought patterns such as "good and bad" and "permitted and banned" in the minds of subsequent generations. The covering up of Muslim women is part of this religious practice, with its moral yardstick for "strong and weak faith." Yet this man-made yardstick has little to do with what is understood as faith within Islam. Nowhere is it written that God or the Prophet Muhammad want rules on clothing. It is the scholars who once stipulated traditions in the so-called "Sharia," the religious laws that are observed to this day.[30]

A SILENCE ACROSS THE MUSLIM WORLD

A few critics of Islam have ventured far outside the fold. One highly polemical German voice is Hamed Abdel-Samad, author of *Der islamische Faschismus (Islamic Fascism)*, who portrays Muhammad as a terrorist and Islam as fascism, pure and simple.[31] Other thinkers are more aggressively reformist or secular minded, while remaining within the fold of Islam. Such thinkers have not historically organized into political movements, precisely because they are uncomfortable accepting the religious label as their primary identifier. They have rather affiliated to mainstream secular parties, generally on the left, which means that most self-identified Muslim organizations are generally conservative, and often extremist. To counter the idea that Islam necessarily implies Islamism, some liberals have now organized into avowedly reformist movements, like Denmark's Democratic Muslims, founded by a Syrian-born member of that country's parliament. Though such movements are presently sparse, they have a substantial potential for future growth.

Although I will not seek to list all the major thinkers who constitute Europe's Islamic modernism, some names demand attention. One is French literary figure Abdelwahab Meddeb, who died in 2014, and who ferociously criticized backward, reactionary Islam. Abdennour Bidar, meanwhile, is a

---

[30]Emel Zeynelabidin, "On Muslim Women and the Islamic Dress Code," *Qantara.de*, 2015, en.qantara.de/content/women-and-islam-on-muslim-women-and-the-islamic-dress-code.
[31]Hamed Abdel-Samad, *Der islamische Faschismus: Eine Analyse* (Munich: Droemer, 2014).

French writer and philosopher who after the Charlie Hebdo massacre of 2015 wrote a much-publicized "Open Letter to the Muslim World." It demands careful reading for its direct challenge to Muslims whose intolerance has inevitably generated the fanaticism of groups like the Islamic State.

> There is a silence across the Muslim World, and in the western media one listens to specialists on terrorism who daily aggravate the general short-sightedness! Oh my dear friend, *do not delude yourself into believing that when one is rid of the Islamic terrorism, that Islam will have solved all its problems!* Because all that I have just called to mind—a tyrannical, dogmatic, literalist, male chauvinist, conservative and regressive religion—is too often the ordinary Islam, the every-day Islam, which suffers and causes the suffering of so many consciousnesses, the Islam of an outdated past, the Islam deformed by all those who abused it politically, the Islam who ends again and again by hushing up all the "Arab Springs" and to hush up also the voices of its young who are asking for something different. So when are you going to at long last make this Revolution happen so that in societies and consciousnesses will definitely associate spirituality and freedom? . . .
>
> This refusal of the right of freedom as regards to religion is one of the *roots of evil* of which you suffer, oh my dear Muslim World! One of the dark stomachs where for some years now, monsters with frightening faces grow that are set free all over the world. Because this "Religion of Iron" imposes upon all your societies an unbearable violence. It has enclosed too many of your girls and boys in a cage of good and evil, of lawfulness (*halâl*) and of unlawfulness (*harâm*) which no-one chooses but under which everyone suffers. It imprisons willpower, it conditions minds, it impedes or hinders all choice of personal life. In too many of your regions, you still associate religion and violence—against women, against the *"bad believers"* / *"unbelievers,"* against the Christian or other minorities, against thinkers and all free spirits, against rebels, whereby this religion and this violence ends up being confused, by the most unbalanced and the most fragile of your sons, as the monstrosity of the *jihad* war![32]

Far from remaining in the world of academic theory, liberal ideas have been popularized by leading clergy, who have a potent influence over the Muslim community. One of France's best-known Muslim clerical leaders is Soheib

---

[32]Abdennour Bidar, "An Open Letter to the Muslim World," January 14, 2015, www.resetdoc.org/story/00000022484. Italics in original.

Bencheikh of Marseille, who praises secularism as a means of defending the rights of all minorities, including his own faith: "Due to secularism, Islam can stand equally with Catholics in rights and duties. . . . We can interact with the French culture that has a background of Catholicism, while holding on to our own spirituality and Islamic values."[33] But far from being simply defensive in character, he believes, secularism actually benefits Muslims:

> The separation between religion and politics will clarify Islam as a divine spiritual doctrine, not as an instrument which (can) be misused to gain power. Moreover, due to that, Islam can return its original formulation, meaning it will return as the *promoted* teaching . . . not as a forced teaching . . . as the Koran affirms—"Anyone who will believe may believe, and anyone who will be an infidel may be an infidel!"[34]

For Muslims to accept these principles in France would mark a milestone; applying them to many Muslim nations would constitute a revolution.

The same media that allow the propagation of extremist doctrines also spread more innovative ideas. One vital figure in contemporary Islam is Amr Khaled, an Egyptian preacher whose whole style and presentation powerfully recalls Christian televangelists, and who has an enormous following among Muslims in Europe as well as the Middle East. His image is thoroughly modern and progressive, and he makes huge use of contemporary media and technology—the Internet, as well as satellite television. Khaled's website is the third most popular Arabic website in the world. Wherever he travels, his avid followers fill stadiums to hear him. He encourages his listeners to accept Islamic principles not on the basis of traditional authority, but on the principles they discover through their own inward journeys. Like Ramadan, Khaled has been accused of clandestine ties to the Muslim Brotherhood and other hard-line organizations, while his glitzy presentation often accompanies a conservative theological message. But he too proclaims the need for a thorough renaissance, a *nahḍah*, which would free the Muslim world of its backwardness. Increasing his potential impact in Europe itself, Khaled has relocated his main base of operations to Birmingham, in England.

---

[33]Interview by Novriantoni with Soheib Bencheikh, "Islam and Secularism," *Qantara.de*, April 2004, en.qantara.de/content/interview-with-soheib-bencheikh-islam-and-secularism.
[34]Ibid.

LONDON'S MAYOR

As I have made clear, many of the reformists are deeply concerned about the prospects for a reformist Islam—I have already quoted Tibi and Bidar. But perhaps the most significant figure of all is an individual who is anything but an otherworldly academic. This is Sadiq Khan, who in 2016 was elected mayor of London, and who may well be a future prime minister of Great Britain—whatever form that country may take in the coming years.

In his professional past, Khan undoubtedly had connections with militant Islamists, and made some harsh and controversial statements. (The very well-informed Maajid Nawaz has published quite extensively on his alleged "sucking up to extremism.")[35] In later years, though, he gravitated away from those views to become an outspoken advocate of social liberalism and interfaith tolerance. He has been resolute on such core issues of potential controversy as homosexuality and same-sex relationships, women's rights, and especially relationships with Jews. More important, he has done all this while never compromising his own identity as a faithful Muslim.

It is hard to overestimate the significance of someone like Khan, who may not offer sophisticated theories about Islamic modernism, but just lives it in practice. As an example of practical modernism, and the total rejection of militancy and terrorism, he is by far the most dangerous force in the world to the extremists and jihadis, and the greatest threat they could imagine. I believe, and I hope, that this is the example that will be followed by the present generation of Tariqs I mentioned earlier, who could potentially choose so many different directions in faith and activism.

THE ROLE OF GOVERNMENTS

I have made some optimistic claims about the possible directions that European Islam might follow, but those face multiple objections and limitations. One of the most significant, paradoxically, is the role of European governments themselves, which one might think would have such a powerful vested interest in preventing violence and radicalization.

The problem can be easily stated. Facing threats of unrest and social division, European governments have understandably tried to build relationships

---

[35]Maajid Nawaz, "The Secret Life of Sadiq Khan, London's First Muslim Mayor," *The Daily Beast*, July 5, 2016, www.thedailybeast.com/articles/2016/05/08/the-secret-life-of-sadiq-khan-london -s-first-muslim-mayor.html.

with groups and federations that claim to speak for the "Muslim population." Often, though, these organizations are much more pious and orthodox than the people they claim to speak for, and many follow a traditional and hardline kind of faith, which is reactionary in matters of gender and sexuality. When governments recognize particular clerical and religious groups as the official spokesmen for their communities, they are treating ordinary people as members of collective religious/cultural entities, holding rights as members of those groups, not as citizens and individuals.

Moreover, people of Muslim background are by definition now seen as Muslims, and presumed to operate under religious and clerical authority. While that assumption might not be true at first, it could easily become so over time. The media assist this process when they report on ethnic communities through the lens of religious leaders, who naturally have their own agendas. Ethnic or class issues become religious problems, and viewers and readers tend to see them in that guise. Minority communities themselves are more likely to frame their grievances in religious terms.

Europe's Muslims represent a huge diversity of practice and devotional styles, to say nothing of social and political attitudes. Yet treating all under the single inflexible label of "Islam" encourages a sense of supranational religious identity that runs flat contrary to goals of assimilation. It also consecrates the role of religious leadership within those communities. Could Muslim fundamentalists have designed things more to their purpose?

This issue is most acute in the sponsorship of European mosques, most of which are funded by various foreign governments and agencies, and that situation is commonly supported by the European states themselves. Across Europe, faithful congregations ingeniously shop around between the various charitable organizations to find donors who will attach the fewest strings to their benevolence: Moroccans are least interventionist, Saudis the most intrusive. But once a mosque is built, many believers find it difficult to escape from the interfering hands of Muslim governments who want to shepherd their former citizens now living overseas.

While the Saudis are famous for projecting their militant agenda, other governments like those of Algeria and Turkey have a vested interest in reducing extremist influences among their communities abroad. Western governments are happy to promote such foreign dabbling as a means of preventing the upsurge of radicalism among immigrant communities. To accomplish their goal, states and their ministries for religious affairs become closely involved in choosing the imams who will teach in such mosques and prepare teaching material for children in religious schools. What the various foreign-controlled networks have in common is a shared desire to prevent migrants from assimilating too easily into European societies, so that they commonly oppose attempts to integrate Muslim children fully into public schools.

In the name of multiculturalism and "engagement," then, governments insist on relating to communities through a variety of hard-line organizations linked to the Muslim Brotherhood, or else to foreign governments. If a French group wishes to establish a mosque for local people, the answer is "Certainly! Do you want to work through the agency connected with the Saudi, Moroccan, or Turkish governments?" It is almost as if they want to delay the coming of a new Euro-Islam, or else prevent it altogether. That is very bad news for our lukewarm Tariqs.

CONCLUSION

At present, hopes for a liberal European Islam face many obstacles. But I would stress the time frame involved: just how long is it since Europe has had to deal with a significant Muslim population? Historical trends of this kind can take three or four generations.

Having said this, two highly practical parts of my story do fill me with hope, much more so than the academic theorizing about Euro-Islam that receives so much attention. One is the solidly practical achievements of pragmatic everyday cooperation represented by someone like Sadiq Khan. The other is the impact of Europe on demographics, both of migrant communities in that continent and in their home countries. Such statistics can seem technical and off-putting, but in a sense, the story they tell deals with the most important issues of all: family structures, gender roles, and the impact of religion in daily life. Critically, it also shows us how contacts with a different culture can resonate across a wider world, spreading those new ways and beliefs.

If even family structures can change so fundamentally, why not doctrines and creeds?

Christian-Muslim Relations and the Ethos of State Formation in West Africa

Nimi Wariboko

In this chapter, we will focus our analysis of the nature and dynamics of Christian-Muslim relations on the implications of the logics of Christianity and Islam intersecting and intertwining in state formation. I have delimited our task in this way for three important reasons. First, we want to shift scholarly attention away from the overused academic paradigm for studying Christian-Muslim relations.[1] Second, we need to set the analysis of Muslim-Christian relations within a long view of history and place it on a broad sociopolitical platform. Finally, from the earliest encounters of West Africans with either Christianity or Islam—and continuing even to the present day—the state and state formation have loomed large in the relationships between the adherents of these imported religions.[2] It is within the parameters of this

---

[1]For instance, see Marinus C. Iwuchukwu, *Muslim-Christian Dialogue in Postcolonial Northern Nigeria: The Challenges of Inclusive Cultural and Religious Pluralism* (New York: Palgrave Macmillan, 2013), 149-50; Akintude E. Akinade, "Introduction: Sacred Rumblings: Reflections on Christian-Muslim Encounters in Nigeria," in *Fractured Spectrum: Perspectives on Christian-Muslim Encounters in Nigeria*, ed. Akintude E. Akinade (New York: Peter Lang, 2013), 6-7; Matthew Hassan Kukah and Kathleen McGarvey, "Christian-Muslim Dialogue: Social, Political, and Theological Dimensions," in Akinade, *Fractured Spectrum*, 14.

[2]There is an alternative perspective that does not consider Islam as an imported or imposed world religion in the generalized West African context. To the extent that the Sahel and Savanna regions of West Africa were historically connected to the wider Maghreb world, Islam has had deep social and political implications on governance for many centuries. Since large swaths of West African communities were integrated into a universe of Muslim and indigenous religious possibilities, especially in the Sahel, according to this alternative perspective, mission Christianity

shift of scholarly attention that we will examine the missiological implications of Christian-Muslim relations in West Africa.

Let me begin by unpacking what I mean by an "overused paradigm" of analyzing Muslim-Christian relations. The paradigm in question is often about any of the following:

1. Comparison of doctrines and theological ideas

2. History of conflicts and tensions

3. Examination of how adherents team up on projects for a common good that will benefit society

4. Analysis of how the adherents of both religions live peacefully in the same neighborhood

5. Interfaith marriage

6. Provision of Western-style education to Muslim students by Christian missions

7. Examination of Muslims and Christians working harmoniously in the same office

8. Analysis of Muslims and Christians doing business together or serving in the same political party

9. Investigation of how various political classes have exploited the divisions between the two religions to support political interests or mobilize collective actions

10. The subjugation and domination of one religious group by the other

It is not too far-fetched to say that scholars who have focused on any of these ten dimensions are often looking at Muslim-Christian relations in terms of interreligious dialogue, the reality or possibility of pluralism, and the promotion of active engagement with plurality or the fundamental ethos of pluralism. This methodology is inadequate for a rigorous understanding of the missiological implications of Christian-Muslim relations in West Africa.

---

is the new world religion that is engaging indigenous religions and Islam with far-reaching implications for politics and governance since the imposition of colonialism at the turn of the twentieth century. I thank Professor Olufemi Vaughan for reminding me of this alternative scholarly perspective.

At the very least, it should not be executed at the expense of the new methodology I am advocating in this essay.

No doubt the concerns of pluralism are important for missions, for creating spaces for missionaries of both religions to thrive, and for mutual understanding between the two religions. But the regnant paradigm or methodology does not provide a robust or sophisticated perspective on the nature and logic of the Muslim-Christian relationship in West Africa as it has played out at a common site of intense and broad political engagement over the *longue durée* of history. The state and its history is a kind of transcendental condition that frames the reality of religious social structures and sets the horizon of meaning that not only conditions how Christians and Muslims perceive the reality of their interactions, but also how that reality has been changing in the context of their living together. In a certain sense, the state in West Africa is the audacious site in which religious leaders and their allied political classes conceive of the entire society (nation) as being sacredly significant. This is especially important if we consider Christian mission as *missio Dei*. This is to say that Christian mission is broadly interpreted as the dynamic partnership of *evangelism* (personal conversion), *reconciliation* between human beings and between humanity and God, and *social transformation* for human flourishing. Considered in this way, mission is always imbricated in the political processes within any society, the social basis of political competition, and the political engagement of religions.

Thus, as an alternative to the regnant models of missiology, I propose an approach that links the intricate dynamics of Christian-Muslim interactions to the political structure and ethos of state formation. Central to my discourse is the argument that the role of religion in state making produced the enduring patterns of Christian-Muslim relations in West Africa. Missiology is thus nudged to recognize, appreciate, or evaluate its nature as a theory of political life, how people (believers and nonbelievers) collectively live together in the light of certain normative assumptions founded on Christian Scripture, thought, and traditions.

Following Olufemi Vaughan, eminent Nigerian historian and political theorist, I will examine how the indigenous structures of Islam and Christianity in West Africa have shaped the evolution of the state in Nigeria, but along the way I will also draw examples from Ghana and Gambia to buttress my arguments.[3] Vaughan argues that Muslim and Christian structures set the foundation on which the state was grafted in the nineteenth and twentieth centuries. But it is also important to immediately add that the state itself also acts to set the stage on which structures of Christianity and Islam are interacting and developing; the two religions and the state are mutually shaping one another, and the trio together shape society's configuration of power.

The intersections and competitions of Islam and Christianity, which are decisive and integral for state formation, are important for understanding how interactions of Christianity with the state have shaped the philosophy of mission and patterned the evolution of Christian missionary praxis in West Africa. No scholar of theology and ethics of mission in West Africa who wants to sound credible can afford to exclude the interplay of state formation and mission from serious consideration. Thus, this essay investigates Christian-Muslim relations in West Africa as situated within the matrix and ethos of state formation.

Christian-Muslim relations, especially as they relate to missions, are also conditioned by another religious force: African traditional religions (ATR). The next section of this essay will offer an overview of the relationship between Christianity, Islam, and ATR. We will see how, in their competition for converts, the two Abrahamic faiths demonize ATR. Here I will principally rely on the work of the late brilliant anthropologist and religious historian John D. Y. Peel. His excellent 2016 historical and ethnographic report *Christianity, Islam, and Orişa Religion: Three Traditions in Comparison and Interaction* offers one of the best analyses of the interactions between the three religions and how the three-way relationship affected missions in southwestern Nigeria.[4] I will rely on it to map out how the relationships between the religions affected not only Christian mission but also the ethos of state formation.

Following this I will offer a summary characterization of the colonial state in Nigeria, which sets us up to examine how the structures of Islam and Christianity have shaped the evolution of the state and society in postcolonial

---

[3]Olufemi Vaughan, *Religion and the Making of Nigeria* (Durham, NC: Duke University Press, 2016).

[4]John D. Y. Peel, *Christianity, Islam, and Orişa Religion: Three Traditions in Comparison and Interaction* (Oakland: University of California Press, 2016).

Nigeria. Finally, I will investigate the missiological implications of the ethos of state formation in Nigeria.

CHRISTIANITY, ISLAM, AND AFRICAN TRADITIONAL RELIGIONS

As stated earlier, Christian-Muslim relations, especially as they relate to mission, are conditioned by African traditional religions. In the early periods of Islam's and Christianity's entry into African societies, the ATR in various communities actively set the rules on how these outsider faiths competed and often drew them into mutual antagonism or emulation. Drawing converts from ATR, who often were still somewhat committed to the visions and pragmatic notions of empowerment and protection, the priests of the Abrahamic faiths were always trying to make further inroads by reminding African Christians and Muslims how imperfectly they practiced their faiths. So not only were Christianity and Islam struggling against each other, but they also had to learn to negotiate their ways into the host cultures. The description of this tension in Yorubaland (Nigeria) by Peel is emblematic of the overall situation in West Africa:

> Islam and Christianity . . . have to engage in a paradoxical struggle: against each other to win converts, a struggle that impels them to make compromises with the ambient religious culture of the Yoruba; and against the same culture, as they strive to realize their own distinctive religious ideals.[5]

Part of this struggle involved the "invention" of the category of ATR against which Islam and Christianity cast themselves as superior alternatives. Precolonial ATR emerged as a discursive construct created by Christians and Muslims for the purpose of conversion or mission. Before this delineation and homogenizing conceptualization, what scholars now label as ATR was a series of local cult practices. It was not a generalized religion.[6] The adherents of Christianity and Islam came up with the notion of religion to cover a body of divergent practices in various communities.[7] Such a unified and now-bounded entity of practices was then

[5]Ibid., 173.
[6]Ibid., 153.
[7]Peel makes this point repeatedly in his *Christianity, Islam, and Orişa Religion*. For the same argument as it relates to other communities, see Peter van der Veer, *The Value of Comparison* (Durham, NC: Duke University Press, 2016), 147-48.

derisively designated as heathenism. As Peel specifically states about the Yoruba in Nigeria,

> The word *esin*, which means "religion" in modern Yoruba, was introduced by Christians and Muslims to refer exclusively to their own self-consciously held faiths. It was not its adherents but missionaries who first discursively constructed YTR [Yoruba traditional religion] as such (initially under the rubric "Yoruba heathenism").[8]

As Christianity and Islam entered sub-Saharan Africa, they drew their converts from adherents of the so-called ATR. Their success in winning converts greatly depended on the ethos of ATR, the live-and-let-live ethos that the various local cult practices had fostered as cultural traits in most African communities. There were even cases wherein priests of ATR—for instance, those of the Yoruba Ifa divination cult—advised their clients to convert to Islam or Christianity, as being Muslims or Christians were their God-given destinies on earth.[9]

The tolerance of ATR toward the Abrahamic faiths was not unconditional.[10] In many places members of the Abrahamic faiths were both persecuted when they were seen as threatening the worship or practices of local gods that were important for human flourishing in the communities and marginalized for their absolutist, exclusivist claims. And there were many cases of local elites and chiefs—such as the Asante in present-day Ghana—who opposed their kings' or states' adopting Islam or Christianity either because of the fear of annoying the ancestors or because the traditional religion was considered the most important key to the political integration of the communities.[11]

In a few cases, the discrimination and persecution of the adherents of the Abrahamic faiths led to religious wars. Take the case of the communities living around the Gambia River. In the early 1800s, the majority of the citizens of

---

[8]Peel, *Christianity, Islam, and Orişa Religion*, 217.

[9]T. G. O. Gbadamasi, "Odu Imale: Islam in Ifa Divination and the Case of Predestined Muslims," *Journal of the Historical Society of Nigeria* 8 (1997): 88-92. On the tolerance of ATR, see also Jacob Kehinde Olupona, *City of 201 Gods: Ilé-Ifè in Time, Space, and the Imagination* (Berkeley: University of California Press, 2011), 274-80. The born-again Olori, wife of the Ooni of Ife, was allowed to build her own "church" next to a very sacred shrine in the palace.

[10]Peel, *Christianity, Islam, and Orişa Religion*, 126, 133.

[11]Ibid., 133.

the various kingdoms in the riverine region were adherents of ATR, though Islam had entered the region in the fourteenth century. Muslims were in the minority in the early 1800s and faced persecution: they were not allowed to own land or hold important offices of state. By the 1840s there were open conflicts between Muslims and the adherents of ATR (called the Soninkes) in the kingdom of Kombo. In 1861 Maba Diakhou, a member of the ethnic group Fula Torodo, launched a jihad and routed the Soninke ruling class in the kingdom of Baddibu, and soon in the other parts/kingdoms of the riverine region Muslims came into control of both society and state.[12] In the words of Arnold Hughes and David Perfect,

> Muslims were thereafter in the ascendancy in most of the area, which was to become the Protectorate in 1894 and, by early 1990s, accounted for four out of five persons in the Protectorate. Almost all the rest were animists (or "pagans") as they were described in the census returns; there were few Christians in the Protectorate. . . . By 1993, only 800 people admitted to being followers of "traditional" religions. The decline of traditional religions was thus more complete in the Gambia than in some other countries in West Africa.[13]

Jihad or conquest was not the usual way Islam spread in West Africa.[14] It predominately made its way in traditional societies through its merchants and clerics. (Take, for instance, the Senegambia Jakhanke clerical tradition and its astute promotion of pacifism from about the eighth to the sixteenth century. The Jakhanke clerics, pacifists averse to militancy, spread Islam among the Mande people through religious study, education, farming, charms, and travel.)[15] As minorities, these purveyors of their faith would call upon the traditional institutions of authority: kings, chiefs, and courts. They were thus provided patronage and protection as guests or vulnerable strangers by the institutions of the state. Thus in many cases Islam grew from

---

[12]Arnold Hughes and David Perfect, *A Political History of the Gambia, 1816–1994* (Rochester, NY: University of Rochester Press, 2006), 24-25.

[13]Ibid., 25.

[14]Lamin Sanneh eloquently makes this point in his recent book, *Beyond Jihad: The Pacifist Tradition in West Africa* (New York: Oxford University Press, 2016).

[15]Lamin Sanneh, *The Jakhanke: The History of Islamic Clerical People of the Senegambia* (London: International African Institute, 1979). See also his *Beyond Jihad* for a history of the Jakhanke people. It is important to mention that some of the pacifist clerics in Gambia turned militant (such as Fode Kaba, Maba Diakhou, already mentioned, and Momodou-Lamin); see *Beyond Jihad*, 201-14.

below, under the protection of religiously tolerant states.[16] According to John Azumah, "This crucial role played by political patronage in the Islamization of Africa was evidenced by Islam having made more gains amongst ethnic groups with chieftaincy institutions than those without them."[17]

In the midst of this precolonial culture of tolerance, supported on the whole by the state in most of the kingdoms and societies in West Africa, membership in Christianity and Islam grew. This growth continued during the colonial era under the supervision of the colonial state controlled by predominantly Christian imperial countries. Christianity, which came into West Africa later than Islam, saw very impressive growth during the colonial period. Now the question is this: Did membership in Islam or Christianity grow due to the success of mission? This is the question that preoccupied the famous anthropologist Robin Horton in the 1960s. Horton argues that it was the expansion in social scale that precipitated conversion; as the horizon of Africans expanded as a result of increasing spheres of commerce and communications, it precipitated a search for God or gods that could explain the larger world. Colonialism and the Abrahamic faiths only acted as mere catalysts for a process of cosmological and cognitive adjustments that were already underway in the indigenous religions.[18] Traditional African religions functioned very well when the people lived in localized, small-scale communities, but as their social experiences and social relations expanded beyond this level, notions of God that would help explain, predict, and control events on a much wider scale began to surface. Since the idea of a supreme being that controls the whole world was implicit in the indigenous faiths but was given relatively less attention, in the change from the concerns of microcosm to macrocosm Islam and Christianity became the only readily available local sources of monotheism. The increase in social scale that colonialism precipitated only delivered converts to Islam or Christianity, depending on which of them was more accessible in any given locality. The general opinion is that though both religions benefited from the colonial condition in accelerating their growth in West Africa,

[16]John Azumah, "Patterns of Christian-Muslim Encounters in Africa," in *The African Christian and Islam*, ed. John Azumah and Lamin Sanneh (Carlisle, UK: Langham Partnership, 2013), 41-44; see also Iwuchukwu, *Muslim-Christian Dialogue*, 35.
[17]Azumah, "Patterns of Christian-Muslim Encounters in Africa," 44.
[18]Robin Horton, "African Conversion," *Africa* 41, no. 2 (1971): 85-108.

"Christianity's overall rate of expansion, starting from a much smaller base, was undoubtedly greater."[19]

Though colonialism generally created the expanded social scale that accelerated conversion to Islam and Christianity, we should not forget the role of the ethos of state formation in traditional African societies in explaining conversion to the Abrahamic religions. This is the argument of Peel, who maintains that we have to also factor in the ethos of state formation and the political role of indigenous religions in maintaining the integrity of the whole society. In his comparison of Asante and Yoruba, he discovered that expansion in social scale alone does not explain the differential rates of conversion to Christianity in these two communities. The Asante, who long retained, he argues, "a lively sense that the integrity of their society depended on the sanctions of the traditional religion," were slow to convert to Christianity compared to the Yoruba.[20]

According to Peel, the Yoruba were more open to religious change, as it was a "less geared-up society" and much more open to religious diversity and novelty in the precolonial period.

> Whereas, after *Asantehene* Osei Kwame's flirtation with Islam in the late eighteenth century, the Asante authorities quarantined Islam and effectively prevented its further spread, in the Oyo empire at the same time Islam made such strides that Muslims became a key component in its overthrow; and Islam grew steadily in Oyo's successor states in the nineteenth century.[21]

This reluctance toward religious innovation should not be construed to mean that the Asante society was religiously static. As Peel puts it,

> I have argued that the relative reluctance of the Akan, especially Asante, to embrace the world religions had much to do with their sense that the integrity of their society depended on sanctions bound up with the old religion. Asante society was not religiously static; but the world religions could not be subjected to local chiefly control as other imported cults were. The Asante knew their political community was founded on human agreement, though also given spiritual sanction by the Golden Stool. McCaskie brilliantly conveys the Asante sense of the fragility of their achievement, speaking of their "abiding

---

[19]Peel, *Christianity, Islam, and Orisa Religion*, 131.
[20]Ibid., 33; see also 34-36.
[21]Ibid., 33; see also 36.

fear that without unremitting application and effort, the fragile defensible space called culture would simply be overwhelmed or reclaimed by an ir-ruptive and anarchic nature."[22]

The comparative case Peel has made between the Yoruba society and that of the Asante supports my argument that any serious attempt to understand mission in West Africa must pay attention to the ethos of state formation or the common ground of state-society relations on which Islam and Christi-anity function. Even the colonialism that expanded the social scale of West Africans from microcosm to macrocosm, as Horton maintains, in a sense further clarifies my thesis. The modern state that was created under colo-nialism and its roles in affecting labor migration, expanding trade networks, promoting production of cash crops for the global capitalist markets, and expanding education, transportation, press, and so on are important for understanding the cognitive adjustment that hugely benefited the Abra-hamic religions. Our next section turns to the colonial state proper to ex-amine how the nature of the state and its relations with the bourgeois elites in Islam and Christianity shaped the understanding of missions in Nigeria.

THE COLONIAL STATE IN NIGERIA

What was the nature of the colonial state, especially aspects of it that throw light on the issue at hand, the ethos of state formation? The colonial state in Nigeria started as a commercial concern—the Royal Niger Company, which was also given charge of the overall economic development of Nigeria. The company not only acted as a *state* in this regard, it also helped to extend British imperialism with coercion. Thus, the state in Nigeria started as a crude tool of capital. The primary function of the colonial state was to create and maintain the political and economic conditions under which the ac-cumulation of capital could proceed through the extraction and exploitation of Nigeria's resources by the metropolitan bourgeoisie. This task was to be carried out at minimal cost to the colonizers.[23]

The colonial state needed to carry out its mission and to survive in the face of the hostility of the colonized. Its power was not only absolute but also

---

[22]Ibid., 35-36; cf. T. C. McCaskie, "Accumulation, Wealth and Belief in Asante History," *Africa* 53, no. 1 (1983): 23-24.
[23]Claude Ake, *A Political Economy of Africa* (London: Longman, 1981).

arbitrary. The state accelerated the destruction or restructuring of any local institution that did not serve its purpose, rejected any restrictions on its power, and extended its rights to power. Thus, in parts of vast Northern Nigeria, where Hausa-Fulani had established a viable administrative system, the colonial government, dictated by pragmatism and biases, quickly co-opted the system for its needs. Colonial administration tended to favor ethnic groups that it thought were superior or more advanced in civilization. The British saw the Hausa-Fulani Muslims as bearers of a higher degree of civilization than non-Muslims. This attitude or inherent preference by the colonizers affected the ethos of state formation in the colonial period. As Matthews Ojo, a Pentecostal scholar, argues, "The British constructed the framework of state formation based on nineteenth-century anthropological thinking of superiority of certain ethnic groups."[24]

The colonial system, as would be expected, denied Nigerians political freedom and choice of state managers. Colonization in Nigeria did not provide liberal democracy, as the political correlate of capitalism instead imposed a state that was not a product of society.[25] The Nigerian state enjoyed a narrow base of support, as it was essentially hostile to the bulk of its populace. The state was often an instrument of class struggle. After independence in October 1960, the state was co-opted for the service of the dominant factions of the elite. There was, and continues to be, an undue emphasis on capturing political power and an intense fear of losing to rival parties. For this reason, Claude Ake argues that political competition assumes the character of warfare and has become a zero-sum game, "an anarchy of dedicated self-seeking."[26] The state's dependence on petroleum rents and the dangers involved in trying to create and sustain wealth independent of prebendal politics and the protection of the state make political competition even more lethal.[27]

---

[24]Matthews A. Ojo, "Competition and Conflict: Pentecostals' and Charismatics' Engagement with Islam in Nigeria," in Azumah and Sanneh, *African Christian and Islam*, 157.

[25]Claude Ake, *Democracy and Development in Africa* (Washington, DC: Brookings Institution, 1996), 1-3; Peter Ekeh, "Social Anthropology and the Two Contrasting Uses of Tribalism in Africa," *Comparative Studies in Society and History* 32, no. 4 (1990): 683-86.

[26]Ake, *Democracy and Development*, 129.

[27]For an excellent discussion on the connections between politics, entrepreneurism, and corruption, see Steven Pierce, *Moral Economies of Corruption: State Formation and Political Culture in Nigeria* (Durham, NC: Duke University Press, 2016).

Let me now give concrete examples of how this particular nature of the state affected religions and how Islam and Christianity interacted. In 1804 Usman dan Fodio (1754–1817), a Fulani Muslim cleric and scholar, successfully waged a jihad in Northern Nigeria, and the influence of his brand of Islam spread rapidly in the region before turning southward. He established the Sokoto caliphate with several states under its rule. Then in 1903 the British army (which included Muslim foot soldiers), under the command of Colonel Frederick Lugard, conquered Sokoto and other states in the caliphate and subjugated them to British authority. This subjugation of the caliphate and the presence of the colonial authority halted the rapid spread of Islam in Northern Nigeria, "but there are statistical evidences to show that there remained constant growth and spread of Islam in northern Nigeria, through the entire era of the colonial rule albeit through peaceful means."[28]

Much more telling about the relation between the state and religion during the colonial period is the oath of office that the Sultan of Sokoto, Shehu Muhammad Attahiru II, the spiritual head and political leader of the caliphate, had to swear. He swore an oath of loyalty to His Majesty King George after his subordination to the British Empire.[29] Based on the sultan's fealty and prospects of the Sokoto caliphate helping Britain maintain its grip on power, the two sides reached a mutual understanding to protect each other's interests.

As part of this understanding between the colonizing British power and the caliphate, Lugard promised to prevent the proselytization of Muslims by Christians in the caliphate's area of influence. This pledge was driven by at least two factors. First, British administrators assumed that the indigenous non-Muslim population of Northern Nigeria would eventually become Muslims. Second, the British administrators, based on the interest of their colonial project, believed that a truly African-style civilization grounded on Islamic principles was already underway and did not want Christianization to disrupt this process and produce subjects who would reject African traditional ways in favor of a Western lifestyle.[30] This stratagem had an effect

---

[28]Iwuchukwu, *Muslim-Christian Dialogue*, 34.

[29]Ibid., 33-34.

[30]Andrew E. Barnes, "'The Great Prohibition': The Expansion of Christianity in Colonial Northern Nigeria," *History Compass* 8, no. 6 (2010): 441; see also Elom Dovlo, "The African Christian and Islam: Insights from the Colonial Period," in Azumah and Sanneh, *African Christian and Islam*, 88-90.

on Christian mission. "Invariably, Lugard and subsequent colonial administrators ensured the protection of this pledge, which by implication suggested that Christian mission and activities of missionaries were not required in northern Nigeria."[31]

The foregoing does not tell the full story of how the ethos and process of state formation in Nigeria defined the mission fields for both Christianity and Islam. Lugard and his fellow colonial administrators wanted to use the political and administrative structures of the caliphate for their purposes, which included control of the people and resources of the vast areas (7 million people and 300,000 square miles) under the administration of the Islamic leaders of Northern Nigeria. To accomplish this, Lugard set up the indirect rule system, whereby the British ruled Nigerians indirectly through existing local structures of power and authorities.

Another dimension of the story is that the colonial administrators were highly interested in preventing interreligious and political conflicts in Nigeria so as not to harm the interests of their exploitation project. The state was in the service of the capitalist and imperialist project of extracting raw materials from Nigeria for British industries and opening and sustaining markets for British goods. Most of the British merchants in Nigeria also adopted the same attitude and hence became known for their hostility to Christian missionaries and any project to convert Muslims to Christianity.

In order to secure its power, the colonial administration adopted the policy of divide and rule: it planted seeds of conflict and division between Islam and Christianity, exacerbated ethnic identities by the differential treatment of ethnic groups, and, by its severe alienation of the governed, drove most Nigerians to their ethnic and religious collectivities for recognition and support. These processes promoted the development of large-scale ethnonational identities that were later deployed for the political mobilization of ethnoreligious consciousness and the interelite competition for scarce resources of the modern state. In Northern Nigeria, the Hausa-Fulani aristocracy used ethnoreligious identity to mobilize Muslim consciousness. In the south, as Peel has shown, it was the Church Missionary Society (CMS)

---

[31]Iwuchukwu, *Muslim-Christian Dialogue*, 15. On the general issue of British colonial authority's attitude to Christian missionaries, see also Shobana Shankar, *Who Shall Enter Paradise? Christian Origins in Muslim Northern Nigeria, c. 1890–1975* (Athens: Ohio University Press, 2014).

missionaries and their early converts who forged a pan-Yoruba ethno-national consciousness.[32] Thus, recurring violence, whether religious, political, or ethnic, cannot be fully grasped if we do not pay attention to the history and ethos of state formation in the colonial time and their endurance in the postcolonial period.[33]

This is the nature of the state that oversaw the terms of competition between Islam and Christianity and conditioned the mission field. This mission field, conditioned by rapacious colonialism and an exploitative state, was characterized by two seemingly opposing factors: colonial-state hostility to the two faiths and growth in their memberships. These two opposing factors have taken different forms in the postcolonial era. The postcolonial state is no longer hostile to the two faiths as before, but it is still hostile to its people. Like the colonial state, it is not serving the common good. The growth in the number of Christians and Muslims has continued into the postcolonial period, even as the two Abrahamic faiths have been increasingly co-opted by the state in their quests for political power.[34] The state in Nigeria is not only a strategic site for conflicts and collaborations between Christianity and Islam, but it also co-opts them to steadily attack its citizens.

THE INFLUENCE OF CHRISTIANITY AND ISLAM ON STATE AND SOCIETY IN POSTCOLONIAL NIGERIA

Here I want to examine the dynamics of Christian-Muslim relations to show how the forces, logics, and ethos of Christianity and Islam intersect and intertwine in state formation during the postcolonial era. This way of studying Muslim-Christian relations as they impinge on mission was inspired by the work of historian Olufemi Vaughan. His historical discussions and incisive analyses demonstrate that Muslim and Christian movements have flourished in Nigeria; that is, they have decisively shaped the processes

[32]J. D. Y. Peel, *Religious Encounter and the Making of the Yoruba* (Bloomington: Indiana University Press, 2003); see also J. D. Y. Peel, *Ijesha and Nigerians: The Incorporation of a Yoruba Kingdom, 1890s–1970s* (Cambridge: Cambridge University Press, 1983).
[33]Thaddeus Byimui Umaru, *Christian-Muslim Dialogue in Northern Nigeria: A Socio-Political and Theological Consideration* (New York: Xlibris, 2013), 46-51.
[34]Ebenezer Obadare, "The Muslim Response to the Pentecostal Surge in Nigeria: Prayer and the Rise of Charismatic Islam," *Journal of Religious and Political Practice* 2, no. 1 (2016): 75-91.

of state-society formation "because their institutions and doctrines are consistently embedded in the structures of society, shaping social relations and the configuration of power."[35] As more ethicists and theologians read his excellent book, Vaughan's scholarship will help to reshape how they understand or interpret Christian-Muslim relations with regard to mission. It will move their gaze from theological quarrels, spectacular maneuvers, and "street fights" to the grand and *longue durée* process of state formation, institution building, and the search for state legitimacy. In the preceding pages, I have already utilized his approach toward understanding Christian-Muslim relations and its imbrication in Christian mission. Put differently, I have tried to show how Christian mission, standing against the shadow of a strong Islamic presence in the same sociopolitical landscape, shaped the formation of the Nigerian state and society.

I do not have the space to go into a more detailed account of how the complicated histories of Islam and Christianity in the formation of the Nigerian state and society impacted mission in the postcolonial era. So I will limit this discussion of Christian-Muslim relations in the postindependence era to the issue of expanding shari'a (Islamic law). The goal is to show how this sore point of contention between Christians and Muslims is in a sense attributable to the structural imbalance or the configuration of power in the formation of the postcolonial Nigerian state.

When Britain put together various kingdoms, states, and ethnic groups to create what we know today as Nigeria, the nation began with various forms of imbalance that have since bedeviled its politics. In 1914 Britain amalgamated two very unequal and dissimilar protectorates (north and south) to form Nigeria. The south contained two regions, east and west; the north had only one. The Northern Protectorate, dominated by the Sokoto caliphate, was almost twice in land mass and population compared to the whole south. The north was and still is dominated by Muslims, but there is a portion of it called the Middle Belt that is dominated by Christians. The south was and still is predominately made up of Christians. In the western region of the south, the area of the Yoruba, the population is split almost equally between Christians and Muslims.

---

[35]Vaughan, *Religion and the Making of Nigeria*, 2.

When the British granted Nigerian independence in October 1960, the country went through its first republic in less than six years. This was followed by a military coup in 1966 and a civil war that lasted from 1967 to 1970. As the military prepared to hand over power to the civilians in 1979, beginning the second republic, a Constitution Drafting Committee (Constituent Assembly) was set up in 1976. In the process of drafting the constitution, the majority of the northern (Muslim) delegates to the constitutional conference wanted to expand the role of shari'a in the political and legal affairs of the country. The pro-shari'a delegates wanted a federal appeals court that would preside over both criminal and civil matters. Under this proposal there would be two courts of appeal under the Supreme Court: the regular Federal Court of Appeal operating under common law and a Federal Shari'a Court of Appeal to adjudicate on appeal cases from any state Shari'a Court of Appeal.

The south and northern-minority Christians resisted this, and the ensuing debates and conflicts dangerously exposed the ethnoreligious-regional fault lines of the country. Christians saw the Muslim request to establish a Shari'a Court of Appeal with jurisdiction over the country as a ploy to Islamize the whole nation. The Hausa-Fulani Muslim elites used the issue of shari'a as the medium to coalesce and articulate their interests and accused Christians of being unsympathetic to their religious needs. It is important to mention that the debate did not always fall along the usual religious fault lines. There were progressive Muslims that opposed the establishment of the Shari'a Court of Appeal.[36]

When the pro-shari'a members could not have their way, they staged a walkout from the Constituent Assembly. Those left behind worked out a compromise such that, instead of establishing a Federal Shari'a Court of Appeal, the Constitution Drafting Committee established both Shari'a and Customary Courts of Appeal, which had limited authority in civil and criminal matters and were restricted to the northern states.

The shari'a issue has never gone away. The debates continued in the second republic (1979–1983) and progressed in the ill-fated third republic (1991–1993). In 1999, at the beginning of the ongoing fourth republic, Governor

---

[36]Iwuchukwu, *Muslim-Christian Dialogue*, 58-62.

Ahmed Sani of Zamfara, a northern majority-Muslim state, authorized shari'a courts to have jurisdiction over criminal and civil cases. This was the first time in the Federal Republic of Nigeria that any state would have a shari'a court system with powers over criminal and civil cases. Hitherto, the power of shari'a courts was limited to personal matters among Muslims. Not long after this bold, unprecedented move, nine other northern states followed suit, with two other states adopting shari'a in a limited fashion— making a total of twelve states out of the nineteen northern states and thirty-six states in the whole federation. These strict religious measures enjoyed popular support among the northern masses.[37]

The euphoria over and insistence on shari'a cannot be attributable only to Muslim religious sensibility or an Islamic vision of society. There are at least five other ways of interpreting it. First, we must also see it as related to the process of state formation amid competitive Muslim-Christian relations. Advocates of shari'a argued that the common law system, which derived from Christian sensibility, eroded or restricted Islamic law under the British colonial system. But as this was going on, British authorities co-opted the Sokoto caliphate and its aristocracy of emirs, alkalis, and ulamas to keep power and to exploit the masses. The masses viewed the compromises the Hausa-Fulani Muslim elites made under the Britain-imposed common-law legal system as a sellout of core Islamic principles for the elites' own political gain.

Second, the Muslim masses' support for shari'a was also a form of protest or repudiation of the colonial state-formation process that had further entrenched the Hausa-Fulani elites over them. The masses even believed that the adoption of shari'a could lead to wealth redistribution through the *zakāt* tax (2.5 percent on liable assets) on the affluent.[38] The "overwhelming Northern Muslim support for expanded sharia," according to Vaughan,

> was hardly a blind allegiance to the Hausa-Fulani political class. The erosion of the moral authority of the emirate political elite . . . had left the masses of Northern Muslims disaffected with the Sokoto Caliphate's power structures.[39]

---

[37]For an excellent account of the shari'a crisis, see Brandon Kendhammer, *Muslims Talking Politics: Framing Islam, Democracy, and Law in Northern Nigeria* (Chicago: University of Chicago Press, 2016), 117-79.

[38]Vaughan, *Religion and the Making of Nigeria*, 174.

[39]Ibid., 177.

Third, for the Hausa-Fulani elites, expanding shari'a was a way to distract the masses from their political and economic failures and part of the ethnoregional and ethnoreligious machinery of controlling state power.[40] It is important to also mention that some of the northern Muslim elites were ambivalent about the expansion of shari'a, seeing it as a policy that could potentially destabilize the country and also undermine their age-old strategy of constructing multiethnic coalitions to capture and hold state power for primitive accumulation.[41]

Fourth, the shari'a controversy raises the urgent matter of how to deal with a section of Nigeria with (arguably) overwhelming advantage in population and hence majority seats in the parliament and whose citizens insist that they have a democratic right to choose the law that will govern the region's religious members. Thus, the Nigerian president at that time, General Olusegun Obasanjo, a born-again Christian, was tardy in responding to the shari'a-induced legal imbroglio but eventually managed to avoid raising the conflict to the level of a constitutional crisis or existential threat to the survival of the country.

Finally, the shari'a proposal and resistance to it must also be situated within the parameters of the struggles of the factions of the ruling class and the Christian-Muslim competition to manipulate religion in order to capture state power for primitive accumulation. As stated earlier, the Nigerian state is an instrument of class struggle. The state is often co-opted for the service of the dominant faction (or coalition of factions) of the elite. There is an undue emphasis on capturing political power and an intense fear of losing to rival parties. For this reason, political competition, as Ake reminds us, assumes the character of warfare and has become a zero-sum game.

In this anarchy of self-seeking, corruption, and primitive accumulation in the postcolonial period, no faction of the ruling class wants to upset the

---

[40]Ibid.

[41]Primitive accumulation, a Marxian concept, is used here to refer to the process whereby Nigerian elites accumulate capital outside the mechanics of the market; they accumulate wealth without participating in the typical investments and risks of entrepreneurial activities of capitalists (bourgeoisie) but by acquiring and holding state power. Members of the rapacious Nigerian ruling class create and sustain their wealth by stealing, plundering, or directly appropriating public and state resources for themselves, to create and strengthen their material base. Often, they do not invest in or own normal means of production and engage in exploiting wage workers. Access to state power is their means of production. The logic of primitive accumulation demands that the state be captured by a small group of very powerful citizens (civilian and military) and be used for the interests of class and self.

balance of religious adherents and ethnoreligious identities that came down from the colonial era. Each of the Abrahamic faiths watches the other to understand and interpret its capacity for political mobilization, not only to capture state power for primitive accumulation, but also to transform its confessional community into the state.

Indeed, the competition between the ruling elites, the bourgeoisie of both religions, for state power affects the way the two religions interact. The state-bourgeoisie relation served as model for, as well as model of, Christian-Muslim relations. Religious competition, growth, and innovation are integral aspects of the functioning and deployment of state power to master the resources and activities of citizens. The postcolonial state maintains a sense that the two religions are key to the integrity of society. The faiths themselves turn to the state to underpin their authority, and the elites of both religions use the state to shore up their weak material base.

MISSIOLOGICAL IMPLICATIONS OF CHRISTIAN-MUSLIM RELATIONS IN WEST AFRICA

In the foregoing, we have examined the nature and logic of Muslim-Christian relations in Nigeria as they have played out as a significant dimension of state formation over the *longue durée* of history. We have demonstrated that the state and its history frame the horizon of meaning that conditions not only how Christians and Muslims perceive the reality of their interactions, but also how that reality has been changing in the context of their living together. In the dialectics of this interaction, the religious leaders and political classes of both religions conceive of the entire nation as being sacredly significant for their missions.

The dialectics of this struggle have implications for how Nigerian Christians understand mission or what kind of societal arrangement is best suited for the social transformation of a country. Put differently, given the context of the long process of state formation and the competition between ethno-religious groups, any theology of mission in the country has to address the ideological and structural orientations to state and society relations. Muslims fundamentally do not recognize the separation of the political sphere, the state, from religious control and as such advocate for a strong federal state that will centralize religious and social order and then "use the power of the state to its advantage."[42] This much is clear from the debates over shari'a since the mid-1980s—at least from Muslim extremists. Christians, especially Pentecostal groups, which some Muslims consider as extremists, have advocated for a decentralization of the political and social order. Matthews Ojo, one of the few Pentecostal scholars who understands how the process of state formation impacts Christian mission, has this to say about Nigerian Pentecostals' ideological orientation to state and society:

> Pentecostal groups have favoured a decentralization of the political and social order. Such decentralization has in the past favoured religious creativity that has stimulated more Christian growth. Decentralization is more suited to Pentecostalism, which, with its emphasis on the personal empowerment of the Holy Spirit, has created alternative centres of power to solving human needs against the background of the failure of the centralized state.[43]

Given the importance of the process of state formation in the relation between Christian and Muslim, what are the missiological implications for finding solutions to the problems of modern life? There are at least three options. One approach is to remove the dysfunctions, corruption, and inefficiencies of the modern state and make it responsive to its society. Ojo argues that this is the preferred approach of Islamic groups in Nigeria.[44] But some Christians also share this position. For instance, the brilliant historian Toyin Falola expressed the same idea in his own words without, of course, implying a religious control of the state:

> What can prevent the tension from degenerating to prolonged violence and the breakup of Nigeria is better political and economic management by a patriotic political class genuinely committed to change and the construction of a nation-state that is sensitive to the needs and concerns of a multireligious, multiethnic society.[45]

---

[42]Ojo, "Competition and Conflict," 159.

[43]Ibid. We have to be careful here in accepting Ojo's assumption about the "alternative centres of power." Often these "alternative centres" hardly stand on their own. They tend to be supported by the state or from resources looted from the state by Christians in ways that betray or question the conceits of the Pentecostal elites and their followers.

[44]Ibid.

[45]Toyin Falola, *Violence in Nigeria: The Crisis of Religious Politics and Secular Ideologies* (Rochester, NY: University of Rochester Press, 2002), 303.

Ojo goes on to state that Pentecostal groups are concerned with solving problems confronting the individual.[46] "This contradictory orientation continues to create gaps between Pentecostal churches and Islam," he notes.[47] I contend that the whole schema of state-based approach versus individual-focused approach that Ojo sets up is inadequate to develop a viable missiological theology of social action in West Africa. Elsewhere I have named the two approaches as statecraft versus soulcraft and advocated the need for a different kind of practice.[48] The options before us are not limited to withdrawal into private, individual spaces or the embrace of public space as conditioned by the calculus of capturing state power and dedicated self-seeking. Our choice is not between exclusion and embrace. The church must develop a radical imagining that sutures the public and the private, transgressing the lines that separate statecraft and soulcraft in order to create a distinct kind of theopolitical practice. I have called this radical imagining the *care of the soul* as a third way beyond the two. The care of the soul is not just equivalent to soulcraft or statecraft, but it may be considered as one viable way of integrating the strategies of statecraft and soulcraft. Care of the soul acknowledges that the work of human flourishing must connect the transformative work of public policy and liberatory praxis. Human flourishing must pass, as it were, through the realm of the state. On the other hand, we understand also that human flourishing must move through the subject, the foundation of the person. The paradigm of the care of the soul holds that the step to subjectivation, inner self-presence, is a step toward human sociality, if only to accede beyond to liberating freedom.[49]

What then does care of the soul mean for the work of *missio Dei* in societies where the logic and character of state-society relations are at stake or need to be fashioned? By care of the soul I am not talking about the pastoral technique of preparing the soul to ascend to heaven, preparing the self for an elsewhere. I am interested in the political act of preparing Nigerians for

---

[46]Once again, we have to take Ojo's assumption with a pinch of salt. Yes, the Pentecostals may be concerned with solving problems confronting the individual, but the Pentecostal ethos is no less politically charged for that.

[47]Ojo, "Competition and Conflict," 159.

[48]Nimi Wariboko, *Economics in Spirit and Truth: A Moral Philosophy of Finance* (New York: Palgrave Macmillan, 2014), xi-xii, 168-71.

[49]For a discussion on subjectivation in Nigerian Pentecostalism, see Nimi Wariboko, *Nigerian Pentecostalism* (Rochester, NY: University of Rochester Press, 2014).

the coming event, for political transformation as an infrastructure of economic development. The care of the soul, as the micropolitics of freedom, precedes any order or being, always searching for the crack or line of flight to explode any socioeconomic order that resists human flourishing. Care of the soul in this sense is the praxis of taking on one's own existence always as potentiality, as an unfinished and incompletable project. Missiology in West Africa must endeavor to encompass care of the soul.

We have so far examined two missiological implications of our study of the process of state formation and the state-society relation in Nigeria. We examined the differences between Islamic and Christian ideological and structural orientations to the state, indicating what that might mean for a theology of mission. Next we examined the missiological implications for finding solutions to the problems of modern life as conditioned by the history of Christian-Muslim relations in Nigeria. We offered the paradigm of care of the soul as an alternative to the regnant soulcraft and statecraft. We now have three other possible implications to explore.

Mission theology must address how to prepare Christians not to be sucked into (or be delivered from) Constantinian Christianity or ethnoreligious competitions for power by the corrupt dominant factions of the ruling elites. The competing elites simultaneously mobilize and marginalize the masses of the two faiths for their selfish ends. The elites use religion to mask and convey their personal, economic, and political interests to the corridors of state power. The power, once gained, is used to marginalize and brutalize not only members of the other faith, but also adherents of their own faith because of class differences. This particular deployment of religions in Nigerian polity is a threat to the separation of church/mosque and state and to the ideals of a religiously diverse and plural society. In this sense, missiology must also be a public theology. Such a public theology must be able to revise the public role of religions in the context of state formation, engender ethical reorientation rooted in the interior of the three religious traditions, and empower the elites to govern with high moral standards. Missiology in West Africa must also be a public theology that can heal social wounds.

Given that mission theology is about holistic reconciliation between all of God's children, between humanity and creation, and between humanity and God, the peculiar, predatory nature of the Nigerian postcolonial state warrants theological-ethical attention. The Nigerian state separates and atomizes its citizens, destroys solidarity among the ruled, and feeds the fault lines of ethnic and religious groups. The state is hostile to its people. The colonial and postcolonial state that fought its citizens pushed them to their ethnic enclaves, separating ethnic groups from one another. The postcolonial state that failed to provide basic public facilities pushed Nigerians to become self-sufficient, to be states in themselves. Careless crude-oil production by rapacious, death-dealing multinational corporations pollutes the environment and destroys sources of livelihood for a large proportion of Nigerians, and their own state turns a blind eye to their plight as it is busy collecting petroleum rents from them. The citizens steadily being attacked by the colonial and postcolonial state are alienated from the state. The citizens are not morally linked to the society, and they do not see their lives or duties as moral obligations to benefit and sustain a nation of which they are members. So today we are seeing the evolution of the monistic, self-absorbed person as citizen, the self on a quest for separation, self-sufficiency, and autonomy and in revolt against African personhood. There is thus an urgent need for a viable theology qua missiological theology to aid in the reconstruction of the general ethos (including the ethos of state formation) in ways that will foster senses and practices of human co-belonging and co-humanity in Nigeria.

Our earlier definition of mission has three parts to it: evangelism (personal conversion), reconciliation, and social transformation. In our analysis of the missiological implications of our thesis, we have delved into only two of them. We have yet to talk about evangelism—personal conversion, or "soul winning," as Nigerian Pentecostals are wont to put it. A missiology that is not concerned with winning souls for Christ from within and outside Christianity is a prescription for the slow, painful death of the church. I am not for the death of the church! What do the character of the Nigerian state and the attendant moral decadence of Nigerian society tell us about the future prospects of bringing people into God's kingdom? Let me respond to this crucial question by mapping out the future direction of Pentecostalism. There are likely to be three divergent paths in the future. First, Pentecostalism will likely become the religion of the community and the state; that is, it will be co-opted as part of the ruling establishment. With this will come an extensive rationalism of the priesthood. Second, there will be a vigorous prophetic strand that will critique state and society in the name of social justice. This strand will try to avoid becoming part of the ruling elites, but will seek the social transformation of society. Finally, there will be a revivalist movement that will intend to recapture something of the nature, innocence, and accent on holiness of the movement in the 1970s and early 1980s. But it is likely to turn away from engaging with society. This third path of holiness is the most strategic for personal conversion; but if added to the second, we would come closest to what *missio Dei* should be.

CONCLUSION

This essay has explored the historical dynamics of the modes of Christian-Muslim relationality, accenting their entanglements within the political sociology of state formation. We have emphasized generally the interactions between Muslim-Christian relations and other social institutions and society rather than focusing on the relations in their own right. This is to say we located Muslim-Christian relations in the broader and historical scope of the social organization of power in Nigeria. The approach enabled us to deal with Christian-Muslim relations against the backdrop of the relationship between state and society on the basis of the complex interactions between state, society, and the indigenous structures of religion (Christianity, Islam, and ATR).

The methodology and arguments of this essay have served notice to missiologists that the political, social, and economic institutions in which Christian-Muslim relations are embodied have to be continually studied afresh if missiology is to meet the changes that are going on in the differential articulations of power by the two competing religions in West Africa. The intersections and competitions of Christianity and Islam are important for understanding how Christian mission has shaped state-society relations and how the logic and character of the state have shaped the philosophy of mission and patterned the evolution of Christian missionary praxis in West Africa. This knowledge should be considered important for how we evaluate past and future missionary work.

The point is that while missionaries can always work to transcend or evade the political and economic calculations that frame interactions with the state, the states of affairs between the state and its religions make some responses to the mission field more or less likely than others. No particular state-society configuration is a reliable predictor of the success of mission, but just as important, state-society relations are not interchangeable. Going forward, missiology must pay serious attention to the process of state formation and the state-society relation in West Africa. As we have demonstrated, the state in West Africa is the audacious site in which religious leaders and their allied political classes conceive of the entire society as being sacredly significant for the mission of God. No scholar of theology and ethics of mission in West Africa can afford to exclude state formation from his or her purview and still be considered contextually relevant. Thus, this essay has investigated Christian-Muslim relations in West Africa as conditioned not only by the ethos of state formation, but also as a political theorization of the missiological. To end, let me be so bold as to say that the whole of our discourse gestures toward forging a new path in missiology: political sociology of mission.[50]

---

[50]I am grateful to Olufemi Vaughan of Bowdoin College and Ebenezer Obadare of the University of Kansas for their helpful comments on the original draft of this chapter.

4

Islam in South Asia

Dynamics of Contemporary Muslim Societies in Hyderabad Deccan

David Emmanuel Singh

South Asia accounts for one of the largest concentrations of Muslims whose way of life varies significantly from standard understandings of Islam. Islam has had many local variations here affected through translation, which is often mediated by Sufis.[1] A cross-section of this reality reveals several *maslaks* (schools of thought) unique to this region. The goal here is not just to underline this diversity (which is fairly well-known), but to show that besides being diverse South Asian Islam is also dynamic. I will illustrate this in two cases from Hyderabad Deccan: the first involves a *munazara* (public debate) between two major maslaks, while the second examines a Sufi-inspired community creatively negotiating different fault lines for cohesion.

The main aim of this study can be missiologically understood in very practical and strategic terms, as informed by Johannes Verkuyl (1908–2001).[2] What this means it that there is undoubtedly a theological element to missiology, but this chapter focuses mainly on the manifest sociological

---

[1] I use the term *translation* here in the sense explained by Lamin Sanneh, as the ability of Islam, like Christianity, to shape and be shaped by local culture. See Lamin Sanneh, *Translating the Message: The Missionary Impact on Culture*, 2nd ed. (Maryknoll, NY: Orbis, 2009). See more information on Islam in John Esposito and David Emmanuel Singh, "Islam," in *Worldmark Encyclopedia of Religious Practices*, vol. 1, *Religions and Denominations*, ed. Thomas Riggs, 2nd ed. (New York: Gale, 2015), 453-91.
[2] See Johannes Verkuyl, *Contemporary Missiology: An Introduction*, trans. Dale Cooper (Grand Rapids: Eerdmans, 1988).

reality on the ground and strategies that emanate and/or reflect from here. In the second part of this chapter, I offer my reflections as a Christian. My rationale for the selection of themes for missiological reflection is not entirely subjective: the themes I have included relate to and emerge from the cases. Their appropriateness for missiological reflection is, as I see it, supported by the selected cases. What I offer here, however, are snapshots of Muslim life from different schools; thus my reflections on them do not claim to be comprehensive.

CONTEXT OF HYDERABAD DECCAN

The context of Hyderabad Deccan is unsurprisingly complex given its long imperial, cultural, and political history as a Mughal, Nizami, and Indian state. It is impossible to sketch this and the cumulative impact of history on the identity of the Hyderabad people except to point to one formative event. British rule in India was in many cases indirect, coming as it did through 562 states of different sizes, most of which were incorporated into independent India or Pakistan in 1947. Hyderabad, one of the largest and richest of these states, was an exception. The independent India of 1947 was heterogeneous and majority Hindu, but it was held together by secular forces. Hyderabad was a unique case—not only was it majority Hindu, but it also was ruled by a Muslim (the Nizam Osman Ali Khan [1886–1967]).[3] Whereas most princely states acceded to either India or Pakistan, the state of Hyderabad chose to remain independent. As the state faced its own internal peasants' rebellion, India sought to annex it in what is euphemistically referred to as the "police action." The Majlis-e-Ittehadul-Muslimeen (MIM), which was formed in 1926 "to unite all Muslims" in the state, had cobbled together a private militia of about 200,000 *razakars* (volunteers), who collaborated with the Nizam's army to resist the Indian advance.[4] These conflicts affected a large population as Hyderabad was incorporated into India over five days of combat in 1948.[5] Although MIM was disbanded and its

[3]Khan was the last Nizam (ruler) of the state of Hyderabad and Berar. He inherited a dynasty that ruled over a South Asian region larger than the UK and that had been in existence since 1724.
[4]Anne Vaugier-Chatterjee, "Two Dominant Castes: The Socio-Political System in Andhra Pradesh" in *Rise of the Plebeians? The Changing Face of Indian Legislative Assemblies*, ed. Christophe Jaffrelot and Sanjay Kumar (New Delhi: Routledge, 2009), 285.
[5]A. G. Noorani, "Of a Massacre Untold," *Frontline* 18, no. 5 (March 3-16, 2001), www.frontline

leader, Qasim Razvi (1902–1970), exiled to Pakistan, today the group has reinvented itself as a political party known as the AIMIM.[6]

The seizure of the Hyderabad state proved to be doubly challenging for much of the Nizam's personnel because they were "foreign" (many had Arab, Afghan, or African backgrounds) and "Muslim." Most found creative ways to integrate with Indian Muslims and in their own broader social lives within the new state, and their descendants continue to do so even today. There is a fairly large population of Indian Muslims in Hyderabad, representing about 25-27 percent of the 7 million people who live in the region, but these Muslims are local converts or from other parts of India, and they belong to different schools of thought, or maslaks. Despite their apparent integration, those that are descended from Arab, Afghan, and African backgrounds appear to carry memories of the past as well as the creative ways in which their predecessors sought to belong and secure privileges when Hyderabad was first incorporated into India.[7] Their descendants, evidence shows, continue this process in different ways—some seek to address what they see as divisions within Indian Islam, while others seek to maintain broader affiliations with all Muslims, Hindus, and Christians.

The first case below comes from this melting pot of Indian and "foreign" Muslims in Hyderabad and focuses on two prominent maslaks. It is meant to illustrate an aspect of the diversity and dialogue present in this region. The second case involves the descendants of these foreign Muslims, who seek not just to assert an Indian Sufi identity but a different sort of dialogue.

MUNAZARA BETWEEN AHL-E HADITH-DEOBAND

I have argued before (as also others, for instance Sikand) that a cross-section of Islam in Hyderabad reveals many different maslaks.[8] It is not necessary

.in/static/html/fl1805/18051130.htm; Mike Thomson, "Hyderabad 1948: India's Hidden Massacre," BBC News, September, 24, 2013, www.bbc.com/news/magazine-24159594.
[6]All India Majlis-e-Ittehadul-Muslimeen is headquartered in the city of Hyderabad and represents Muslims both in the state legislature and in federal parliament.
[7]Taylor C. Sherman, "Migration, Citizenship and Belonging in Hyderabad (Deccan), 1946–1956," *Modern Asian Studies* 45, no. 1 (2011): 81-107.
[8]David Emmanuel Singh, *Islamization in Modern South Asia: Deobandi Reform and the Gujjar Response* (Berlin: Walter de Gruyter, 2012); David Emmanuel Singh, "Diverse Muslim Populations in India: Re-evaluating Our Approach," *Journal of Asian Mission* 15, no. 1 (2014): 43-56; and Yoginder Sikand, *Bastions of the Believers: Madrasas and Islamic Education in India* (New Delhi: Penguin Books India, 2005).

to list all of the various maslaks here, though these broadly range from the Salafi-inspired Ahl-e Hadith (AH)[9] to the Sufi-inspired Barelwis.[10] Deoband, one of the most prominent maslaks in India, falls somewhere near the center of this spectrum. This is because, like the Barelwis, the Deobandis follow a liberal school of law (Hanafi) but are also immersed in both philosophy and Sufi practice, which have helped shape their identity as Indian Muslims as open to working with Hindus, supportive of a united India, and so on.[11]

There is deep suspicion and even conflict between the maslaks, but in recent times the Deobandis and AH have often appeared together in gatherings for public debates. AH's aim in these debates has been to transform the locally informed Indian-Muslim maslaks into a single community living in "the exclusive light of the Qur'an and the Hadith."[12] It is unclear what the Deobandi agenda is, and they seem to take a rather defensive position in most gatherings. Despite provocations (even humiliations), the Deobandi are quite willing to associate with AH, seeing munazara as a means for relating to their ideological challengers.

Both the AH and the Deobandis see intermaslak debates as an extension of the arguments and reasoning with *ahl-al-kitāb* encouraged in the Qur'an (e.g., "And argue not with the People of the Scripture unless it be in (a way) that is better" [Q 29:46, Pickthall], and, "Say: O People of the Scripture! Come to an agreement between us and you" [Q 3:64, Pickthall]). But the flourishing of interfaith and intermaslak debates also reflects the heightened sense of identity resulting from interreligious interactions in nineteenth-century India.[13]

We know from the context of the debate in view and from wider observation of intermaslak relations that there are different issues keeping the two maslaks apart. These issues reveal contrasting positions on the nature and

---

[9]This maslak is aligned with the Saudi-Salafi movement, which has relatively few followers in India. However, when combined with Deoband (as in Pakistan), this group could become a force to reckon with and remains quite visible in India despite its smaller size.

[10]One of the largest maslaks in South Asia, the Barelwis maslak was founded by Ahmed Raza Khan (1856–1921) in the town of Bareilly, from which it received its name.

[11]See Singh, *Islamization in Modern South Asia*, Chap. 1, esp. 16-29.

[12]"Ahl-i Hadith," in *The Oxford Dictionary of Islam*, ed. J. L. Esposito (Oxford: Oxford University Press, 2014).

[13]For more on this period, see Kenneth Jones, *Socio-Religious Reform Movements in British India* (Cambridge: Cambridge University Press, 2006), and Kenneth Jones, *Religious Controversy in British India: Dialogues in South Asian Languages* (Albany: SUNY Press, 1992).

needs of the Muslim community. When engaging in dialogue, the maslaks seek to debate issues related to these positions. The case I am highlighting took place at an AH-affiliated house owned by Shaykh Fasih Hyderabadi.[14] Shaykh Fasih, an earnest young scholar of AH, is deeply motivated to propagate AH as the only true vision of Islam and permits no compromise: "There is one religion before God and that is Islam." The reality of interschool diversity represents a serious problem for him.

The three rooms in Shaykh Fasih's house fill up with Muslim youth wanting to see the performance. Most are nominally Deobandi, but there are supporters of AH and other maslaks as well. It takes about two hours to agree on the agenda containing the claims (*dawa*) and counterclaims, even though the outline of the debate had been settled previously via email. Emotions range from light-hearted laughing to stern warnings against humor as the issues at hand are said to be serious. It is organized chaos. A lot of time is wasted in unsettling others through frequent interruptions.

Shaykh Fasih is the host and has the stage for making any introductory remarks. His position, which is simple and unambiguous, sets the tone for the debate: there are different maslaks because each follows its own traditional authority (or disciples, or disciples of disciples) instead of simply following the Qur'an and hadith. He distinguishes AH from the others in its obedience to no authority save God (Qur'an) and the Prophet (hadith). Since the Deobandis follow Imam Abu Hanifah (ca. eighth century CE; the eponymous founder of the Hanafi, or the *hanafi muqallid*), they rely on a series of authorities following Hanafi to help contextualize their faith. This is *taqlid*—following an authority of a *mujtahid* other than the Qur'an/hadith—and to Shaykh Fasih this amounts to *kufr* (unbelief).

The Deobandi debater is on the defensive right from the start. Despite endless interruptions and accusations, including that Deobandis subscribe to a *khichdi madhab* (syncretistic position), he tries to stress that *taqlid* does not allow for complete freedom in contextualizing Islam. It is practiced only in those aspects of faith and practice where there is no possibility of finding

---

[14]"MUNAZARA or DEBATE b/w AHLE HADEES & DEOBANDI on TAQLEED," YouTube video, 5:28:11, from a debate between Shaykh Fasih Hyderabadi of Ahl-e hadith and Deobandi scholars in the home of Shaykh Fasih on November 9, 2014, posted by "DISQ SHAIKH FASIH," December 3, 2014, www.youtube.com/watch?v=nP49G_MBCYc.

a scriptural solution to a modern issue. In any case, he asserts, it is not about following a single authority (*taqlid-e shakhsi*) but about the consensus of a school (*maktab-e taqlid*) and its reasoning (*ijtihad*). In his own graceful manner, the Deobandi then manages to ask a key question of Shaykh Fasih: "Do you not do *taqlid*? How then do you address issues of modern times? We do *taqlid*, but how can you simply follow the Qur'an/hadith on questions for which there are no answers in these books?"[15] No answer is given. The entire process takes five and a half hours. Both groups claim victory and leave amicably enough, causing no damage except for some bruised egos. The aim of the entire conference (as was repeatedly asserted) was to influence not just those at the performance but also anyone who would later watch it on their computers, and several times during the course of the debate the onlookers were challenged to "convert" by moving to opposing sides of the room.

This munazara may not appear on the surface to serve any useful purpose other than being simply a performance. There is evidence from various reports (e.g., *multaqa ahl-e hadith*), however, that while AH still remains a united front against the Barelwis and others, they are now often divided on the Deobandis. The munazaras and the frequent opportunities these give for face-to-face interaction connect disparate lives and ideologies in silent ways. For example, on the important issue of "praying behind" an imam belonging to another school, some from AH have begun to suggest the Deobandi should be allowed to lead prayers.[16] This suggests rapprochement as the boundaries between certain schools in the broader context of the "intra-Sunni rivalry"[17] are beginning to break down. Unlike in interreligious debates, where identities become more sharply defined, in intrareligious debates mutual "crossing over"[18] and the engendering sense of a single community are more easily facilitated due to the presence of the overarching

[15]Ibid.

[16]See the discussion at "Multaqa Ahl al Hadeeth: Meeting Place of Students of Knowledge," www .ahlalhdeeth.com/vbe/archive/index.php/t-6346.html (accessed September 11, 2016).

[17]Yoginder Sikand, "Wahabi/Ahle Hadith, Deobandi and Saudi Connection: Ulema Rivalries and the Saudi Connection," *Sunnicity.com* (blog), April 14, 2010, https://sunninews.wordpress.com /2010/04/14/wahabiahle-hadith-deobandi-and-saudi-connection/.

[18]See Henry Hughes Presler, *The Mid-India Practice of Toleration Within Islam, Christianity, Hinduism: Eight Ways Incompatible Co-Religionists Preserve Their Brotherhoods* (Delhi: ISPCK, 1996), for the idea of "crossing over."

reality of Islam to which all belong. One can see these coalescing identities both in Pakistan and Britain, where the term *Deobandi* is often used interchangeably for the Salafis of South Asia.

Afro-Indian Muslim Performances

No consensus exists on the number of Afro-Indians (the descendants of African immigrants, also called Siddis) present in India today. The estimates range anywhere from thirty thousand to half a million.[19] Part of the difficulty with these estimations stems from Afro-Indians themselves, who often choose not to reveal their African connections. Most live in the state of Gujarat, and about ten to twelve thousand reside in the southern city of Hyderabad. Hyderabad's African Cavalry Guards (AC Guards) is home to the majority of self-identifying Afro-Indians. In another Hyderabad locality, Chinthal Basti (the *basti* or *siddi risala*), about one hundred families identify themselves as Afro-Indian.[20] They live among Indian Muslims of Arab or Afghan descent (40 percent) and Adi-Hindu descent (50 percent)[21] as well as Catholics (10 percent).[22]

Writing about the descendants of the Nizam's African guards, Ababu Minda Yimene argues that their self-identity moved in "divergent directions" through the adoption of either Indian or Arab affiliations. The conflict here involved these two groups accusing each other of "Islamic" or "Hindu" nationalism, the argument being that a single community was

---

[19]See David Emmanuel Singh, "The Roles of Religious Procession Among the Afro-Indian of the African Cavalry Guards in Hyderabad," *Journal of African Diaspora Archaeology and Heritage* 4, no. 1 (2015): 92–114; "Siddi Lore Mentions Nigerian Ancestor," *Times of India*, July 19, 2011, http://timesofindia.indiatimes.com/city/ahmedabad/Siddi-lore-mentions-Nigerian-ancestor/articleshow/9278391.cms.

[20]Alexander Francis (local Catholic of the Roch Memorial Church and Our Lady of Health), interview with the author, December 12, 2012; Abu bin Almaz (principal of Mawlana Azad Memorial High School, African Cavalry Guards), interview with the author, December 10, 2012; Ayaz bin Mahmood (local Majlis-e Ittehadul Muslimeen member and Pace Committee member), interview with the author, December 15, 2012.

[21]Those of Adi-Hindu descent largely consist of Dalits previously identified as *panchamas* (untouchables). The reinvention of their identity took shape in the early twentieth century. Bhagya Reddy Varma (1888–1939) is credited with being the reformer behind this transformation. As a group, the Adi-Hindu abhor the ancient Hindu law (*manusmrit*) but represent their identity in terms of the Sanskritic notion of the "Hindu."

[22]Largely of Tamil origin, the Catholics here served in the Nizam's army and were awarded grants in land, where two schools, a hospital, and a church thrive even today. These Christians appear to "punch above their weight" despite being a minority in the region.

being polarized into ideologically opposing groups.[23] After ten years of research, what I have found here is surprisingly different from Minda's position. The Afro-Indians in this case were predominately affiliated with Sufism and experienced different intrareligious and interreligious fault lines with the AH, Deoband-Tablighi Jama'at (a preaching pavement affiliated with Deoband), Adi-Hindus, and the Catholics.[24]

Observation and interviews conducted in the *basti* over two years highlighted three different methods for addressing these fault lines:[25] the procession, the *darbar* (royal court), and the *aman* (peace) committee.

The procession. The processions in Hyderabad and especially in the AC Guards are a martial hangover from the period of the Nizam. Their role then was to project power, keep challengers away, and celebrate warfare and victory. In the particular case below, an idiom of war has been translated into an open invitation for a fragmented community to join in the celebration of Sufi saint Khwaza-Gharib-Nawaz (KGN).[26]

The procession starts on the road in front of the KGN Arabic Daff Company.[27] The *daff* performers are especially enthusiastic in maintaining the vigorous rhythm of sounds from the three different types of instruments in use: the Arab *daff*, a small semicircular container covered with parchment or some plastic substitute and played with a stick; the Indian drum, a cylindrical device (larger than the *daff*) covered on two sides with parchment or plastic, hung on the neck, and played with one or two sticks; and a steel water container generally found in many Hyderabadi homes and used in storing water for cooking or drinking. The steel container doubles as an instrument and as storage for money offered by people on the way. The procession is accompanied by drums and a style of dancing incorporating

---

[23] Ababu Minda Yimene, "Dynamics of Ethnic Identity Among the Siddis of Hyderabad," *African and Asian Studies* 6, no. 3 (2007): 321-45; and Ababu Minda Yimene, *An African Indian Community in Hyderabad: Siddi Identity, Its Maintenance and Change* (Göttingen: Cuvillier Verlag, 2004).

[24] See Singh, "Roles of Religious Procession," 92-114.

[25] David Emmanuel Singh, video 1, from the procession and performance in AC Guards, Hyderabad, on May 5, 2013; and David Emmanuel Singh, video 2, from the procession and the performance in AC Guards, Hyderabad, on May 5, 2013.

[26] Khwaza-Gharib-Nawaz, often referred to as KGN, literally means "the benefactor of the poor." KGN was a thirteenth-century Muslim mystic (Sufi) affiliated with the Chishti order (also referred to as the Moinuddin Chishti).

[27] One of the three "*daff* companies" based in the *basti*. Each of these companies employs a group of about fifty to sixty performers for special events.

both martial movements (thrusting, piercing, slashing, chopping) and celebrations of the Indian festival of *basant* (harvest). As the procession passes
the streets, everyone in the community is invited to participate: Catholics,
Hindus, and Muslims from different schools of thought.

The centerpiece of this procession is the *chador* (an embroidered carpet)
in honor of KGN. Originally from somewhere between Iran and Afghanistan, KGN is depicted as *khwaja-e hind* (the Master of India) and is understood by the organizers as a benign rallying point for the divided community. The *chador* is displayed over a four-wheeled hand-propelled cart
with a flat top commonly used by poor vendors in South Asia for selling
fruits and vegetables. The cart has been reengineered to hold the *chador*
vertically so that most of it—rising fairly high above the *daff* players, the
impromptu dancers, and others in the procession—remains visible even
from far ahead of the procession. A map of India (with some artistic license taken in its creation) is displayed prominently in the middle of the
chador. The entire *chador* is fabricated and embroidered using both the
color of Islam (green) and the color of India (yellow for the festival of
basant). The procession swells as it winds through the narrow streets and
up to the function hall (usually reserved for weddings), where the *darbar*
has been set up.

The darbar. KGN is reimaged as a king in his court, complete with
courtiers. The difference here is that, although the setting replicates the
image of a court, its aims are devotional and inclusive. As the smoke of the
incense continues to grow, the *chador* and a Chishti Sufi standing in for
KGN have the pride of place in the hall, which is now full of men, women,
and children from the community.

The *darbar* here is a different sort of royal court—not the court of the
Nizam, but that of KGN.[28] In this *darbar*, KGN is embodied as a young man
dressed as a prince but bearing the name of a mysterious Islamic saint (Khizruddin). His *darbar* is not a place for passing judgments, punishing the
guilty, excluding the poor, or privileging the elite. Instead, it is a place for

---

[28]See Ibn ʿArabi, the thirteenth-century theologian-philosopher whose ideas permeate all Sufi
orders in South Asia, including KGN. Cf. David Emmanuel Singh, "Adam and Muhammad:
Models of Human Epistemic Potential," *Muslim World* 94, no. 2 (2004); and "The Possibility of
Having Knowledge of *Al-Wujud al-Mahd*: 'Sheer Being' According to Ibn ʿArabi's *Kitāb al-Jalāl
wa-ʾl-Jamāl*," *Islam and Christian-Muslim Relations* 10, no. 3 (1999): 295-306.

devotion, friendship, and hospitality. This is symbolized by both garlanding visitors and covering them with yellow scarves.

No one in need or who wants to be admitted into his presence is turned away: "O Lord of Hind [India], this is your high court," sing the *qawwals*. Those who come seeking gifts must have hearts expansive enough to receive, for otherwise, the *qawwals* remind those in attendance, their hearts would break open! The khwaja as king is reminded too that he should not change from being a *mawla* (protector) to a traditional king. People flock to him because he is different. The *qawwals* chant, "Sing in praise of your *mawla*; though the world has changed around us, we do not mind it; what we do mind is if our *mawla* changes! O my *mawla*, O my *mawla*, do not change, do not change." These ideas are repeated by the *qawwals*:

O *shahenshah* [king of kings], the *sultanate* [kingdom] is yours; the *nizam* [government] is yours; you are my *aka* [master], and I am your *ghulam* [slave]. Thousands of *badshah* [kings] come and go, but your *hukumat* [rule] lasts forever. My khwaja's sultanate is eternal; my khwaja is a *badshah*; he is our *murshid* [teacher]. *Lakhs* [hundreds of thousands] of *murids* [disciples] rely on him—I live because of him, and I have no *gham* [sadness].

Another *qawwal* sings, "My *pir* [lit. old person; refers to a Sufi master] is before me, I will not lack; my khaja [khwaja] is king."[29]

As those gathered feel a rush of deep emotion, cash begins to float through the hall, and Khizruddin is kept busy dispensing gifts and cash on behalf of the people. Those wanting to offer their gifts to the *qawwals* bring their cash to Khizruddin, who sometimes rises from his seat regally and walks along with the donor to the platform as the cash is gifted to the singers, after which he returns to his seat. Occasionally donors come to his presence, roll the cash around his majestic cap, and then offer this to the singers as a gift from the king.

Aesthetics of performance. Theoretically, the ideas of the procession and the court may be explained as a sort of "aesthetic revolt." Two brief examples of similar "revolts" will help to explain this concept. First is the "decollation of St. John." John the Baptist is the patron saint of French Canadians and has been a national icon there since the mid-nineteenth century. In 1969, there

---

[29]Singh, video 2.

was a public beheading of his statue by believers in an annual procession in his honor in Montreal. This event has been described as an "aesthetic revolt" because of how key symbols of identity were invoked when insiders perceived a threat, in this case fear over the exercise of absolute power.[30] Second is the "Kano *darbar*." This example of aesthetic revolt straddles local Nigerian politics and Islam. The *darbar* in question is an annual event (coinciding with the Id) celebrating the powerless nineteenth-century emirate. It involves different performances, including prayers, processions, and martial rituals, in several northern cities of Nigeria. In the main event at Kano, the emir receives tributes from horsemen who pass through the city and reach the palace in a procession, as in the past. In this theater, a disparate audience feels reconstituted as "a single cultural community" around the emir, who has no real power.[31]

In the first example, the exercise of absolute power was critiqued through a public performance, and in the second, a symbol of absolute power has been reinvented to publicly relive a counter reality. Here the processions are used not as a military exercise but as an invitation to belong to the emir's spiritual sphere. They offer a veiled critique of the representations of God that make him appear distant and severe. If God moves among people, invites them to him, shares bread with them, and offers gifts to them, then those who follow him should do the same for their neighbors. This is where the idea of hospitality emanates from, which I shall say more about later. Humor, song, and good-natured conversation in such public performances juxtapose the benign and the dangerous (that which causes fear).[32] In the case of the performative *darbar*, the presence of God—or someone representing him in the theatrical backdrop of an alternative *darbar*—enables participants to rise above their personal, religious, or denominational differences. It also enables them to share this space with even their ideological challengers and reflect on God together.

---

[30]See more in Geneviève Zubrzycki, "Beheading of the Saint: Aesthetic Revolt and the Remaking of the National Identity in Quebec 1960-69" (lecture, Workshops in Cultural Sociology 2011–2012, Centre for Cultural Sociology, Yale University, September 30, 2011).

[31]Wendy Griswold and Muhammed Bhadmus, "The Kano Durbar: Political Aesthetics in the Bowel of the Elephant," *American Journal of Cultural Sociology* 1, no. 1 (February 2013): 125-51.

[32]"Jimmy Carr and the Science of Laughter," *Horizon BBC*, www.bbc.co.uk/programmes/b07vxkbv (accessed October 12, 2016).

Aman *(peace) committee.* Postcolonial Indian historians acknowledge the colonial construction of religious identities. These historians also suggest that many Indians themselves have internalized these identities[33] and demanded "allegiance" from others in their communities to actively further their interests.[34] For example, the Sanyasi Rebellion, featured in the nineteenth-century novel *Anandamath*,[35] was characterized as a revolt led by "Hindu" monks against the British, with "Muslims" also being identified as adversaries.[36] The novel likely found inspiration from the first recorded conflict characterized as "Hindu-Muslim." This 1853 conflict began over the sixteenth-century "Babri Masjid," a simmering symbol of "communal" identities eventually demolished in 1992 by Hindu nationalists. Since the 1853 event, several other conflicts have been characterized as "Hindu-Muslim," including a few in Hyderabad.[37] In the context of a wider memory of such conflicts, interviews reveal many local fissures.[38] Apart from the public performances (outlined above), Afro-Indians seem adept also at peacemaking through proactive community organization.

As I looked for familiar faces in the performances described above, I noticed the conspicuous absence of some prominent Afro-Indians I knew. They were uninterested in sacred performances, envisioning instead a different (more proactive and direct) route to addressing fault lines, one that involved a different definition of self-identity. For example, Abu-bin-Almaz (principal of a school and a congressman) believed that popular religious beliefs and practices were not something to be flaunted but kept private.

---

[33]See Gauri Vishwanathan, "Colonialism and the Construction of Hinduism," in *The Blackwell Companion to Hinduism*, ed. Gavin Flood (Malden, MA: Blackwell, 2003).

[34]See Romila Thapar, "Imagined Religious Communities? Ancient History and the Modern Search for a Hindu Identity," *Modern Asian Studies* 23, no. 2 (1989): 209-31.

[35]Bankim Chandra Chattopadhyay, *Anandamath, or The Sacred Brotherhood*, trans. J. J. Lipner (Oxford: Oxford University Press, 2005).

[36]William Pinch, *Warrior Ascetics and Indian Empires* (Cambridge: Cambridge University Press, 2006), 94.

[37]Hendrik Vroom, Henry Jansen, and Jerald Gort, eds., *Religion, Conflict and Reconciliation: Multifaith Ideals and Realities* (Amsterdam: Rodopi B.V., 2004); see also "Communal Clashes Breakout in Hyderabad," *Hindu*, April 9, 2012, updated July 13, 2016, www.thehindu.com/news/cities/ Hyderabad /communal-clashes-break-out-in-hyderabad/article3295782.ece; Abhishek Sharan, "Huji, Not Hindu Group Behind Mecca Masjid Blast," *Hindustan Times*, September 23, 2010, www.hindustantimes.com/delhi/huji-not-hindu-group-behind-mecca-masjid-blast/story -mUeqmUUahKnuyTlxwox3NJ.html.

[38]I am still transcribing these recordings, but this position is also based on years of observation living in AC Guards with family and on my own research.

Celebrating a mainstream Sufi spirituality was fine, but not when it was disengaged from or prioritized over other more relevant layers of what made them who they were: Indian first, Muslim or African second.[39] Public performances were lower down on his list of priorities; more important was proactivity in assuming agency. Peace-committee initiatives were evidence of this agency. In this reimagination, the emphasis was more directly on community building and reordering a sense of self, so that in public discourse the "Indian" preceded the "Muslim" (Sufi or traditional) and the "African." Another prominent person absent from the performance was Ayaz-bin-Mahmood (a local Afro-Indian political activist belonging to the Majlis-e-Ittehadul-Muslimeen and a local peace-committee member).[40] He also believed in direct engagement through active peacemaking among Muslims, Catholics, and Adi-Hindus of the *basti*.

As illustrated before, the context of South Asia is quite fractious, yet there are opportunities for public expressions of faith. The need is to carefully remain within the sanctioned limits tacitly allowed for all players. Here local Catholics are not excluded, though in practice they often (but not always) prefer to keep their faith private. A more outgoing and outwardly visible faith can be seen by all as a player in overcoming fault lines (provided it restricts itself to the unspoken limits). Several specific cases of the role played by this committee in Chinthal Basti came to light as I spoke to the representatives from different maslaks and from Adi-Hindus and Catholics. There is no space here to detail these narratives, but suffice it to say, their efforts in this microcosm seem amplified by the recognition by both politicians and the police of their contribution to peacemaking. In a region of India where people live and express their vision of faith publicly (literally on the streets), the potential for interreligious conflicts and violence is huge. Managing such vitality through active peacemaking appears to be no mean feat.

MISSIOLOGICAL REFLECTIONS

In my description above, I used two cases from Hyderabad. These cases highlight three different strategies Muslims from different schools have adopted: performative debates, processions and court scenes, and peace

---

[39]Almaz, interview.
[40]Mahmood, interview.

committees. As a Christian observer, I wonder if there is something for the church to learn from this.

I highlighted first the role of debates in encouraging interschool encounters by looking at two of the many schools of thought that are often in bitter conflict with each other. I then described three different ways in which a local community of Sufist Muslims (like most South Asians) reconnect over intrareligious/interreligious fissures they experience locally: first, through a reinvented martial procession adapted as an open invitation to a sacred performance involving a Sufi saint from history; second, through the enactment of an alternative court scene complete with a living Sufi roleplaying an unusual king, his courtiers, and their unreserved hospitality to guests; and third, through the more proactive and direct route of peacemaking and managing conflict.

I chose the case involving the interschool debates to speak about the continuing relevance of debates in mission, something I have failed to appreciate in the past. My interest in this was sparked while supervising a student working on a nineteenth-century interfaith debate in India. The case I described above, however, also lends itself to reflection on the continuing relevance of debates as a mission method: first, the form of the intrafaith/interfaith debates used by Muslims in South Asia is modeled arguably on the nineteenth-century missionary approach in vogue among Muslims from that period; and second, even though most missionaries have given up on this approach, fresh evidence suggests that debates might not have been futile after all. There is some evidence to suggest that the debates, while not resulting in mass movements among Muslims, resulted in secret believers.

I chose the case involving the procession, the royal court scene, and the peace committee to draw attention to the following items. First, there is a need for freer public expressions of the Christian faith (where possible) as an invitation not only to meet Jesus but also to publicly experience his followers' hospitality. Christians are often ill-informed about the faiths of others and often do little to express their own faith freely for others to learn from or participate in Christianity; this may be easier to address by adopting a performative route immersed in devotion and humor. Second, the church must reemphasize the importance of the activist route in witnessing to Jesus. Christian minorities are often too occupied in their own concerns or too fearful of other peoples' conflicts to fulfill their roles as peacemakers. The manner in which Christians mimic public expressions of faith may help in this regard.

DEBATES AND SECRET BELIEVERS

Public debates. Since my recent discovery of the massive nineteenth-century text *Collected Works of an Aryan Pilgrim* [41] and my supervision of a doctoral student[42] researching a nineteenth-century Muslim convert, Imaduddin (1830–1900), I have learned that intrafaith/interfaith debates in South Asia owe much to two nineteenth-century debating legacies. Though considered spiritual battles by some, these debates were clever public performances meant to expose the weaknesses of debating partners and encourage listeners to switch camps, occasionally openly but mostly privately, to minimize offense.

First, the debates were spectacles, the nineteenth century's Great Agra Debate a primary example of this.[43] The format of such debates theoretically allowed both parties to present their arguments on issues where there was difference of opinion. The goal was to expose those who "lost" the argument in full view of interested viewers, who would then (at least in theory) follow the natural course of "converting" to the victors' position. Clearly both parties believed they were absolutely right, and with no groups officially conceding defeat, there were hardly ever any open conversions. The show was therefore not only to make the disputants feel good for fulfilling certain obligations, but also to influence viewers in their personal beliefs. Second, the debates were understood also as "prayer duels." Take, for instance, the case of Scottish minister John Alexander Dowie and South Asian Ahmadi Mirza Ghulam Ahmad, on the one hand, and Arya Samaj (a Hindu reformist group), Pundit Lekhram, and Mirza Ghulam Ahmad, on the other.[44] Here the challenge was not to defeat the opponent in argument but to expose their "falsehood"

---

[41] Pundit Lekhram, *Kulliat-e-Arya-Musafir* (Saharanpur: Satya Dharam Parcharak, 1904); cf. Kenneth W. Jones, *Socio-Religious Reform Movements in British India* (Cambridge: Cambridge University Press, 2006).

[42] Maqsood Kamil, a Pakistani Christian scholar, is working toward a PhD studying Imaduddin's role in completing "the unfinished agenda" of the Great Agra Debate.

[43] Avril Powell, *Muslims and Missionaries in Pre-Mutiny India* (Richmond, UK: Curzon, 1993).

[44] See Lekhram, *Kulliat.*

enough for God to do the rest. Thus, those who subscribed to falsehood were expected to die.[45] It was presented as a spiritual battle, complete with an elaborate public performance meant to make an effect upon viewers.

Thankfully, prayer duels are not happening today, but the debates modeled on the Great Agra Debate are still fairly common. We have, however, little evidence of these ever leading to significant levels of conversion. In her "sociology of conversion" from selected Arab contexts (and especially from among women), Kathryn Kraft notes some reasons for the lack of expected conversions: the enormous difficulties converts face in relating with churches and missionaries, and, more importantly, the notions of "Tawhid and Umma."[46] Missionary writings from the nineteenth century recognize these difficulties too: for instance, Burgoyne, a missionary with the Bible Churchmen's Missionary Society in India, wrote of Islam being the most "persistent challenge" for "the missionary enterprise" for a hundred years. He portrayed Islam as a "virile" and "fanatical" religion embedded "behind a wall of law and tradition."[47]

Burgoyne also wrote about a handful of exceptional cases where "stalwart converts . . . were won to Christ by such argumentation," but such converts were clearly few in number.[48] Another report in Louise Creighton's (1850–1936) work, purportedly based on a paper written by a convert, suggested too that "converts from Islam to Christianity have come"[49] but never in large numbers. Such "conversions from the Moslem faith in India have always been individual—there has never been anything of the nature of a mass movement."[50] Of these individual converts, Creighton claimed that the number of learned converts ("men of real intellectual mark") from Islam was far greater than that of those who were not learned. The reason for this was said to be the strategy of missionaries, who focused their efforts on "Moslem students," hoping to "influence Muslim thought" through them.[51] The prime example

---

[45]Dowie died in 1907, a year before the Mirza; Pundit Lekhram was murdered in 1897, about six years after his duel.

[46]Kathryn Ann Kraft, *Searching for Heaven in the Real World: A Sociological Discussion of Conversion in the Arab World* (Oxford: Regnum, 2013).

[47]S. R. Burgoyne, *The Christian Church and the Convert from Islam* (Lucknow, India: Lucknow Publishing House, 1999), 1.

[48]Ibid., 17.

[49]Louise Creighton, *Missions: Their Rise and Development* (London: Williams and Norgate, 1912), 137.

[50]Ibid., 136.

[51]Ibid., 136-37.

of such rare conversions was Mawlawi Imaduddin, who was present at the
Agra Debate in 1854, baptized in 1866, and ordained in 1868. He has been
hailed as "the great literary champion of the church at Amritsar."[52]

The actual number of baptized converts then (as today) was low, and
where such conversions took place, they were largely among scholars. Ordinary Muslims, it appears, remained untouched by these methods, and if
they were influenced, the power of "the wall of law and tradition," combined
with what Gairdner calls "insecurity and political pressure," discouraged
conversion to Christianity.[53] This "wall" was an invincible fort that, for Burgoyne, neither the soft approach of personal friendships nor institutional
debates had been able to breach.[54] As I outline below, however, Burgoyne
was only partially right, and this is why I think there is value in public debates if conducted respectfully and with integrity.

Secret believers. Zwemer alluded to a phenomenon among Muslims of his
time that we are now familiar with both from testimonies of mission practitioners and some academic works: "[There are] Moslems who would secretly
assert themselves as Christians, but make no open statement because of the
danger attending."[55] Gairdner too wrote of Muslims seeking freedom and
called upon all Christians to pray for those "who have secretly believed."[56]
Imaduddin, who I referred to above, should be at the heart of the discussion
on mission among Muslims. In my modest effort here, I merely wish to point
to the evidence we have from his autobiography, which, like an honest testimony, mentions the presence of a large number of secret believers in Islamic
circles.[57] As a convert who scaled the "wall of law and tradition," his testimony
is significant even though he makes this reference only in passing.

The published version of his autobiography contains two parts. The first
part was written immediately following his baptism in 1866. The second part,
written in 1873, contains, as expected, a more reflective account of the evidence of "the grace of God" for someone who had successfully scaled "the

---

[52]Church of England, National Assembly, Missionary Council, *The Call from the Moslem World*
(Westminster: Press and Publications Board of the Church Assembly, 1926), 46.
[53]William Temple Gairdner, *The Rebuke of Islam* (London: United Council for Missionary Education, 1920), 196.
[54]Burgoyne, *Christian Church*, 1.
[55]Samuel Zwemer, *The Law of Apostasy in Islam* (London: Marshall, Morgan & Scott, 1924), 24.
[56]Gairdner, *Rebuke of Islam*, 197.
[57]Mawlawi Imaduddin, *Waqi'at-i 'Imadiyya* (Lahore: Punjab Religious Book Society), 1957.

wall of law and tradition" and faced the threat of dire consequences. One such consequence included estrangement from his wife, who was deeply offended by his decision to be baptized. As part of his commitment to transcend "the wall," he was even willing to "leave her behind for the sake of Christ"; this, however, did not happen, as she herself had an "encounter with Christ" and followed him into Christianity. This led to his five daughters and four sons following suit and receiving baptism. All of his sons except for one, who passed away, became "servants of God" (*masih ke bande*) with him.[58] His autobiography then delves into a theological discourse on the true knowledge of God for Muhammad's ummah, which is "bereft of the *injil* and the *torah*,"[59] and makes a passing reference to secret believers.

Imaduddin acknowledges that even those who understood Christianity often did not take the final step toward conversion, as Safdar 'Ali (another product of the Great Agra Debate) and he had done: "They [Muslims] said to me clearly that they know *din-e muhammdi* cannot be true (*haqq*) but we cannot help; we do not wish to lose *izzat* (honour) in our world." Some of them advised him too not to reveal his new faith: "*Zahir mein musalman kahlao; dil men masih par aitiqad rakkho*" (Remain a Muslim externally, but in your heart have faith in Christ). Some of them said to him that the religion of the Christ (*masih ka madhhab*) was reliable (*durust*) and intellectually satisfying (*muwafiq-e 'aql*) but that they did not understand the Trinity and Jesus as the Son of God as well as some Christian practices (and hence were unable to take the risk of becoming openly Christian).[60]

Kraft's qualitative research among women in Lebanon and Egypt shows that the notion of secret believers as mentioned by nineteenth- and early twentieth-century missionaries and in Imaduddin's autobiography was not a figment of their imagination.[61] It is as real today as it was then. One of my students is currently researching secret believers in Southeast Asia using empirical evidence gathered from five different locations. These believers choose to reveal themselves selectively in order to relate with Christians and allow Christians access to their world. Duane Miller's recent PhD work from

[58]Ibid., 25-26.
[59]Ibid., 10-11.
[60]Ibid., 22-23.
[61]See Kraft, *Searching for Heaven*.

the University of Edinburgh encourages the church to search for theology making emerging from secret believers who identify themselves as "ex-Muslim Christians."[62]

Henry Presler's work[63] throws some theoretical light on the mechanism involved in the "crossing over" of ordinary people from one denomination, sect, or faith to another without openly converting. Such undercurrents among Muslims raise big questions about the nature of belonging, the church as an institution versus the people of God, kingdom- versus church-centric mission, theology making by insiders versus contextualization, and so on—all of which requires further thought.

PUBLICLY PERFORMED PRACTICE

Inviting strangers to Jesus' **darbar.** Our second case highlighted public expressions of religious life in Hyderabad, much of which occurs on the streets. I described there the adaptation of a military march as inviting people to a "*darbar*," a public space used for the creative enactment of a royal court scene. While we will discuss later the expressions of faith on the streets, I focus here on the court scene to highlight specific elements that may be relevant for thinking about Christian mission.

The first point to underline is that the court scene serves as a deliberate departure from the image of a prophet-king. In our story, the young Sufi saint dressed as a king was named Khizruddin, which is significant. The qur'anic account of Moses is, as is well known, generally in accord with the Bible. The exception to this is Qur'an 18:60-82, which contains an extraordinary story of Moses and his mysterious travel companion, who is called the Khidr (lit. the Green One) in Muslim tradition.[64] Unsurprisingly, this mysterious person has been acknowledged as an individual with high prophetic office.[65] Any other identification here would be tricky, as Moses was a prophet-messenger and could not conceivably be taught by anyone from below his station. The Sufi orders represented in South Asia, not least the

---

[62]Duane Miller, "Living Among the Breakage: Contextual Theology-Making and Ex-Muslim Christians" (PhD diss., University of Edinburgh, 2014), 1-17 and 217-50.

[63]See Presler, *The Mid-India Practice.*

[64]*The History of al-Tabari,* vol. 3, *The Children of Israel,* trans. William Brinner (Albany: SUNY Press, 1991), 1-18.

[65]Brannon Wheeler, *Prophets in the Qur'an* (New York: Continuum, 2002), 40.

Chishtiyya, which is particularly relevant here,[66] accord a special place to Khidr, who is represented as a saint and an heir of the prophet.[67] Clearly, the Sufis offer a new exposition for Qur'an 18, which emphasizes a new phase or dispensation of the saints and sainthood inaugurated by the Saint of saints, the Khidr.[68] God speaks and does so directly through Khidr to the faithful.

Second, the court scene serves also as a departure from the dominant narrative involving a distant God. God relates with humanity not just through the prophets but also through the saints. To Sufis, the Khidr is the very embodiment of the saints, as he is from God and journeys to God. He is also an heir of the prophet (thus providing continuity), albeit a different kind of heir—a spiritual one, as he is from the Spirit (or Light). Arthur Jeffery, who translated a treatise attributed to one of the greatest Sufis, Ibn ʿArabi (who deeply influenced Sufism in South Asia; 1165–1240),[69] suggests that the purpose of the treatise was to make a Muslim contribution to the Christian idea of *logos*.[70] The notion of the Spirit was, therefore, consciously equated with the *logos*. The Khidr represented this Spirit. Sufis drew on Islamic philosophy, where a distinction was made between God-for-us and God-in-Himself.[71] One way of characterizing God was to speak of him in terms of the Spirit or *logos*, the source of all creation and wisdom/revelation.[72] So the saintlike king that they exalted symbolized the Creator, who relates with his creation as a friend and guides those that choose to follow him.

The third point again relates to the idea of the mysterious companion of Moses, the Khidr. In the Hebrew-Christian tradition, the figure of Melchizedek

---

[66]The Chishtiyya Order was originally from Afghanistan but came to India through Moinuddin Chishti (1141–1236) in the twelfth century.

[67]See more on the idea of the "heir" in Arthur F. Buehler, *Sufi Heirs of the Prophet: The Indian Naqshbandiyya and the Rise of the Mediating Sufi Shaykh* (Columbia: University of South Carolina Press, 1998).

[68]See more on sainthood in Michel Chodkiewicz, *Seal of the Saints: Prophethood and Sainthood in the Doctrine of Ibn ʿArabī*, trans. Liadain Sherrard (Cambridge: The Islamic Texts Society, 1993), 116-46, and Gerald T. Elmore, *Islamic Sainthood in the Fullness of Time: Ibn al-ʿArabī's Book of the Fabulous Gryphon* (Leiden: Brill, 1999).

[69]See David Emmanuel Singh, "Sainthood and Revelatory Discourse" (PhD thesis, University of Wales, 2002).

[70]See Arthur Jeffery, "Ibn ʿArabi's *Shajarat al-kawn*," in *Studia Islamica* 10 (1959): 44-77, and *Studia Islamica* 11 (1960): 113-60.

[71]Ian Richard Netton, *Allah Transcendent: Studies in the Structure and Semiotics of Islamic Philosophy, Theology, and Cosmology* (London: Routledge, 1989), 213, 221.

[72]Sayyid Husain Nasr, "The Meaning and Concept of Philosophy in Islam," in *History of Islamic Philosophy*, ed. Sayyid Husain Nasr and Oliver Leaman (London: Routledge, 1996), 1:21-26.

perhaps comes closest to the mystery of the Khidr. Melchizedek, who appears from nowhere after Abraham rescues his nephew Lot, is not identified with any prophet in the Hebrew Scriptures. He knows the Most High God, who has given victory to Abraham. In Hebrews 7, this person has been cast as a type of Jesus. Also, the identification of the mysterious person in the Qur'anic narrative, who the Sufis consider to be a high saint (or even God for us), may not be too dissimilar to Paul's acknowledgment of an Athenian "unknown god"—the god the people of Athens worshiped but were ignorant of (cf. Acts 17:16-34).

The fourth and final point is more tangible. In South Asia, the *darbar* is not merely a theoretical idea for a possible Christian mission practice. *Jesu darbar* (the court of Jesus) is a reality in one of India's few Christian universities, Sam Higginbottom Institute of Agriculture, Technology and Sciences (SHIATS).[73] The idea of the *darbar* in this particular Christian mission outreach comes originally from a well-known Brahmin convert, Narayan Vaman Tilak (1861–1919), who sadly did not have enough time or encouragement to apply his experience of Jesus as his king and the fellowship of his followers as the *darbar* of their Lord Jesus.[74] There is need, however, for further investigation into this phenomenon to see whether it is replicable in other contexts in South Asia with a large Muslim population.

Some supposedly marginal Muslim traditions do more than others to nurture ideas that may possibly make it easier for Muslims to follow Jesus. Such ideas like the Khidr, *darbar*, Spirit/Light, and so on appear in such traditions not to be accidental. In line with many Christian theologians writing from the South Asian context, one might suggest that God has not left himself without witness. In his eternal wisdom God is able to use such ideas to prepare the way for people to respond to Jesus, as many Muslims do. Pierre Johanns (1882–1955), Jules Monchanin (1895–1957), Manilal Parekh (1885–1967), and Dhanjibhai Fakirbhai (1895–1967) were some of the many theologians who considered local religious ideas to be "authentic [preparations] for the gospel."[75]

[73]See "The Royal Court of Jesus: Yeshu Darbar; Vision of Gospel and Plough," accessed June 14, 2016, http://shiats.edu.in/yDarbar/yDarbar.asp.
[74]David Emmanuel Singh, "Sunder Singh and NV Tilak: Lessons for Missiology from Twentieth Century India," in *Mission Spirituality and Authentic Discipleship*, ed. Wonsuk Ma and Kenneth R. Ross (Oxford: Regnum Books International, 2013), 128-39.
[75]M. Stephen, *A Christian Theology in the Indian Context* (Delhi: ISPCK, 2001), 22-30.

Hospitality to strangers. Hospitality is one of the underlying themes emerging from the second case. The court scene imagines an all-encompassing community that breaks down the walls between people affiliated with different religious, ideological, or ethnic groupings; here they experience proximity to one another. Sanneh has spoken of freedom as a precondition for peace (more on peace in the next section).[76] In contexts where freedom is lacking, some have concluded that "peacemaking starts with hospitality."[77] Sharing of gifts and food is often the first step toward realizing friendship. Here people start relating with each other not by engaging in polemics but in generous giving. Debates should therefore occur in such an environment of friendship.

Muslim missionary Henry Martyn (1781–1812) believed that hospitality and friendship were the reason for Abdul Masih's (1776–1827) conversion to Christianity. Abdul Masih later became the first native missionary of the Church Mission Society and also the first ordained Indian priest in the Anglican Church.[78] Abdul Masih himself used this approach with Muslims, though expectedly without much success in terms of converts.[79] As a missionary writer, Burgoyne believed personal friendships were not helpful in gaining converts but that they did draw people to Jesus: "Many of them [were] still believers in secret, but finding their spiritual food in this Revelation."[80] The idea of hospitality as a starting point is therefore missiologically significant. Noteworthy too is its ability to influence social, cultural, and political issues of our time and potentially promote broader cohesion in society. The idea is worth theoretical reflection. How is hospitality framed in different disciplines?

In historical works hospitality is usually linked to antiquity, where accommodating guests and safeguarding strangers at one's door were seen to

---

[76]Lamin Sanneh, *Summoned from the Margins* (Grand Rapids: Eerdmans, 2012), 143.

[77]See the post by Alicia Hughes, "Peacemaking Starts with Hospitality," Preemptive Love Coalition, June 28, 2015, www.preemptivelove.org/peacemaking_starts_with_hospitality; see also Matthew T. Lee, Margaret M. Poloma, and Stephen G. Post, *The Heart of Religion: Spiritual Empowerment, Benevolence, and the Experience of God's Love* (Oxford: Oxford University Press, 1972), 158.

[78]Graham Kings, "Abdul Masih: Icon of Indian Indigeneity," *Fulcrum*, April 1, 2011, www.fulcrum-anglican.org.uk/articles/abdul-masih-icon-of-indian-indigeneity/.

[79]Burgoyne, *Christian Church*, 5.

[80]Ibid., 17.

be sacred obligations. Providing food and shelter was also an essential part
of this obligation (cf. 1 Kings 17:7-16; Gen 18:1-15).[81] However, this could
easily be taken to another extreme, as is clear from the story of Lot and his
hospitality to visitors (Gen 19:8). In social anthropology literature, hospitality is viewed more critically, as a mechanism for negotiating both kinships
and friendships.[82] This often contrasts with the hostility one sees from
certain quarters toward the treatment of migrants, refugees, and asylum
seekers.[83] Critical studies on hospitality also helpfully point to the evidence
of "control" and "management" of strangers who might be perceived as
"dangerous" (in some cases for good reasons). Here some might see hospitality also as a means of civilizing strangers.[84] In these contexts, the professional, managerial approach to hospitality contrasts sharply with faith-based
(and largely Christian) interventions. Whereas the management approach
tends to focus on the pragmatic issues of "food, drink and accommodation,"[85]
the faith-based approach often involves a more emotional/relational motivation and an accompanying witness to Christ.[86]

   In speaking of hospitality, the approach of French Catholic scholar Louis
Massignon (1883–1962) to working with Muslims stands out to me. He was
deeply informed by his experience of the sacrificial hospitality of Muslims.
But hospitality to Massignon was not merely about doing good to others,
nor was it simply a task motivated by social or moral imperatives. To him it
had deeper spiritual roots and was fundamentally about displacing our ego
to make room within us for the Spirit of God. Hospitality was therefore a

[81]See also "Section CXLVI" of the *Mahabharata*, accessed September, 22, 2016, www.sacred-texts
.com/hin/m12/m12a145.htm; K. O'Gorman, "Discovering Commercial Hospitality in Ancient
Rome," *Hospitality Review* 9, no. 2 (2007): 44-52; and J. Browner, *The Duchess Who Wouldn't Sit
Down: An Informal History of Hospitality* (New York: Bloomsbury, 2003).
[82]See Raymond Jamous, *Kinship and Rituals Among the Meos of Northern India* (New Delhi: Oxford
University Press, 2003); Tom Selwyn, "An Anthropology of Hospitality," in *In Search of Hospitality: Theoretical Perspectives and Debates*, ed. C. Lashley and A. Morrison (Oxford: Butterworth-
Heinemann, 2000), 18-37.
[83]Sara Ahmed, *Strange Encounters: Embodied Others in Post-Coloniality* (London: Routledge, 2000).
[84]Bob Brotherton and Roy Wood, "Key Themes in Hospitality Management," in *The SAGE
Handbook of Hospitality Management*, ed. Roy Wood and Bob Brotherton (London: SAGE,
2007), 35-61.
[85]See David Bell, "Tourism and Hospitality," in *The SAGE Handbook of Tourism Studies*, ed. Tazim
Jamal and Mike Robinson (London: SAGE, 2009), 19-34.
[86]Hany Fouadgirgis, "Immigration and Faith Interaction: An Examination of the Evangelical
Faith-Based Engagements with Muslim North African Immigrants in Spain" (unfinished PhD
diss., Middlesex University).

"spiritual commission," even a "spiritual technique," that enabled one to intercede and sacrifice for fellow humans. If all Christians fulfilled this commission, it could be a powerful witness to Jesus Christ.[87] William Temple Gairdner, who is all but forgotten in my context even though he played a central role in the 1910 Edinburgh World Missionary Conference, draws our attention back to what he calls "the Spirit of Christ." He believed we have nothing of true value to give to Muslims except pointing them to Jesus and doing this in "the Spirit of the Father in Jesus Christ. . . . The Spirit of Jesus is the only asset of the Church."[88]

Publicly performed faith and peacemaking. South Asian Christians are generally not good at expressing their faith outwardly even though a lot of life in this context is lived on the streets. It is commonplace to see children playing on the streets or families temporarily occupying a busy street with a wedding tent. National and religious celebrations are also routine: from Muslim celebrations such as Id Muharram, *miladun nabi*, and Sufi Urs to Sikh and Hindu festivals. Political protests are almost always out on the street or at designated public spaces. Christians often appear too shy to live out their faith in the public forum. Churches seem to most non-Christians as forbidding places whose doors often remain shut during the week (unlike temples and *gurudwaras*). The Catholics in the *basti* are an exception. As a reflection of the religious activism in the *basti*, they stage massive processions in honor of "Our Lady of Health," a miracle-working Mary whose shrine is housed in a tiny chapel in the *basti*. Hundreds of people participate in the procession and the mass on September 8 (the day of her feast); most participants in the procession, according to local testimonies, are often local Muslims and Hindus.

Sadly, however, the church here has also been a source of conflict as it has sought to expand its sphere beyond the tacitly approved practice of processions. Images and icons of deities are a common occurrence in the streets, on staircases, and in public building entrances. A serious conflict was caused when the priest of the Catholic church in the *basti* decided to install an outdoor statue of Jesus and Mary facing a mosque and some

---

[87]See Patrick Laude, *Louis Massignon: The Vow and the Oath*, trans. Edin Q. Lohja (London: The Matheson Trust, 2011), 242.
[88]Gairdner, *Rebuke of Islam*, 136-37.

Muslim homes. Reportedly, the priest's reason for pushing for the instal-
lation of the statue was to prevent passersby from using the area as a
"public spittoon" and "urinal."[89] It is not hard to appreciate this logic. In-
stalling an image of a deity or a sacred symbol in or near buildings is a
popular method across India for preventing people from spitting or uri-
nating in public spaces. However, this is not how most local residents saw
it, instead believing that the socially accepted boundaries of the annual
processions had been exceeded. The projection of Catholic faith through
an annual procession was universally accepted because of its perceived
social gain, but this permanent statue was seen as a means of advancing
Catholicism, not Christ the healer. Interestingly, evidence of conflict ema-
nated from within the Catholic church, and it was a Muslim Afro-Indian,
Ajaz bin Mahmood, who found himself engaged in mediation.[90] In my
interview with him, Ajaz outlined the difficulties: opposition to the statue
of Jesus and Mary from within the church due to a fear of conflict, and
conflict inspired by a rogue element in the *basti* or someone politically
motivated to cause a local disturbance from outside (which was what happened, according to him, in a serious, violent conflict between local
Hindus and Muslims). And if someone were to desecrate the site, this
would hurt the entire community and potentially lead to tension between
Christians and Muslims in a context where not a single recorded episode
of conflict had occurred among them.[91]

South Asian preference for the streets and public expression of faith
presents Christians with great opportunities to celebrate Jesus and lift his
name high. In order for this to work, however, the form of such celebrations
will need to be appropriate and socially sanctioned. The line separating acceptance and violent opposition is thin, and where such lines are crossed,
the church, more than any other community, has the opportunity to be a
positive—and peacemaking—influence.

In contrast to the more publicly expressed route of inviting people to
Jesus and into fellowship with his followers, Christians must not overlook
peacemaking. Peacemaking runs the risk of being dismissed as secular in

[89]Francis, interview.
[90]Mahmood, interview.
[91]Mahmood, interview.

exactly the same way that nation building (which includes education, health, and social justice work) was by many in the nineteenth and twentieth centuries.[92] Peacemaking is a corollary to following Jesus, and Christians are called to be peacemakers. Those that make peace are said to be "blessed," and Jesus promises that they will be called the "children of God" (Mt 5:9). Meekness characterizes peacemakers, and Jesus says "they will inherit the earth" (Mt 5:5). For those following Jesus, peacemaking will not be an end in itself; it is important that people understand that Christians are imitators of Jesus. This principle of peacemaking, rooted in Jesus' teaching from the Beatitudes, is clear: "Blessed are the peacemakers, for they will be called children of God" (Mt 5:9). But by and large this principle has not been understood uniformly by Christians.

The interaction between Martin Luther King Jr. and certain clergymen reveals this well. King wrote his famous "Letter from Birmingham Jail" to eight white clergymen who on their part discouraged the civil rights movement because they were fearful of conflict. As Jonathan Bass argues, these clergymen were vilified as "misguided opponents of King" seeking a "gradualist approach to racial justice."[93] Bass argues that King skillfully used the mass media and the meticulous planning, editing, and distribution skills of his associates for the same end: justice. I do not think any one of them was right or wrong. King intended peace to prevail as much as the clergymen. The clergymen hoped it would happen through passive means, while King wanted to make it happen by activism. Both approaches seem appropriate, but not at the expense of Jesus.

CONCLUSIONS

I have described both the role of debates between schools of thought in South Asian Islam and the role of publicly performed practices of Muslim communities living in socioreligious contexts that are intrareligiously/interreligiously fragmented. Besides illustrating diversity among Muslims, this chapter has attempted to show the following points.

---

[92]Carolyn Goffman, "From Religious to American Proselytism: Mary Mills Patrick and the 'Sanctification of the Intellect,'" in *American Missionaries and the Middle East: Foundational Encounters*, ed. Mehmet A. Doğan and Heather J. Sharkey (Salt Lake City: University of Utah Press, 2011), 84-121.

[93]Jonathan Bass, *Blessed Are the Peacemakers: Martin Luther King Jr., Eight White Religious Leaders, and the "Letter from Birmingham Jail"* (Baton Rouge: Louisiana State University Press, 2001), 224, 1.

First, debates are often elaborate acts designed to minimize distinction and facilitate "crossing over." In relating this to Christian mission, I drew attention to the rich legacy of nineteenth-century debates. Largely neglected for their perceived futility, I pointed to evidence that debates resulted in people secretly believing without belonging. While I was formerly critical of the use of debates in mission, I am beginning to realize that they might not be as futile as I thought, especially if they draw people to Jesus and are conducted in performative spaces as a sort of creative theater.

Second, reinvented processions shed martial and protesting intent and are used as an invitation to all, even those who are religiously, ethnically, linguistically, and ideologically different. This is a mesmerizing practice for both those who process toward the court and others who contemplate the call to participate. This happens quite literally on the streets. South Asian Christians are akin to their European counterparts in being more reserved and private in matters of faith and thus are less able to use the streets as a stage for inviting people to Jesus. Usually their faith is limited to personal, family, and community events behind closed doors; churches too are forbidding places. Some fresh thinking on how to make the Christian faith and its practice more public in culturally appropriate ways is therefore needed.

Third, celebrating a living saint publicly as an immanent God enables participants to introduce invitees, even strangers, to meet the one who represents their God and offers their hospitality to them in his name. They use poetic license (expressed in singing) and dramatic enactment of the court scene to softly and indirectly challenge an alternative vision of Islam (AH/Deoband). Humor highlights the benign aspect of God and his followers. Here believers do not relate with God as servants but as friends. There are possibilities for Christians to draw from this sort of culturally sanctioned and publicly expressed faith that uses indirect means of theater, indigenously appealing songs, and local humor to welcome people and be hospitable to everyone in Jesus' name. *Jesu darbar* is a possible replicable model.

Last, South Asia suffers from deep fissures. Some of these are serious and conflict generating. Peacemaking acquires a special significance in such a context. Christians are a minority but are generally much better placed in every way to take the lead in peacemaking as a missionary activity. It is hard to shed the image of such activism as being different from mission. This dimension of mission needs to be recovered so that Christians can again do their part in nation building, education, health, and social justice without the guilt of being unfaithful to Jesus.

PART II

Thematic Analyses

5

Negotiating from the Margins

Women's Voices (Re)Imagining Islam

Cathy Hine

Nothing has really changed. Muslim women continue to be the subject of the salvific endeavors of foreign governments, nongovernmental organizations (NGOs), and Christian mission,[1] who use the image of a veiled woman to tell the story, one that has been written by almost everyone but Muslim women themselves. Islam continues to be considered the domain of men, who are viewed as the interpreters and definers of all things Islamic, the voice that qualifies and quantifies what it means to be Muslim today. Using this contextual lens, mission says that if we focus on men, we will reach the community.[2] Missiologies, mission strategies, and mission practice follow this path, interpreted and defined by a focus on men as the center of Islam and therefore the agents for change in their communities.

---

[1]Spivak challenges the imperialist discourse of "white men saving brown women from brown men." Gayatri Chakravorty Spivak, "Can the Subaltern Speak?," in *Colonial Discourse and Post-Colonial Theory: A Reader*, ed. Patrick Williams and Laura Chrisman (Hertfordshire, UK: Harvester Wheatsheaf, 1994). Lila Abu-Lughod has more recently given focus to our failure to engage Muslim women's agency in her book *Do Muslim Women Need Saving?* (Cambridge, MA: Harvard University Press, 2013).

[2]Parshall's work gives focus to prioritizing male community leaders: "In our context, young persons, or women of any age, would not be appropriate as an initial direction for evangelism. It was hoped that they would follow in the faith of their husband/father." Phil Parshall, "Contextualization," in *Toward Respectful Understanding and Witness Among Muslims: Essays in Honor of J. Dudley Woodberry*, ed. Evelyne A. Reisacher (Pasadena, CA: William Carey Library, 2012). Woodberry said that for a movement to be born, family and community decision makers must be the focus. J. Dudley Woodberry, "A Global Perspective on Muslims Coming to Faith in Christ," in *From the Straight Path to the Narrow Way: Journeys in Faith*, ed. David Greenlee (Waynesboro, GA: Authentic Media, 2005), 11-22. Evans's research in Pakistan affirmed this rationale. Edward Evans, "'Coming to Faith' in Pakistan," in Greenlee, *From the Straight Path*, 167-86.

Everything has changed. Muslim women today are (re)negotiating what it means to be Muslim: challenging male interpretations and the rules of tradition in order to live their faith with integrity; fighting the violences[3] of discourse and practice that marginalize and isolate, that promote their subjectivity and deny their agency; and seeking to be "true Muslims."[4] Increased literacy, greater access to education, more opportunities to participate in employment, and access to technology and information have all contributed to creating change for women.

Focus on traditional discourses, norms, and practices obfuscates the changing patterns of Muslim women's participation in contemporary societies. It ignores the empirical evidence of change negotiated from the margins and relies on the victimhood of their exclusion to silence them. As bell hooks has proposed, the margins should not be seen as a place of deprivation, rather as "the site of radical possibility, a space of resistance . . . a central location for the production of a counter-hegemonic discourse that is not just found in words but in habits of being and the way one lives."[5]

Hooks's work on marginality opens up scope for elaborating how Muslim women are negotiating changing identities, authorities, and social formulations as they (re)claim the margins as their site of resistance. This calls for recognition of the margins as a place of agency. This chapter explores how Muslim women are exercising their agency to (re)negotiate the boundaries of their participation in the ummah.[6] Undeterred by their marginality in religious discourse and tradition and spurred on by their desire for wholeness and justice, they are redefining what it means to truly live their faith, by

---

[3]The use of the word *violences* is deliberate in the recognition that there are many forms of violence perpetrated against women, of which physical violence is but one. Bennett and Manderson speak of the "myriad of violent technologies [that] reinforce women's subordination." They elucidate social injustices such as sexual and other physical violence, economic and psychological violence, civil and local wars that play out across women's bodies, and political, structural, and social inequalities. Lenore Manderson and Linda Rae Bennett, eds., *Violence Against Women in Asian Societies* (New York: Routledge, 2003). Young has described the five faces of oppression: exploitation, marginalization, powerlessness, cultural imperialism, and violence. Iris Marion Young, "Five Faces of Oppression," in *Oppression, Privilege, and Resistance: Theoretical Perspectives on Racism, Sexism, and Heterosexism*, ed. Lisa Heldke and Peg O'Connor (Boston: McGraw Hill, 2003).

[4]Elisabeth Buergener, "'Becoming a True Muslim': Syrian Women's Journey to Devoutness" (unpublished PhD diss., University of Birmingham, 2013).

[5]bell hooks, *Yearning: Race, Gender and Cultural Politics* (Cambridge, MA: Southend Press, 1990), 341.

[6]*Ummah* means community and in Islam most often refers to the community of all Muslims.

whom and how their faith is interpreted so that it is more gender inclusive, and the practices of their faith for a just and inclusive society. The margins from which they act shape their discourse and negotiations.

Their place at the margin creates a multiplicity of vulnerabilities: to manipulation and control through their exclusion from the center of religious life, interpretation, and practice; to the subjectivities of this positioning that denies them the right, capacity, or equality of participation; to further marginalization through the denial of alternative renderings of religion, shutting the door to their exploration of faith in the twenty-first century; to being entrenched at the margins by religious authorities determined to maintain the status quo and protect their leadership; to the discourses of Christian mission that uses their marginality to further their subjectivity, both in the ways it acts upon them and in denying their agency in (re)imagining Islam. Christian mission, in accepting the dominant discourse of Islam, relegates women to a footnote in missiology, strategy, and practice, intensifying their marginalization.

We will consider three movements among Muslim women who are (re) imagining Islam today. Women of the piety movement, alternatively called the mosque movement, are seeking a more life-encompassing expression of their faith. They want their faith to radically inform the way they live every day, refusing to allow modernist political discourses and the perceived secularization of their societies to determine their lived experience of Islam. The growth of this movement has seen a concomitant rise in the number of female preachers and teachers who operate inside certain mosques and teach in gatherings in homes. They are articulating Islam through a woman's lens, reshaping its discourses in the light of the lived experiences of women. Women of the piety movement are a growing voice in defining what society should look like as they strive to be true to the demands of their religion.

The second movement of women is calling for a new, gender-inclusive interpretation of the Qur'an. These women fall along a broad continuum. Some self-identify as (Muslim) feminists, while others reject that identification and any association of their work with Western, feminist, Christian, Jewish, or any other women. Some want their work to be accepted as a legitimate work of Islamic *tafsir* (interpretation or exegesis), while others are considered to be outside of Islam even though they self-identify as Muslims.

They hold that Islam is a nonpatriarchal religion that has been badly inter-preted, declaring their works as a return to what the texts truly say. In their desire for acceptance as legitimate exegetes and for the reform of Islam, their work is (re)imagining Islam by challenging established boundaries and guidelines.

Women activists are also redefining Islam, being voices of conscience in societies where women are victimized by the use of religion to entrench laws and customs that enact violence against them. They bring human rights and equality discourses to bear on laws and practices that discriminate against, marginalize, and abuse women, challenging the hegemony of religious scholars and leaders. Their work is creating tensions in societies where Islam is the proclaimed raison d'être for existence. Women's activism is a dynamic player that publicizes violences and calls into question prevailing social con-structs and their perceived religious legitimacy.

LIVES OF DEVOTION: PIETY MOVEMENTS

Once a week, in the quiet heat of late afternoon, one can see a stream of women—either singly or in small groups—making their way up a narrow staircase tucked away on one side of the large . . . mosque complex. . . . The women making their way discreetly to the top floor of the mosque are here to attend a religious lesson . . . delivered weekly by a woman preacher/reli-gious teacher. . . . Between fifty and one hundred women sit for two hours in an air-conditioned room listening to Hajja Faiza provide exegetical com-mentary in colloquial Arabic on selected passages from both the Qur'an and the ḥadīth[7].[8]

3:10 p.m. and all is fairly quiet upstairs in the mosque, though as always there's an undercurrent of activity. I see four women just sitting, another one praying, and a few having their *tajwid*[9] of the Qur'an heard. Three groups of young women, each eight to twelve people, are on the inner balcony sitting in circles, and there's a computer class in the library. Children pass through rapidly. People stand upstairs in the ablution area, talking. A woman puts her bag at the end of the mattress I'm sitting on, steps back and

[7]Hadith(s) are the collected traditions of the sayings of the Prophet Muhammad.
[8]Saba Mahmood, *Politics of Piety: The Islamic Revival and the Feminist Subject*, 2nd ed. (Princeton, NJ: Princeton University Press, 2012), 40-41.
[9]*Tajwid* refers to the correct pronunciation of the Qur'an.

begins praying. I've greeted a couple of women, sat with one for a little while she practiced reciting. Anisah Huda sits in the front middle of the room, and others behind her.

3:30 p.m. Anisah Huda begins *du'a'* prayers.[10] A girl squats beside her to ask something—she nods, without stopping in the invocation, continues with another one. She asks "the sisters" to close the doors and windows and continues to whisper quietly. A woman is reading the Qur'an. Others are sitting with their palms open, or with prayer beads. . . . There is silence, broken only by the noise of children upstairs, and Anisah Huda murmuring "*Allah*" about ten times.[11]

Saba Mahmood's ethnographic study of piety movements in Egypt and Moyra Dale's study in Syria are a window into this growing phenomenon. They highlight some of the unique aspects of these movements. Piety movements are gendered, with women claiming a space that has been the domain of men for much of Islam's history. They are for and by women. They have opened new opportunities for Muslim women to participate in the ummah by creating acceptable roles within Islam. A new generation of scholars and teachers has emerged, empowering women to infuse new life into faith. Religion has been brought into women's everyday lives, giving them a framework from which to negotiate the many challenges of their changing societies. Piety movements have opened an inclusive religious space for women, confronting the ambivalence around women's belonging.

Participants in the piety movements want to see their faith directly impact their daily living. Mahmood describes the emergence of the mosque movement as a "response to the perception that religious knowledge, as a means of organising daily conduct, had become increasingly marginalised under modern structures of secular governance."[12] Sadaf Ahmad, who studied the Al-Huda movement in Pakistan, explains that the aims of the movement are to

equip individuals with authentic knowledge of Qur'an and Sunnah . . . so that they may apply it in all aspects of their lives . . . be better equipped to

---

[10]*Du'a'* prayers are prayers of supplication, calling out to God, a conversation with God.
[11]Moyra Dale, *Shifting Allegiances: Networks of Kinship and of Faith* (Eugene, OR: Wipf & Stock, 2016), 21.
[12]Mahmood, *Politics of Piety*, 3.

revive the humanitarian spirit of Islamic teachings and to invite others to
Islam in a peaceful and non-aggressive manner . . . to help them develop
their personality, character and self-confidence, and to prepare them for
their future roles as wives, mothers and sisters and beneficial members of
their society.[13]

Buergener has described the desire of Syrian women to live devout lives,
what they call "becoming a true Muslim,"[14] as essential to understanding
piety movements.

Women's expressed desire for being true Muslims, and their aspiration
that faith be a lived experience, has shifted the focus of Islam from its
outward form and structure to the experiential. Women strive for the integration of life and faith. While this is arguably within orthodox articulations
of Islam, the code of conduct governing all aspects of human existence, the
longings of women expressed in their pursuit of devotion go further. Women
of the piety movements want integrity between life lived and desires expressed, a wholeness in religious dogma and practice. They refuse to draw
distinctions between their religious anthology and the practice of faith.
Buergener notes that the women she interviewed were primarily concerned
with practicing Islam, living pious lives rather than seeking the acquisition
of knowledge according to the highest traditions of Islam.[15]

As Muslim women pursue lives of devotion, are they impacting Islam and
their societies today? Outward manifestations of their influence are seen in
styles of dress and speech, standards regarding what is deemed proper en-
tertainment for adults and children, patterns of financial and household
management, provision of care for the poor, and how public debate is conducted. In the case of Egypt, Mahmood argues, their influence is impacting
the sociocultural ethos of Egyptian public life.[16] Ahmad agrees, saying that
Al-Huda is committed to "transforming themselves and influencing others
around them within a particular Islamic framework. . . . They play an active
role in attempting to change the very culture of society."[17]

---

[13]Sadaf Ahmad, *Transforming Faith: The Story of Al-Huda and Islamic Revivalism Among Urban Pakistani Women* (New York: Syracuse University Press, 2009), 2.
[14]Buergener, "Becoming a True Muslim," 7.
[15]Ibid.
[16]Mahmood, *Politics of Piety*, 4.
[17]Ahmad, *Transforming Faith*, 197.

These outward manifestations of change are occurring alongside signif-icant internal shifts in the discourses of Islam brought about by women re-reading the texts of the Qur'an and hadiths from a woman's perspective and applying them to their daily lives and lived experiences. Women's inter-pretive practices are brought to bear on the male exegetical tradition in new ways. Some women leaders within the piety movement are less inclined to make determinative pronouncements, preferring to offer a number of readings of the text and allow women to make the final application them-selves. Women are also more willing to openly challenge something they disagree with from the teaching. Mahmood describes interactions in a summer class discussing prescribed limitations on women's interactions with males, particularly focusing on eye contact between the sexes. One young woman found the limitations restrictive and untenable in today's world and openly challenged the teacher, declaring that certain verses were not relevant today. Of interest in the exchange was the young woman's use of a hadith to validate her position.[18]

Moyra Dale's perceptively titled book *Shifting Allegiances: Networks of Kinship and Faith* alludes to changes being effected within Islam. Two are of particular note here. "The growing presence of Muslim women teachers is offering Muslim women a new mimetic ideal, a new shape to their aspira-tions and identity."[19] While Muslims talk of following the example of Mu-hammad, what that means is being reinterpreted by this new group of women leaders. The second observation highlights the transfer of women's faith from being defined in maternal and familial terms to placing it in the line of succession to the caliphs in a role that mediates between God and his people.[20] This is a titanic shift in the place of women within Islam.

These women are labeled as conservative in their dress, the limitations they place on their social interactions, the acceptance of discourses that appear to marginalize them, and the observance of religious practices that exclude others. In the unreached-people-group language of mission they are an unreached group, hidden by their desire for a life of devotion. We have done little work on a missiology of hiddenness or on one of piety and

---

[18]Mahmood, *Politics of Piety*, 102.
[19]Dale, *Shifting Allegiances*, 103.
[20]Ibid., 103-4.

devotion. Cathy Ross, in advocating a more gender-nuanced missiology, speaks of a missiology of emptiness and hiddenness. Her theme of women's witness being carried out in weakness and selflessness, in women's hiddenness and invisibility, provides a starting point for articulating a missiology that engages the reality of this group of Muslim women. At the same time, Ross warns of the dangers in pursuing a missiology that has the potential to reinforce women's oppression or socialization and diminish the fullness of women's identity and life in Christ.[21]

A further challenge cast upon mission and missiologies by the dynamic of the piety movements has to do with subjectivity and agency. By denying the modality of the actions of women searching for devotion, we divest them of agency. Mahmood urges us to see how women's actions reinscribe instruments of oppression with new meanings, even in the midst of their oppression. "Agency . . . is understood as the capacity to realise one's own interests against the weight of custom, tradition, transcendental will, or other obstacles (whether individual or collective)."[22] We have a problem with ascribing agency to those whom God seeks after, particularly women whose acting bewilders our understanding of subordination and agency.

Jesus' interaction with the Samaritan woman reveals how the place of oppression becomes the fabric of agency. Acknowledging the fact that she has been married five times and that the man she is with now is not her husband becomes the place of revelation both to her own identity and need and to who Jesus is. The Samaritan woman cannot hide behind her brokenness, remain in isolation, or stay socialized as the helpless victim. Having come to the well to be away from others, after meeting Jesus she runs to them with the good news of the Messiah. In this interaction Jesus models what Kenneth Bailey calls "a profound theology of mission."[23] He humbles himself and expresses great vulnerability, acknowledging his need for help from this woman. "To serve from a position of power is not true service but beneficence."[24] Ross, quoting Indian Christian P. T. Chandapilla, says,

---

[21]Cathy Ross, "'Without Faces': Women's Perspectives on Contextual Missiology," in *Putting Names with Faces*, ed. Christine Lienemann-Perrin, Atola Longkumer, and Afrie Songco Joye (Nashville: Abingdon, 2012), 363-67.
[22]Mahmood, *Politics of Piety*, 8.
[23]Kenneth E. Bailey, *Jesus Through Middle Eastern Eyes: Cultural Studies in the Gospel* (Downers Grove, IL: IVP Academic, 2008), 203.
[24]Ibid., 203, quoting David T. Niles.

Servanthood is entirely voluntary. Servanthood is for those like Jesus Christ, who laid aside his privileges, and who choose to act on it. There is no pressure, no recruitment, no inducement. True servanthood shows whether we are really sons and daughters of God. "He who is rich became poor." The bene-factor becomes the beggar. The one who has everything opts for nothing. This is a paradox. Where this does not occur there is no servanthood.[25]

Voluntary submission as servanthood releases a dynamic of agency for those who are otherwise the subjects, or even victims, of social power structures and their abuses. In a world where power dynamics in relationships with Muslims are burdened with history, we need a theology of agency and sub-jectivity that vests our mission with the power of servanthood modeled in Jesus' ministry among us.

Reform from Within: Women (Re)Interpreting Islam

"Islam needs transforming" is a regular mantra from a cross-section of Muslims. Women who call for and practice a (re)interpretation of the Qur'an are seeking to (re)claim what they believe is the nonpatriarchal, egalitarian nature of Islam. Their desire has been fueled by the violences of gender in-equalities that many women across the Muslim world experience. Aysha Hidayatullah describes "feeling alienated as a woman by a religious tradition to which I was deeply devoted."[26] Women want to reinterpret the texts that are used to declare their subordination. They desire inclusion as fully par-ticipating, contributing members of the ummah. They challenge the disso-nance between Islam's supposed gender reforms and equality for women and women's subservience and control, which is declared lawful according to particular interpretations of the Qur'an. Across the world, women are pursuing issues of concern to their well-being at a greater rate than at any other time in history, and this includes Muslim women, who seek to do it from within the boundaries of Islam.

The work of these women exegetes emerged with developments in the discourses of Islamic feminism(s), the growth in international human rights activities, the United Nations conference on women in Beijing in 1995, and

---

[25]Ross, "Without Faces," 367.
[26]Aysha A. Hidayatullah, *Feminist Edges of the Qur'an* (New York: Oxford University Press, 2014), vii.

the discussions that emerged as a result of the development of the Convention on the Elimination of All Forms of Discrimination Against Women (CEDAW). Feminism's arrival in the Middle East and other Muslim-majority countries was linked to projects of colonization in the nineteenth century, while the latter twentieth century saw significant developments in Islamic feminism as part of the reaction against the apparent failures of postcolonial states.[27] The advances women had won during the struggles for independence were over-written by conservative articulations of religion, entrenching their second-class status. Increased opportunities for education, including access to some of the highest levels of religious education, equipped women to participate in rearticulating the meaning of religion. Advances in information technology transmitted information and ideas freely and quickly, creating global conversations and networks of action. Women reformers were committed to situating their claims for transformation firmly within Islam.

Women's call for reinterpreting the Qur'an is not new; however, since the late 1980s there has been a growing body of work from women exegetes. Many seek to distance themselves from the feminist label, afraid that others will exclude them for being Western and secular. Amina Wadud is one such woman. She states that she cannot comfortably be labeled feminist, progressive, liberal, or Islamist, and that she holds to a rigorous expression of faith while wrestling with its apparent shortcomings and challenges. Wadud is at pains to reiterate her pro-faith position. "[I] consider myself a believing Muslim who works for justice on the basis of my faith. I consider myself a pro-faith, pro-feminist Muslim woman."[28] Asma Barlas situates her work in opposition both to Islamic conservatism and to feminism.[29] In spite of such nuances in self-identification, these women are seeking a central place within Islam. They see the Qur'an as containing a call to justice for women and equality in gender and describe it as nonpatriarchal. Women exegetes want to increase the volume of discussion around the dissonance between what they believe the Qur'an says about women and the traditions and social conditions that contradict those interpretations.

[27]Margot Badran, "Between Secular and Islamic Feminism/s: Reflections on the Middle East and Beyond," *Journal of Middle East Women's Studies* 1, no. 1 (2005).

[28]Amina Wadud, *Inside the Gender Jihad* (Oxford: Oneworld Publications, 2006), 4.

[29]Asma Barlas, *"Believing Women in Islam": Unreading Patriarchal Interpretations of the Qur'an* (Karachi: Sama Editorial and Publishing Services, 2002).

They imagine an Islam that fully includes women, one that breaks down the traditional public/private divide that has excluded women from participation in so many areas of religion and society. They want Islam to be understood in women's experiences and not just from the male experience or by men interpreting how women should experience it. New conceptualizations of leadership in the ummah are being generated by women's work. Gender empowerment, gender mainstreaming, protection of the rights of girls and women, eradication of violence against women, religious authority, and spiritual wholeness are all part of what they are striving for from within Islam.[30] Their work is wresting the right to describe Islam from the place of male epistemic privilege and from the formally ordained interpretive community, or clergy.[31]

They pursue a fresh *tafsir* through the application of what Hidayatullah has summarized as three principles: the historical, contextualization principles that demand that verses be read in light of their historical context; the intratextual method, which requires for verses to be read and interpreted as part of the whole story of the Qur'an and not in isolation; and the Tawhidic paradigm,[32] which applies the unity or oneness of God to emphasize his otherness so that no one and no thing stands between the individual and God. While other reformist scholars have developed these tools of *tafsir*,[33] it is the application of challenging masculine readings of the Qur'an that is the particular contribution of this new generation of women scholars. In this light Wadud suggests that "no record exists, in our Islamic legacy, of a meaningful discourse between the perceptions, experiences and reflections of women and men about both their different and similar understandings of the text."[34]

Much of the exegetical work of these women focuses on the verses routinely used to subjugate and control women. They argue against interpretations that suggest women are of lesser value than men (Q 24:31; 2:228, 282) or reliant on men for their faith and relationship with God (Q 44:54; 37:48),

---

[30]Wadud, *Inside the Gender Jihad*, 3.

[31]Barlas, "Believing Women in Islam," 209-10.

[32]*Tawhid* is the indivisible oneness or unity of God.

[33]Notably, the thinking of men like Fazlur Rahman has shaped the ideas of these women exegetes.

[34]Amina Wadud, *Qur'an and Woman: Rereading the Sacred Texts from a Woman's Perspective* (New York: Oxford University Press, 1999), 96.

that men have authority over women (Q 2:222-23), that men can beat their wives (Q 4:34), and that women have limited inheritance rights (Q 4:11). They prioritize verses that carry notions of equality for women (Q 48:5-6; 49:13; 9:71-72; 4:1), using them as their interpretive measure for less helpful verses.

Women exegetes are committed to demonstrating "how to transform Islam through its own egalitarian tendencies, principles, articulations, and implications into a dynamic system with practices that fulfill its goals of justice."[35] Although they seek to self-identify within the mainstream of Islamic religious scholarship, that position is tenuous. Patterns in their arguments and thinking can clearly be linked to the discourses of feminism, leading to the charge that they are promoting Western ideologies. However, their reticence to acknowledge the social and intellectual heritage of their work seems to be a denial of their own journey and plays into obscurantist tactics of marginalizing and isolating the other[36] both within Islam and in broader gender discourses. Their desire to see nonpatriarchal readings of the Qur'an accepted into the dominant discourses of Islam is tempered by realism. As Barlas says, "I remain aware that such a possibility is remote. . . . The nature both of most Muslims states and my own standing in the Muslim community will make this difficult."[37]

However, their work is impacting society. Conservative scholars have felt it necessary to speak out against them. Hasan Mahmud ʿAbd Al-Latif Al-Shafiʿi, a scholar of the Qur'an at the University of Cairo, says,

> This movement seeks to take the Western "hermeneutic" methodology and apply it to the Noble Qur'an and Islamic religious texts in general, with complete indifference to the principles of Qur'anic exegesis and rules of interpretation established in our Arabic-Islamic heritage. . . . The dangers of this phenomenon may not be obvious today; but as this "intellectual" output continues, the cultural environment will become polluted by its by-products until future generations are left unable to breathe clean air. . . . I ask Allah—Most High—to bring these bright minds back to the vastness of their culture and heritage, and the origins and reality of their existence.[38]

---

[35]Wadud, *Inside the Gender Jihad*, 2.
[36]"Othering" reinforces and reproduces positions of power and domination. The other is marginalized, excluded from the mainstream and from participation as an equal.
[37]Barlas, *"Believing Women in Islam,"* 209.
[38]Quoted in Hidayatullah, *Feminist Edges of the Qur'an*, 1.

The work of female exegetes is now being described as a movement that has "grown by now into an identifiable field of Qur'anic interpretation with which increasing numbers of Muslims are beginning to grapple."[39]

The second generation of Muslim women pursuing a fresh interpretation of the Qur'an is now at work. They acknowledge and build on the pioneering work of women who have profoundly reshaped the space of scholarship in Islam. These scholars are taking their questions to new places and asking what would happen for them as women, Muslims, and feminists if the Qur'an did not support a nonpatriarchal understanding of the organization of life and its structures. In testing the boundaries further, they will give new inscriptions of meaning to Islam. Their questions are already creating tensions within communities.

Whereas human-rights and gender-equality discourses have been influential on Islam and the work of women exegetes, now there is a desire for gender justice to be read from within Islam, for gender rights and human rights to be reclaimed from their secularization. The discourse of rights is increasingly conceived of as a universal legal code, divorcing it from the grounding of moral and religious ethics. Former Archbishop of Canterbury Rowan Williams has spoken of the need to "reconnect thinking about human rights and religious conviction—more specifically, Christian convictions about human dignity and human relatedness, how we belong together."[40] Herein lies a challenge and an opportunity for Christian mission. Mission needs a new theology and missiology of rights and human dignity. In a world where violence and abuse are perpetrated with abandon because of the regression to attitudes of suspicion and harshness, we need to demonstrate the kingdom of God among us. It is an opportunity to respond to the desire of Muslim women seeking to ground justice and equality in religious convictions.

Jesus' interaction with the Syrophoenician woman in Matthew 15:21-28 subverts theologies that promote marginalization of the other. He lays bare the inequities of an egocentric view of belonging premised on an exclusivity of culture, tradition, and religion. He demonstrates that the coming of the kingdom of God breaks down barriers, that he is revealed and his kingdom

[39]Ibid., 1-2.
[40]Rowan Williams, "Human Rights and Religious Faith," *ABC Religion and Ethics*, February 29, 2012, www.abc.net.au/religion/articles/2012/02/29/3442363.htm.

is made know as dividing barriers are removed. Given that mission among Muslims is often happening in the midst of profound brokenness and the disfiguring of human dignity by violence and injustice, a desire for justice and equality must feature prominently in our mission and missiologies.

Jesus' own description of his ministry, as he read from the scroll in the synagogue, roots justice and righteousness in the Scriptures: "The Spirit of the Lord is on me, because he has anointed me to preach good news to the poor. He has sent me to proclaim freedom for the prisoners and recovery of sight for the blind, to set the oppressed free, to proclaim the year of the Lord's favor" (Lk 4:18-19). This is not new. Justice and compassion are described as foundational to God's people living in society, who were to do as God had done for them (Deut 10:10-19; cf. Mic 6:8). There are theological foundations for understanding and practicing human rights and justice.

Muslim women's pursuit of gender equality and justice through a reinterpretation of the Qur'an is reimagining what Islam could be. Their desires imagine a world of justice and righteousness, community and belonging, healing and wholeness, compassion and mercy. This is how Jesus described and demonstrated the kingdom of God among us. There is a "God-centeredness" in Muslim women seeking after a new reality, even if the teachers of the law and religious authorities oppose them. Their search for equality and justice, authenticated by religious texts, opens the door for companionship in the journey.

SOCIAL JUSTICE: WOMEN ACTIVISTS

While calls for reinterpreting the Qur'an are one response to the discourses of rights and equality by Muslim women, a parallel response is the growth of Muslim women's activism. This activism is visible in large, international networks such as Women Living Under Muslim Law (WLUML); in national initiatives like the Women's Action Forum (WAF) in Pakistan or Karama in Egypt; in grassroots projects like the Association for the Protection of the Environment (APE), which works among the garbage-collecting community in Cairo; and in individuals like Asma Jahangir and Hina Jilani of Pakistan, Tawakkol Karman in Yemen, Razan Ghazzawi from Syria, and Manal al-Sharif in Saudi Arabia.[41]

---

[41]There are multiple lists of activist organizations for women. For instance, see "Directory of

Women's activism is not new. Muslim women have a rich history of fighting for their rights, for positive social change, and for the renewal of their communities. They have opposed implementation of shari'a[42] laws based on particular interpretations of the Qur'an and hadith. They have fought for independence, challenged cultural norms and traditions, sought constitutional and legal rights as well as protection, and worked for the welfare of women marginalized and victimized in their communities. The early growth of women's activism was linked to modernizing projects and gained momentum during the colonial period. Huda Sha'rawi, Doria Shafik, and Zainab al-Ghazali in Egypt; Amat Al-Alim Alsoswa in Yemen; Labibah Thabit, Rose Shihaa, and Evelyne Bustros in Lebanon; Shaista Suhrawardy Ikramullah in Pakistan; and Raden Adjeng Kartini in Indonesia are just some of the early activist women who fought for women's full participation in society and state.

I understand women's activism broadly to include a spectrum of activities that, in various ways, "aim at empowering women and advancing their situation—by increasing their participation, their agency and/or their authority in various situations and sectors of society."[43] This notion of activism recognizes that women approach their work through various lenses: as scholar activists, lawyer activists, rights activists, philanthropic activists, political activists, feminist activists, and Islamic activists. These lenses help to give attention to the different developments, priorities, and achievements of women's activism in contemporary Muslim societies.

The success or failure of women's activism is regulated by its ability to frame its challenges in symbols and actions that compel others to join the work. This is complex in contemporary Muslim societies, where competing voices, histories, power dynamics, identity issues, nationalisms, religious conservatisms, and global spotlights jostle to dominate how issues and solutions are framed. Fareeda Shaheed explains how activists in Pakistan have framed the challenge for women's change:

Women's Organizations/Campaigns," Women's Islamic Initiative in Spirituality and Equality, www.wisemuslimwomen.org/activism (accessed July 7, 2016).

[42]Shari'a law is Islamic canonical law derived from interpretations of the Qur'an and the sayings of the Prophet Muhammad.

[43]Julie Elisabeth Pruzan-Jørgensen, "Islamic Women's Activism in the Arab World: Potentials and Challenges for External Actors," Danish Institute for International Studies Report, January 12, 2012, 15.

Women are neither uni-dimensional—defined only by gender or religious
identity—nor silent passive victims. Therefore women's strategic responses to
the complex web of influences that modulate their lives are as diverse as their
realities. Strategies range from theological interpretations to a radical rejection of religion, from individual strategies of personal assertion and career
development to formal lobbying and—sometimes—armed struggle. Some
put primacy on class struggle, others on other factors. Many women identify
with the larger global women's movement that, itself, consists of multiple
strands and tendencies; others reject such integration.[44]

Religious discourse as a frame for activism has always been contentious.
When laws are proposed or enacted on the basis of Islam, they assume an
aura of religious sanctity that makes challenging them difficult. If they are
challenged by the language of rights, then change is often hindered. Khawar
Mumtaz and Fareeda Shaheed argue that, in the case of the implementation
of shari'a law in Pakistan under General Muhammad Zia-ul-Haq, "in order
to expose the proposed laws or measures for what they were and to divest
them of religious sanction it was necessary to argue from within the parameters of Islam."[45] But even as activists seek to frame their calls for change
using the rhetoric of Islam, their actions and activities are condemned in the
name of Islam. Some have decided to move outside this framework because
of the slowness of change and the rise of political Islam, which they believe
creates a frame that is difficult to challenge. Some activists consider even
progressive interpretations of Islam problematic, asserting that they "mask
social cleavages, and differences among women, behind the assertion of a
shared Muslim identity."[46]

Feminism as a frame for Muslim women's activism is perhaps even more
contentious. Activists have often been slow to declare their feminist leanings
because they fear the alienation of supporters, alignment with the West, the
cultural imperialism of some feminist discourse, and the disconnect between

---

[44]Farida Shaheed, "Asian Women in Muslim Societies: Perspectives and Struggles" (keynote address, Asia-Pacific NGO Forum on Beijing+10, in Bangkok, Thailand, July 1, 2004, www.wluml
.org/node/1557).

[45]Khawar Mumtaz and Farida Shaheed, eds., *Women of Pakistan: Two Steps Forward, One Step
Back?* (London: Zed Books, 1987), 131.

[46]Fauzia Gardezi, "Nationalism and State Formation: Women's Struggles and Islamization in
Pakistan," in *Engendering the Nation-State*, ed. Neelum Hussain, Samiya Mumtaz, and Rubina
Saigol (Lahore: Simorgh Women's Resource and Publication Centre, 1997), 101.

feminist discourse and women's daily lives. There is often a tension among activists between demands for legal equality and demands for structural change. The feminist framework has been critiqued for an elitism that privileges developed feminist understandings and international linkages while failing to connect these with the daily experiences of many women.[47] Although a disputed discourse, the contestations around feminism have led to new developments under the umbrella of Islamic feminism.

Human rights, international conventions, and the law are another set of tools used by Muslim women activists to negotiate change. Hina Jilani, a lawyer and former United Nations Special Representative of the Secretary General on Human Rights Defenders, argues vociferously for legal reform as the basis for improving women's rights and human rights. She says that her hands are tied without laws to fight women's cases in court.[48] Human-rights discourse is not without its problems. Some consider such discourse as an instrument of power and domination in the hands of the West. Activists describe it as a "double-edged sword" that enables "the West to intervene into the personal politics of third world countries."[49] Activists often avoid speaking about rights in order to avoid challenges from religious authorities.

Activism has undergone what some advocates refer to as the NGO-ization of activism. The term describes the professionalization and projectization of donor-funded attempts to promote change. Activists feel that it has detracted from their work[50] because of contests over resources, compromises in their programs due to the agenda of donors, and the marginalization of broader issues for women. At the same time, NGOs have effected significant grassroots-level shifts in the daily lives of women. Microfinance projects in Upper Egypt, for instance, have allowed a woman to raise buffalo calves, sell them, and pay for her daughters' education, opening a new future for them. Literacy and health-education programs in Yemen have given women the

---

[47]Farida Shaheed, "The Other Side of the Discourse: Women's Experiences of Identity, Religion, and Activism in Pakistan," in *Shaping Women's Lives: Laws, Practices and Strategies in Pakistan*, ed. Farida Shaheed et al. (Lahore: Shirkat Gah, 1998), 438-39.

[48]Catherine Hine, "Untying the Hard Knot of Her Subjugation: Women Activists Negotiating Change in Pakistan" (PhD diss., Australian National University, 2010), 227.

[49]Ibid., 229.

[50]Nighat Said Khan, "The New Global Order: Politics and the Women's Movement in Pakistan," in *Pakistan: The Contours of State and Society*, ed. Sofia Mumtaz, Jean-Luc Racine, and Imran Anwar Ali (Karachi: Oxford University Press, 2002).

opportunity to make significant choices about the way they manage their
families and their own lives. Cottage industries among vulnerable women
imprisoned in North Africa have created changes in the prison system,
given dignity to women and helping them become contributing members
of their families.

Muslim women's activism is an undeniable part of contemporary Muslim
societies. Multidimensional, it is reinscribing the discourses of state, society,
and religion with an awareness of the abuse and marginalization of women.
It is creating a space for dialogue and action that confronts traditional, cultural, and religious norms. Powerful political, social, and religious structures are being moved by the multifaceted challenges of women to the entrenched status of such structures. Grassroots interventions are empowering
women to become dynamic participants in their societies.

Christian mission is being granted new opportunities through the work
of these activists. Whereas in early mission history the missionary had to
open up space for activity, Muslim women activists have now created a space
where activity and intervention are expected and experimented with. Their
calls for change resonate with the heart of the good news of the kingdom of
God: justice for the oppressed and needy, dignity for all whom God has
created, inclusivity to all individuals as fully participating members of society, improved social conditions for everyone, and welfare for the whole of
society. What would it look like for Christians to work in partnership with
Muslim women activists, meeting them in the space they have created and
bringing the leaven of the kingdom of God into that place?

Justice and compassion are among the overarching themes of God's engagement with the world, and the Scriptures echo these themes again and
again (Mt 5:6; 6:23; 23:23; Mic 6:8; Is 58:6-8; 61; Acts 4:32-35; Gal 2:10; Jas
2:14-17). Christopher Wright argues that in Abraham God shows us that
righteousness and justice are actions we actually do, not just concepts we
think about and theorize on. He suggests that the Old Testament words
righteousness and *justice*, when paired together, are best expressed as "social
justice."[51] Contestations over the discourses of human rights and equality
call for a new vision and expression of justice and righteousness, a renewed

---

[51]Christopher J. H. Wright, *The Mission of God's People: A Biblical Theology of the Church's Mission* (Grand Rapids: Zondervan, 2010), 164.

moral compass, one that Christians should be well placed to address. Williams has stated that human rights cannot exist without a Christian foundation.[52] Human rights are a contested discourse, but the work of Muslim women activists calls for a fresh theology and for wrestling with the missiological implications of such activism.

FROM A WOMAN'S VIEW

Of all the different oppressions we suffer as women living under Muslim laws, one of the worst is that we are denied the right to even dream of a different and alternative world. We have always fought for the right to dream our dreams, to link hands, to challenge those who isolate us, and to have the courage to reach out for those dreams. Finally, we must continue to honor and seek justice for those who lose their lives in reaching for their dream.[53]

Women within Islam are influencing cultures from the edge, away from where the balance of power is held at the center of contemporary Muslim societies. They have created places of resistance, those "sites of radical possibilities."[54] Mission would do well to recognize that innovation and creativity within Islam is moving the balance of traditional structures and powers and that women hold the key to this dynamic of change. Not only are Muslim women the keepers of tradition within Islam, they are also among the most radical voices giving momentum to change. As Ross asserts, "Women see the connections, operate on different levels simultaneously, build bridges to reality, notice resonances and echoes, and tend to think holistically."[55]

Women in the Bible so often occupy a marginal position, but it is from this place of marginality that they recognize and point to the new things that God is doing. Think of Ruth, Naomi, Esther, Rahab, the Samaritan woman at the well, the Syrophoenician woman, and Mary, who anointed Jesus' feet with a pound of pure perfume: each of these women—and many others in the Bible—left behind insights into the nature of God and his mission that

---

[52]Rowan Williams, "Religious Faith and Human Rights," Dr Rowan Williams: 104th Archbishop of Canterbury, May 1, 2008, http://rowanwilliams.archbishopofcanterbury.org/articles.php/1161/archbishop-religious-faith-and-human-rights.

[53]"Farida Shaheed—Pakistan," World-Wide Asian-Eurasian Human Rights Forum, *World People's Blog*, April 20, 2007, http://word.worldcitizenship.org/wp-archive/1222.

[54]hooks, *Yearning*, 341.

[55]Ross, "Without Faces," 377.

illuminate our faith and practice, the nature and power of forgiveness, and God's providence. These women radically reshaped understandings of religious life, reinterpreting traditional views of faith life in the light of an enlarged vision of God and his kingdom.

Seeing God at work in the margins points to the possibility that mission can be reinscribed with the powerful, subversive dynamic of the kingdom of God. Themes of emptiness and hiddenness, faithfulness and devotion, subjectivity and agency, power and servanthood, justice and compassion are writ across Jesus' pronouncements that the kingdom of God is among us. These themes enlarge the work of Muslim women activists, giving fuller expression to the dynamic of change and the vision of the future they are pursuing.

However, Christian mission faces more profound questions about its theology and missiology, ones that are critical to the shape of its work in light of the changing dynamics of women's participation in contemporary Muslim societies. How will it include those places where God is at work in Muslim societies as integral parts of participating in God's mission? Whose voices will Christian mission include in reshaping the missiologies, strategies, and practices of ministry with Muslims? What does a contextual missiology look like that includes women and their role in and experience of Islam? How will mission be prophetic in engaging the structures and power dynamics of Islam, particularly with respect to the marginalization of women in state, society, and religion? How can mission include all of the gifts that God has invested in it in order to reach Muslim women and men? What sort of mission is needed in contemporary Muslim societies for living out the declaration that the kingdom of God has come among us?

Mission—in its theology, missiology, strategy, and practice—must include women's perspectives: women's experiences of God and readings of Scripture and theology; women's daily negotiations of life; women's experiences of the world, its structures, and its power dynamics; women's journeys to and in faith. Not only must the contributions and stories of women in mission be acknowledged and told, but women must also be included as shapers of theology and missiology, mission strategies and practices. Their voice must become more than a token inclusion. The role of women in shaping missiology and mission practices is underacknowledged, what

Young Lee Hertig calls "without a face,"[56] which Cathy Ross explores in "'Without Faces': Women's Perspectives on Contextual Missiology."[57] Muslim women and the dynamics of their pursuit of God through a life of devotion, a gender-inclusive reading of texts, and the demand for a just society must inform the development of contextual missiologies.

The Christian church, mission, and missiology must reflect on the a priori assumptions that shape the missiologies and mission strategies directed toward the house of Islam. The dynamic of women within Islam challenging the hierarchies and hegemonies of their societies heralds a call to confront traditional views on contextualization that reify cultural norms and deny women's agency. As we recognize the distinct and emerging trend of women's agency in Muslim societies, mission faces questions about how it will recognize and affirm the work of women missionaries, missiologists, and theologians. Concomitant missiologies will be more gender nuanced, moving away from managerial missiology premised on the language of management and military terminology.[58] A renewed missiology of the kingdom of God provides a framework for responding to this changing dynamic in societies confronted by the reality of Muslim women's agency.

The recent history of mission in Muslim communities has often failed to make the gospel equally available to women. It has been built on the flawed assumption that we will influence the whole community by first reaching the men. It is interesting to note that research by men affirms this assumption[59] while that of women suggests this conclusion is false.[60] This demonstrates the need for further examination of how the kingdom of God is being and will be made evident in Muslim communities.

---

[56]Young Lee Hertig, "Without a Face: The Nineteenth-Century Bible Woman and Twentieth-Century *Jeondosa*," in *Gospel Bearers, Gender Barriers: Missionary Women in the Twentieth Century*, ed. Dana Robert (Maryknoll, NY: Orbis, 2002), 185-99.

[57]Ross, "Without Faces."

[58]Ibid.

[59]Parshall, "Contextualization"; Woodberry, "A Global Perspective on Muslims Coming to Faith in Christ"; Evans, "'Coming to Faith' in Pakistan."

[60]Yvette Wray, "Using Qur'anic Themes for Apologetics and Witness," in *A Worldview Approach to Ministry Among Muslim Women*, ed. Cynthia A. Strong and Meg Page (Pasadena, CA: William Carey Library, 2006); Victoria Lindhal, "Stories Along the Silk Road: Reaching Muslim Women in Central Asia, Russia and China," in Strong and Page, *Worldview Approach*; Beth Stricker, "Communicating Christ in Contexts of Persecution," in Strong and Page, *Worldview Approach*; LaNette W. Thompson, "How Will They Hear? Reaching the Muslim Women of Sub-Saharan Africa," in Strong and Page, *Worldview Approach*.

Mission must wrestle with the complexities of cultural and religious traditions and the way they are being inscribed with new meanings in contemporary Muslim societies. It must look for where God is at work in these
societies and engage with the internal tensions that dynamics of change are
creating. It must reflect God's heart for women as well as for men.

The Islamic Punishment
for Blasphemy

Diversity in Sources and Societies

Gordon Nickel

During the month of Ramadan in the summer of 2016, two gunmen shot and killed a popular singer in the city of Karachi in Pakistan. As the story developed, the reason for the killing was not immediately clear. Some media reports said that the gunmen killed the singer, Amjad Sabri, because they accused him of blasphemy. But to many this would seem strange, because Amjad was a singer of *qawwali* and *naʿt*, which generally praise Allah and especially the messenger of Islam.

On the surface, the story indicates a diversity of practice and perhaps theology among the Muslims of South Asia, who together make up about a third of the global Muslim community. Songs of praise to the messenger of Islam are widely—and wildly—popular and a characteristic part of the culture of South Asian Muslims. How could other Muslim views about the practice be so different as to motivate murder?

In the same country, Pakistan, the media were trying to account for another event earlier in 2016. A reported one hundred thousand people attended the funeral of a convicted killer in Rawalpindi. Mumtaz Qadri had publically assassinated his employer, the governor of Punjab province, Salman Taseer.[1] Qadri was charged and convicted of the murder, for which

---

[1]Carlotta Gall, "Assassination Deepens Divide in Pakistan," *New York Times*, January 5, 2011, www.nytimes.com/2011/01/06/world/asia/06pakistan.html. Cf. Paul Marshall and Nina Shea,

he was eventually executed. So why the outpouring of popular approval for what he had done? The answer concerns the efforts of the Punjab governor to defend a Christian woman, Asia Bibi, who had been accused of blasphemy against the messenger of Islam. Again, these were signs of a diversity so significant and so deeply felt among Muslims that murder could be popularly approved.

Our observations about diversity among Muslims and within Islam can lead us, on the one hand, to study more attentively the reasons for these differences and, on the other hand, to consider missiological responses to a range of situations that the church faces in her encounter with Islam. The observations offered in this chapter come out of academic study of the sourcebooks of Islam and a felicitous acquaintance with Muslim societies in the majority world, especially South Asia.

We should not be too surprised that Western non-Muslims do not understand the nature and extent of diversity in the Muslim world. Most Muslims themselves are not too sure about it. An August 2012 Pew Research survey asked Muslims in Muslim-majority countries whether they believe there is only one true way to understand Islam's teachings or if multiple interpretations are possible. In 32 of 39 countries surveyed, half or more Muslims said there is only one correct way.[2] In most Asian countries, only about 1 in 5 believed Islam is open to multiple interpretations. In sharp contrast to this, 57 percent of Muslims in the United States said Islam is open to multiple interpretations, compared to the global median of only 27 percent.[3] The only two Muslim countries close to the American percentage were Morocco and Tunisia.

An American Muslim, therefore, is much more likely to talk about diversity within the Muslim community than most Muslims in Muslim-majority countries. This seems worth noting, because it is generally the voices of American Muslims that we hear on subjects like diversity. We are thankful for those voices. But we could reasonably ask whether on this

---

Silenced: How Apostasy and Blasphemy Codes Are Choking Freedom Worldwide (New York: Oxford University Press, 2011), 99.

[2]Pew Research Center, "The World's Muslims: Unity and Diversity," August 9, 2012, www.pewforum .org/files/2012/08/the-worlds-muslims-full-report.pdf, 11.

[3]Pew Research Center, "The World's Muslims," 108-9. "Unlike Muslims in most countries surveyed, American Muslims are inclined to see their faith as open to interpretation" (108).

subject they represent the majority of Muslims in contexts where Christians serve Jesus in Asia or Africa. (Here, ironically, diversity in the sense of different Muslim American voices may actually mislead our examination of Islamic diversity. We may need to ask how preferring or prioritizing Western Muslim voices would influence both our research and our missiological reflection.) Even so, some 37 percent of American Muslims believe there is only one true way to understand Islam.[4]

This essay will focus on one particular Muslim practice, punishment for blasphemy, as a way of inquiring into the nature of Muslim diversity. It will set modern diversity against the background of the Islamic source documents. Muslims around the world agree on their twin sources of authority: the Qur'an and the *sunna*. What then would account for the diversity observable among various Islamic groups today?

DIVERSITY IN SOURCES AND SOCIETIES

Traditional Muslim accounts of the first centuries of Islam tell about a number of famous splits in the Muslim community, chief among them the Shi'a-Sunni split. We read about the differences between the Khārijites and the Murji'ites, the Mu'tazila and the Traditionists. The Shi'a split seems to have occurred because of a struggle for political authority in the rapidly expanding Arab conquest. But other differences raised issues of what it means to be a Muslim. The Khawāraj, for example, had a much more rigorous concept of adherence to orthodox belief and practice than the Murji'a, who were content with a simple confession of faith. Differences of approach between these early groups seem to have continued to the present day, and we can certainly look to see whether these differences affect the diverse approaches to the Islamic practice in focus in this essay.

Helpful characterizations of Muslim diversity have been advanced by Andrew Rippin and Tariq Ramadan. Rippin gives a basic division into Traditionalist, Islamist, and Modernist.[5] Ramadan further separates these divisions into a range of "Salafi" varieties. Interestingly, Ramadan distinguishes Sufism from what he calls the other five "major tendencies" in Islam,

---

[4]Ibid.
[5]Andrew Rippin, *Muslims: Their Religious Beliefs and Practices*, 3rd ed. (London: Routledge, 2005), 190-99.

and he seems to believe that the majority of Muslims fall into a category he calls "Salafi Reformism."[6]

What would account for the differences among the six groups? Ramadan writes,

> We find a diversity of readings of the Qur'an that can be attributed principally to *the greater or lesser role the human intellect is allowed to play* and, consequently, to the scope for interpretation that is permitted as an integral part of the Islamic field of reference.[7]

Rippin explores how the response to modernity plays into Muslim diversity and notes that revival movements not only resist the ideology of modernity, but also bring traditional understandings from Islamic source documents into the center of Muslim identity.[8]

Norman Calder offers an analysis of diversity in an important article on Islamic orthodoxy. He notes that Sunnis appeal to the Qur'an and the hadith "when they are expressing and interpreting their faith"[9] and shows by this measure why groups like the Ismailis are judged unorthodox. Calder gives an interesting list of literary genres through which Sunnis define their relationship to Allah and their messenger: *qiṣaṣ al-anbiya* (stories of the prophets); *sīrat an-nabī* (life of the prophet); the Qur'an; the hadith (traditions attributed to Muhammad); *fiqh* (Islamic law); *kalām* (theology); *tafsīr* (commentary on the Qur'an); and *sharḥ al-ḥadīth* (commentary on the hadith).[10]

Many scholars who seek to account for diversity among Muslims will commonly cite the Qur'an and perhaps the hadith. However, our analysis of Muslim diversity in the interests of missiological response should encourage us to consider the other source documents that Calder indicates as well as others not listed here. As we will discover, such study is certainly necessary for our examination of the Islamic punishment for blasphemy.

---

[6]Tariq Ramadan, *Western Muslims and the Future of Islam* (Oxford: Oxford University Press, 2004), 24-28.

[7]Ibid., 22, emphasis mine.

[8]Rippin, *Muslims*, 224-28, 235-38.

[9]Norman Calder, "The Limits of Islamic Orthodoxy," in *Intellectual Traditions in Islam*, ed. Farhad Daftary (London: I. B. Tauris, 2000), 73.

[10]Ibid., 74.

PUNISHMENT FOR BLASPHEMY IN ISLAM

When researching Islamic sources of authority related to the punishment for blasphemy, the scholar finds substantial unanimity in Islamic law, on the one hand, and some ambiguity in Qur'an, *sīra,* and hadith, on the other. This makes the topic ripe for the analysis of diversity. The diversity is evidently not related to what most orthodox Muslims came to accept as the divine law, but rather to their understanding of the sources from which Muslims believe the law was derived.

The punishment for blasphemy in Islam is certainly a small slice of Muslim belief and practice. However, as we will see shortly, it relates to a larger web of concern constituting a considerable part of Islam. The reason for this sharper focus is that it is difficult to get a grasp on generalities, but by studying a particular belief and practice we may hope to gain a better understanding of Muslim diversity.

The virtue of this topic is its connection to stories made familiar by Western media and at the same time its relevance for the daily life of Christians living within Muslim societies. How many in the West had thought much about the topic of blasphemy in Islam prior to hearing reports of the fatwa against Salman Rushdie in 1989? The issue likewise generated extensive discussion after the reaction to the Danish cartoons in January 2006, the Muhammad video of September 2012, and the Charlie Hebdo killings of January 2015. At the same time—though seemingly of much less interest to the West and its news media—Christians in Pakistan have been suffering under Section 295-C of that nation's penal code since 1986.

This essay will not deal with the stories that have drawn the most attention in the West, because all of these stories have been politicized to the point that it has become very difficult to discuss them without prejudice. Rather, this essay will probe the understanding of the sourcebooks of Islam in Muslim-majority contexts for the sake of missiological response. Paul Marshall and Nina Shea have helpfully described and analyzed the better-known news stories in their book *Silenced: How Apostasy and Blasphemy Codes Are Choking Freedom Worldwide,* which "[surveys] the contemporary use and effects of such accusations and threats."[11] However, the basic

---

[11]Marshall and Shea, *Silenced,* 13.

theological questions are the same for both the ancient sources and the latest news stories.

Killing blasphemers is certainly seen as negative and even evil to most people in the modern West. But this punishment is not necessarily seen as negative, and certainly not evil, in a Muslim-majority country like Pakistan or Bangladesh. Investigation of the Islamic punishment for blasphemy is not a matter of saying something negative about Muslims. Evaluations of right or wrong in this case are in the eye of the beholder.

Islamic law—that is, *fiqh* expressed in written form in *furūʿ* ("branches")—is relatively straightforward on the punishment for blasphemy. Most jurists ruled that any Muslim who blasphemes is thereafter considered an apostate and is therefore condemned to death.[12] Some jurists ruled that the blasphemer remains a Muslim but may still be executed for a *ḥadd* crime. As for non-Muslims, blasphemy will also incur the punishment of death.[13]

The question of what actually constitutes blasphemy in these legal sources is interesting and relevant for this study. Blasphemy was understood to apply primarily to Muhammad, and it seems that only later on was it applied to Allah, or to prophets.[14] Lutz Wiederhold excludes blasphemy against Allah from his research because "the sources used mention it only occasionally."[15] The distinction between language judged to be against Muhammad and language against God was based on the concept of the "right of Allah" and the "right of [humans]." In the case of speaking against Muhammad, "Islamic law takes a more severe view than in the case of reviling God," in the words of

---

[12]*Minhāj al-ṭālibīn*, a law manual written by the Shāfiʿī jurist al-Nawawī (d. 1276), considers the blasphemer an apostate. *Minhaj et Talibin: A Manual of Muhammadan Law According to the School of Shafii*, trans. E. C. Howard (London: W. Thacker & Co., 1914), 436-38. Lutz Wiederhold writes that at the latest since the *Minhāj*, "blasphemy against the Prophet(s) is mentioned regularly among the acts that constitute *kufr* in the chapters on apostasy (*riddah*) of the Shāfiʿī manuals of positive law (*furūʿ*)." "Blasphemy Against the Prophet Muḥammad and His Companions (*sabb al-rasūl, sabb al-ṣaḥābah*): The Introduction of the Topic into Shāfiʿī Legal Literature and Its Relevance for Legal Practice Under Mamluk Rule," *Journal of Semitic Studies* 42 (1997): 46.

[13]Abdullah Saeed and Hassan Saeed, *Freedom of Religion, Apostasy and Islam* (Aldershot, UK: Ashgate, 2004), 37-39; Mark S. Wagner, "The Problem of Non-Muslims Who Insult the Prophet Muḥammad," *Journal of the American Oriental Society* 135 (2015): 529-40; Yohanan Friedmann, *Tolerance and Coercion in Islam: Interfaith Relations in the Muslim Tradition* (Cambridge: Cambridge University Press, 2003), 149-52.

[14]Saeed and Saeed, *Freedom of Religion*, 37-38; Friedmann, *Tolerance and Coercion*, 150.

[15]Wiederhold, "Blasphemy Against the Prophet Muḥammad," 40.

Abdullah Saeed and Hassan Saeed.[16] As Muhammad is not in a position to avenge himself, they write, "it is seen to be the responsibility of the Muslim community to seek vengeance on his behalf by imposing the death penalty on the offender."[17]

Muslims believe that Islamic law was expertly derived from four main sources, the first two being the Qur'an and the *sunna*. Do these two sources support the punishment for blasphemy in Islamic law? The basic vocabulary for blasphemy in the Islamic sources is a pair of verbs: *shatama* and *sabba*.[18] *Shatama* does not occur in the Qur'an, while *sabba* appears only once—as part of a commandment to Muslims not to insult the idols of polytheists (Q 6:108). Academic treatments of blasphemy in the Qur'an tend to highlight verses that contain the verbs *iftarā* (invent lyingly, slander), *kadhdhaba* (give the lie to, deny), and *kafara* (disbelieve).[19] In such verses blasphemy would mean denial of standard Islamic views,[20] a concept we shall return to later in this chapter. However, a qur'anic term that seems to be generally neglected is the verb *ādhā* (to harm, hurt, irritate, trouble).[21] A typical occurrence is Sura 33:57: "Those who hurt [*yu'dhūna*] Allah and his messenger—them Allah has cursed in the present world and the world to come, and has prepared for them a humbling chastisement" (Arberry).[22] One can see where ambiguity might arise: the curse here is not only in the world to come but also in the present world, and the verse does not specify when the painful chastisement is to fall. There are other qur'anic passages that specify

---

[16]An interesting detail about these authors that is relevant to diversity is that though Abdullah Saeed and Hassan Saeed are Muslims from the Maldives, their book *Freedom of Religion* is currently banned in those islands. Marshall and Shea, *Silenced*, xv.

[17]Saeed and Saeed, *Freedom of Religion*, 39.

[18]Wiederhold, "Blasphemy Against the Prophet Muḥammad," 40; *Encyclopaedia of Islam*, vol. 12, *Supplement*, ed. P. J. Bearman et al., 2nd ed. (Leiden: Brill, 2004), s.v. "Shatm," 725.

[19]*Encyclopaedia of the Qurʾān*, vol. 1, *A–D*, ed. Jane Dammen McAuliffe (Leiden: Brill, 2001), s.v. "Blasphemy," 235-36; Carl W. Ernst, "Blasphemy: Islamic Concept," in *Encyclopedia of Religion*, ed. Lindsay Jones, 2nd ed. (Farmington Hills, MI: Macmillan Reference, 2005), 2:975; *Encyclopedia of the Bible and Its Reception*, vol. 4, *Birsha–Chariot of Fire*, ed. Hans-Josef Klauck et al. (Berlin: de Gruyter, 2012), s.v. "Blasphemy: Islam," 122-23.

[20]*Encyclopedia of Religion*, "Blasphemy: Islamic Concept," 2:975; Rudolph Peters and Gert J. J. De Vries, "Apostasy in Islam," *Die Welt des Islams* 17 (1976–1977): 3-4.

[21]*Adhiya* form IV. The term can also mean "to abuse (verbally), to revile or to insult" someone. *A Concise Dictionary of Koranic Arabic*, comp. Arne A. Ambros with Stephan Procházka (Wiesbaden: Reichert Verlag, 2004), 23.

[22]The verb *ādhā* is also used in relation to the messenger at Q 9:61 and 33:53 (x2), and in relation to Moses in Q 33:53 and 61:5.

that a painful punishment would come "in the world [*dunya*]," including
Sura 9:74—a verse cited by some Dēobandīs to support the death penalty for
blasphemy.[23]

As for the literary sources of the *sunna*: *Sīra*, *maghāzī*, hadith, and *ta'rīkh*
present stories of Muhammad requesting or agreeing to the assassination of
people who had mocked, insulted, or troubled him.[24] But there are also
stories of Muhammad tolerating insults or leaving the punishment to Allah.

Many of the blasphemy stories come from the *Sīrat al-nabawiyya* of Ibn
Isḥāq (d. 767) edited by Ibn Hishām (d. 833), and from the *Ṭabaqāt al-kubrā*
of Ibn Saʿd (d. 845). Other stories appear in the hadith collections of al-
Bukhārī (d. 870) and Muslim (d. 874). The most common story is that people
who satirize Muhammad through poetry are killed.[25] Several of the poets in
the stories are women, while some are slaves and others are Jews. Kaʿb ibn
al-Ashraf is considered by some Muslim scholars to be the first person executed for speaking against Muhammad.[26] However, one particular story
seemed to capture the epitome of blasphemy in the narrative sources: "In
the eyes of the Muslim tradition, the vilifier par excellence seems to have
been ʿAbd Allah b. Saʿd b. Abī Sarḥ." According to Muslim sources, ʿAbd
Allah b. Saʿd is a scribe of Muhammad who begins to "question the reliability
and accuracy of the Qur'an."[27] He invents his own recitations, then reads
them at the end of the day to Muhammad, who approves them as his own.[28]

There are also stories of Muhammad tolerating insults or leaving the punishment to Allah. These stories tend to appear less frequently in the early

[23]Mufti Obaidullah Qasmi, "Blasphemy in Islam: The Quran Curses and Hadith Prescribes Punishment," *Deoband Online Islamic Portal*, October 16, 2012, www.deoband.net/blogs/blasphemy
-in-islam-the-quran-curses-and-hadith-prescribes-punishment.

[24]Qāḍī ʿIyāḍ, *Muhammad, Messenger of Allah: Ash-Shifa of Qadi ʿIyad*, trans. Aisha Abdarrahman
Bewley (Granada: Madinah Press, 1992), 376-79; Jon Hoover, "Kitāb al-ṣārim al-maslūl ʿalā
shātim al-Rasūl," in *Christian-Muslim Relations: A Bibliographical History*, vol. 4, *1200–1350*, ed.
David Thomas and Alex Mallett (Leiden: Brill, 2012), 854; Friedmann, *Tolerance and Coercion*,
149-51.

[25]Ernst, "Blasphemy: Islamic Concept," 2:975; Friedmann, *Tolerance and Coercion*, 150.

[26]Wagner, "Non-Muslims Who Insult," 533; Abdelmagid Turki, "Situation du 'Tributaire' qui
insulte l'Islam, au regard de la doctrine et de la jurisprudence musulmanes," *Studia Islamica* 30
(1969): 46-48.

[27]Friedmann, *Tolerance and Coercion*, 150-51.

[28]See also *Encyclopaedia of Islam*, ed. H. A. R. Gibb et al., 2nd ed. (Leiden: Brill, 1960), s.v. "ʿAbd
Allah b. Saʿd," 1:51. This is the story that Salman Rushdie tells through his character Salman the
Persian in *The Satanic Verses* (London: Viking, 1988), 363-68.

Muslim narrative sources, but are nevertheless familiar to many Muslims.[29] One of the best-known stories of this kind narrates the resistance that Muhammad faces when he visits the town of al-Ṭāʾif. According to al-Ṭabarī (d. 923), the elders of the town will not help Muhammad, and "their ignorant rabble and their slaves" shout at him and revile him.[30] In this account, Muhammad is alone and has already been rejected by the Quraysh of Mecca. Muhammad finds refuge in a garden, where a Christian slave from Nineveh named ʿAddās brings him a bunch of grapes and converses kindly with him.

In spite of the apparent ambiguity in the sources of the *sunna*, the advocates of the death penalty for blasphemy base their argument on hadith, *sīra*, and *ijmāʿ* (the consensus of Islamic jurists). For example, Mufti Obaidullah Qasmi of the Dr. Zakir Hussain College in New Delhi writes,

> The death punishment assigned for blasphemy is agreed by all Islamic scholars of Ahlus Sunnah wal Jamaʿah and, is normally covered in Kitabul Hudud in Islamic juridical texts . . . , the evidence for blasphemy punishment being based on Ahadith, certain reported incidents during the lifetime of the Prophet (p.u.h.) and unanimous agreement of all Islamic scholars in all the ages (*Ijma*).[31]

If we find in the course of research that a command or practice attributed to Muhammad seems to have taken precedence over the Qurʾan in determining Islamic law, how would this affect our understanding of Islam and our missiological response? Some who write on Islam claim that if a practice or belief cannot be found in the Qurʾan, it is not Islamic. However, scholars seeking to understand worldview in order to formulate missiological response might consider a different angle. What is the place and importance of Islamic law in Muslim belief and practice—that is, in the Islamic worldview? Calder wrote, "Since the topics of the law cover all the major categories of a pious, and a social, life . . . , a work of furūʿ [that is, the written form of Islamic law], formally at least, constituted a literary depiction of

---

[29]For example, Laiq Ahmed Atif, "Blasphemy and the Holy Prophet Muhammad, Peace Be on Him," *Ahmadiyya Muslim Jamaat Malta* (blog), October 21, 2011, http://laiqatif.blogspot.com /2011/10 /blasphemy-and-holy-prophet-muhammad.html.

[30]*The History of al-Ṭabarī*, vol. 4, *Muḥammad at Mecca*, trans. W. Montgomery Watt and M. V. McDonald (Albany: SUNY Press, 1988), 115-17.

[31]Qasmi, "Blasphemy in Islam."

social reality in normative form."[32] In other words, according to Calder, the intention of Islamic law is to both reflect and define culture.

The most extensive legal discussion about the punishment for speaking against Muhammad came from Ibn Taymiyya (d. 1328) at the end of the thirteenth century in a book titled *The Unsheathed Sword Against Whoever Insults the Messenger*.[33] This is an important source for our purposes because the work was evidently sparked by an accusation against a Christian scribe near Damascus. Ibn Taymiyya's thesis was that anyone—Muslim or non-Muslim—who abuses (*sabba*) Muhammad must be killed without further recourse.[34] He built his case largely on episodes from *sīra* literature "that demonstrate that the Prophet dealt harshly with those who insulted him."[35] A Muslim offender becomes an apostate, he wrote, and a non-Muslim offender forfeits the so-called pact of protection; in Ibn Taymiyya's view, this made both kinds of offender worthy of immediate death. Now, Ibn Taymiyya needed to deal with dissenting legal opinion that gave apostates the chance to repent before facing the death penalty. He therefore argued that speaking against Muhammad fell into a special category of apostasy that he called "aggravated apostasy" (*ridda mughallaẓa*).[36] Jon Hoover suggests that the large number of modern editions of *The Unsheathed Sword* indicates considerable interest in Ibn Taymiyya's discussion today.[37]

The punishment for blasphemy seems like a small slice of Islamic belief and practice, but it actually relates to a number of other phenomena that together make up a substantial portion of Muslim life, past and present. These phenomena are united by the Muslim practice of venerating Muhammad. This wider practice includes the decision to call Muhammad the perfect human, and the claim that he was sinless or immune from sin.[38]

---

[32]*Encyclopaedia of Islam*, vol. 9, *San–Sze*, ed. C. E. Bosworth et al., 2nd ed. (Leiden: Brill, 1997), s.v. "Sharīʿa," 323.

[33]*al-Ṣārim al-maslūl ʿalā shātim al-rasūl.*

[34]Hoover, "Kitāb al-ṣārim al-maslūl," 854; Thomas F. Michel, ed. and trans., *A Muslim Theologian's Response to Christianity: Ibn Taymiyya's al-Jawab al-sahih* (Delmar, NY: Caravan, 1984), 69-71; Friedmann, *Tolerance and Coercion*, 151-52; Turki, "Situation du 'Tributaire,'" 39-72.

[35]Wagner, "Non-Muslims Who Insult," 538.

[36]Cf. Hoover, "Kitāb al-ṣārim al-maslūl," on this translation.

[37]Hoover, "Kitāb al-ṣārim al-maslūl," 854.

[38]Lutz Wiederhold assumes that the inclusion of the punishment for blasphemy in the legal manuals "was preceded and accompanied by a theological discourse on the righteousness and impeccability" of Muhammad ("Blasphemy Against the Prophet Muḥammad," 69). A. J. Wensinck wrote that, in turn, "We must assume that [the dogma of prophetic sinlessness] arose out of the

Veneration also advances the life example of Muhammad as the model for all of humankind to emulate, and declares that the sayings attributed to Muhammad in the hadith have authority for human behavior in Islamic law.[39] This illustrates the importance of the *sunna* of the messenger as expressed in *sīra, maghāzī*, and hadith.

Beyond this, veneration includes a wide variety of other popular practices and beliefs: for example, the belief that Muhammad is alive and intercedes before Allah for his community. It includes the claim that the coming of Muhammad is prophesied in the Bible, and the practice of making this claim the criterion for judging Judaism and Christianity (as Martin Accad has explained so well[40] and as Walid Saleh has recently insisted[41]).

Veneration also includes the qur'anic claim that Allah and the angels "pray upon" the prophet (this is the literal sense of the verb *ṣallā ʿalā* in Sura 33:56)[42] and the command to believers to do the same. It is interesting to note that immediately following the command to "pray upon the prophet" comes this statement: "Those who abuse [*ādhā*] Allah and his messenger, Allah has cursed them in this world and the hereafter and prepared for them a humiliating punishment" (Q 33:57, Arberry). This is one of the key verses we indicated earlier that uses the verb *ādhā*.

I list these dimensions in anticipation of the missiological responses to the diversity surrounding my topic. A common feature of all these dimensions is the veneration of Muhammad, which in some of its diverse expressions certainly resembles deification. Muhammad veneration is a topic of academic research exemplified by Annemarie Schimmel's study *And*

growing worship of Muhammad." *The Muslim Creed: Its Genesis and Historical Development* (London: Frank Cass & Co. Ltd., 1965), 218.

[39]al-Shāfiʿī, *al-Risāla fī uṣūl al-fiqh*, trans. Majid Khadduri, 2nd ed. (Cambridge: The Islamic Texts Society, 1977), 109-22.

[40]Martin Accad, "Muhammad's Advent as the Final Criterion for the Authenticity of the Judeo-Christian Tradition: Ibn Qayyim al-Jawziyya's *Hidāyat al-ḥayārā fī ajwibat al-yahūd wa-ʾl-naṣārā*," in *The Three Rings: Textual Studies in the Historical Trialogue of Judaism, Christianity and Islam*, ed. Barbara Roggema et al. (Leuven: Peeters, 2005), 217-36.

[41]Walid A. Saleh, review of *Narratives of Tampering in the Earliest Commentaries on the Qurʾān*, by Gordon Nickel, *Al-Masāq* 28, no. 1 (2016): 104.

[42]*Encyclopaedia of Islam*, vol. 10, *Tāʾ–Uʿ[..]*, ed. P. J. Bearman et al., 2nd ed. (Leiden: Brill, 2000), s.v. "Taṣliya," 359. Cristina de la Puente, "The Prayer upon the Prophet Muhammad (*taṣliya*): A Manifestation of Islamic Religiosity," *Medieval Encounters* 5, no. 1 (1999): 121-29. Constance Padwick found in her study of Muslim prayer manuals that the *taṣliya* accounted for one-third of the total material of all manuals "at the very least" and was "the commonest of phrases on Muslim lips; the commonest of phrases in Muslim books." *Muslim Devotions: A Study of Prayer-Manuals in Common Use* (London: SPCK, 1961), 152.

Muhammad Is His Prophet: The Veneration of the Prophet in Islamic Piety[43] and especially the classic monograph by Tor Andrae from nearly a century ago, *Die Person Muhammads in Lehre und Glauben seiner Gemeinde*.[44] Helpful missiological responses to the punishment of blasphemy would need to take into account the general web of concern surrounding the veneration of Muhammad.

An important primary source that explicitly connects the punishment for blasphemy to these wider dimensions of veneration is the book titled *Healing Through the Announcement of the Rights of the Chosen One* by the Spanish Qāḍī ʿIyāḍ ibn Mūsā al-Yaḥsubī (d. 1123).[45] The *Healing* includes major claims about Allah's praise of Muhammad; for Muhammad's miracles; on the obligation to believe in Muhammad as well as to obey and love him and follow his *sunna*; about praying on Muhammad; and for his sinlessness.[46] Then the book concludes with a long section on punishments for those who think Muhammad imperfect or curse him.[47] Qāḍī ʿIyāḍ is unequivocal about the punishment: death. He presents extensive material from the Qurʾan, hadith, *sīra,* and judgments of famous jurists. He claims that there is no dispute about this punishment among the *ulama* and the *salaf*.[48] Qāḍī ʿIyāḍ also adds that even if people speak against Muhammad without intent, through ignorance, or by a slip of the tongue, they must be killed without hesitation.[49]

This is the understanding of blasphemy that seems to provide the background for the enactment of Section 295-C of the Pakistani Penal Code in 1986:

---

[43] Annemarie Schimmel, *And Muhammad Is His Prophet: The Veneration of the Prophet in Islamic Piety* (Chapel Hill: University of North Carolina Press, 1985).

[44] Tor Andrae, *Die Person Muhammads in Lehre und Glauben seiner Gemeinde* (Leipzig: Otto Harrassowitz, 1917).

[45] *Kitāb al-shifāʾ bi-taʿrīf ḥuqūq al-muṣṭafā.*

[46] Interestingly, the *Shifāʾ* contains "probably the most authoritatively cited refutation" of the truth of the satanic verses incident; cf. *Encyclopaedia of the Qurʾān*, vol. 4, *P–Sh*, ed. Jane Dammen McAuliffe (Leiden: Brill, 2004), s.v. "Satanic Verses," 533.

[47] Qāḍī ʿIyāḍ, *Muhammad, Messenger of Allah*, 373-448; Delfina Serrano Ruano, "Kitāb al-shifāʾ bi-taʿrīf ḥuqūq al-Muṣṭafā," in *Christian-Muslim Relations: A Bibliographic History*, vol. 3, *1050–1200*, ed. David Thomas and Alex Mallett (Leiden: Brill, 2011), 544.

[48] Qāḍī ʿIyāḍ, *Muhammad, Messenger of Allah*, 373-75.

[49] Ibid., 385-86. The *Shifāʾ* made Qāḍī ʿIyāḍ famous throughout the Muslim world and earned him the reputation of being one of the foremost anti-Christian polemicists of his time. Ruano, "Kitāb al-shifāʾ," 544.

Whoever by words, either spoken or written, or by visible representation or
by any imputation, innuendo, or insinuation, directly or indirectly, defiles the
sacred name of the Holy Prophet Muhammad (peace be upon him) shall be
punished with death, or imprisonment for life, and shall also be liable to fine.[50]

Is there, however, any explicit link between classical source and modern
society? In this case, there seems to be a connection. Mark Wagner writes
that the influence of Qāḍī ʿIyāḍ's *Healing* was passed through Ibn Taymiyya's
Unsheathed Sword and his advocate Ibn al-Bazzāz (d. 1424) to the Ḥanafī
scholars of South Asia and the "Islamicization" of law in Pakistan.[51]

What Is the Diversity in This Case?

Returning to the stories of recent killings in Pakistan, the diversity within
Pakistani society seems to be between Muslims who believe (1) that the punishment of death for blasphemy is right and just but should be administered
by an Islamic government, (2) that Muslims may inflict this punishment
individually without the initiative of the government, or (3) that blasphemy
should not be punished in this way. Virtually all Pakistani Muslims would
hold to the veneration of Muhammad and would agree that speaking against
Muslim truth claims for Muhammad amounts to blasphemy.

In orthodox Sunni Islam there is unanimity on the punishment for blasphemy.[52] Islamic interpretation of the Qur'an, hadith, and shari'a tends to
be traditional, building on the authorities of the past rather than proposing
new and creative approaches to the same questions. A recent illustration of
this propensity is *The Study Qur'an*—a 2015 publication that offers interpretations from a thousand years ago but no comments from modern critical
academic scholarship. In the case of blasphemy, tradition prescribes death,
whether immediate or after first giving the offender an opportunity to recant.
Diversity arises over the question of whether blasphemers immediately
become apostates or whether they remain Muslims and are judged for a
ḥadd crime. If apostates, there is also diversity over whether offenders
should be immediately killed or whether they should be given an opportunity to repent. In all of these diversities, blasphemy deserves death.

---

[50]"Pakistan Penal Code (Act XLV of 1860)," Pakistani.org, October 6, 1860, www.pakistani.org/
Pakistan/legislation/1860/actXLVof1860.html.
[51]Wagner, "Non-Muslims Who Insult," 538-40. For more on the influence of Qāḍī ʿIyāḍ on Ibn
Taymiyya, see Ruano, "Kitāb al-shifāʾ," 545; and Turki, "Situation du 'Tributaire,'" 40, 61-63.
[52]Friedmann, *Tolerance and Coercion*, 151.

This chapter has described a number of medieval Muslim works that argue for death. This impulse continues into the modern age, Shabbir Akhtar's book *Be Careful with Muhammad!* being a good example of this.[53] Writing after the Salman Rushdie controversy, Akhtar reviews traditional Muslim thinking on blasphemy to explain the Muslim reaction to *The Satanic Verses.* A test for diversity in this area would be to inquire whether modern Muslim scholars have written books or articles disagreeing with this punishment or the concept of blasphemy upon which it is based.

Muslims generally agree that speaking against Muhammad is serious and deserves painful punishment, but some Muslims do not believe the Qur'an prescribes punishment in this world and therefore disagree with capital punishment. Other Muslims understand the Qur'an to prescribe punishment in this world and find this position affirmed by *sunna* and Islamic law. For example, the Indian modernist Muslim Wahiduddin Khan refers only to the Qur'an,[54] while modernist Laiq Ahmed Atif quotes the Qur'an and adds stories about Muhammad forgiving insults.[55] There is no question that these two writers venerate Muhammad, but neither mentions Islamic law in relation to blasphemy.

The harshest expression of punishment for blasphemy explored in this essay is Ibn Taymiyya's work *The Unsheathed Sword.* Ibn Taymiyya acknowledged only a narrow margin of diversity in cases of blasphemy: the difference between immediate death and the chance for repentance before execution. He argued for immediate death. Even so, in the words of Wagner, "Ibn Taymiyya's draconian version of the law against insulting the Prophet enjoyed great success."[56]

POSSIBLE REASONS FOR THIS DIVERSITY

Some Ḥanafī and Shāfiʿī jurists disagreed with Ibn Taymiyya about the punishment of non-Muslims accused of blasphemy. This suggests a reason for

---

[53]Shabbir Akhtar, *Be Careful with Muhammad! The Salman Rushdie Affair* (London: Bellew, 1989).
[54]Wahiduddin Khan, "Blasphemy in Islam: The Quran Does Not Prescribe Punishment for Abusing the Prophet," *Times of India,* October 2, 2012, http://timesofindia.indiatimes.com/edit-page/Blasphemy-in-Islam-The-Quran-does-not-prescribe-punishment-for-abusing-the-Prophet/articleshow/16631496.cms.
[55]Atif, "Blasphemy and the Holy Prophet Muhammad."
[56]Wagner, "Non-Muslims Who Insult," 538.

Muslim diversity from the four Islamic schools of law. For example, the later Ḥanafī jurist Ibn ʿĀbidīn (d. 1836) argued that "non-Muslims were wont to say things about the Prophet that Muslims would find offensive and should not be punished for it."[57] The predominant school of law among the Sunnis of South Asia is the Ḥanafī school. Wagner explains, however, that though South Asian Ḥanafī scholars revered Ibn ʿĀbidīn, they preferred the approach of a different Ḥanafī jurist, al-Bazzāz, who was an advocate of Ibn Taymiyya and his *Unsheathed Sword*.[58]

There are indeed differences among the schools of law related to the status of blasphemers and the punishment they deserve. Mālik ibn Anas, Aḥmad ibn Ḥanbal, and al-Layth reputedly held that those who speak against Muhammad, whether Muslim or not, must be punished by death. Mālikīs say that blasphemers become apostates; they should be given a chance to repent, otherwise they deserve death. Similarly, Abū Ḥanīfa and Abū Yūsuf are believed to have accepted the repentance of the blasphemer. Shāfiʿīs hold two views: some say that blasphemers apostatize and should be given a chance to repent, while others consider speaking against Muhammad a *ḥadd* offense that should be punished by death and cannot be set aside by repentance.[59] Further, there was disagreement among the four schools—and even within the schools themselves, as with the Ḥanafīs—concerning whether leniency could be shown to non-Muslims accused of blasphemy.[60]

Commentary on the funeral of Mumtaz Qadri suggests a second possible reason for diversity over the punishment for blasphemy, at least in South Asia: the strong (and opposing) Sunni movements in the region. One report noted that Barēlwī Muslims attended the funeral in large numbers and that the execution of Qadri has become a rallying point for Pakistan's Barēlwīs. The Barēlwīs have even established a popular shrine or *mazār* in Qadri's honor. In the South Asian context, the importance given to Muhammad has been a point of contention between the Barēlwīs and other groups like the Dēobandīs and modernists for more than a century. At issue is the strong Barēlwī belief that Muhammad intercedes with Allah on behalf of Muslims

---

[57]Ibid., 540.
[58]Ibid., 538-40.
[59]Friedmann, *Tolerance and Coercion*, 151, summarizing Ibn Taymiyya's *Unsheathed Sword*.
[60]Wagner, "Non-Muslims Who Insult," 530.

at all times.[61] Other important claims of this group's first leader, Aḥmad
Riḍa Khān Barēlwī (d. 1921), included the following: Muhammad's
knowledge of the unseen (and ultimately knowledge of everything); the
preeminence of Muhammad's light; the claim that Allah created the world
for Muhammad's sake; the belief that Muhammad, being created of light,
had no shadow; and so on.[62]

Related to the punishment for blasphemy, however, the distinction
should not be overstated. In a recent public disagreement about the punishment in India, one modernist Muslim writer stated that speaking against
Muhammad "is not a subject of punishment, but is rather a subject of
peaceful admonishment."[63] In this case it was the Dēobandī scholars who
took up the defense of capital punishment, stating that it was supported by
Islamic sourcebooks and the consensus of Muslim jurists.[64]

This recent Indian disagreement in turn points to a third possible reason
for diversity: different opinions about the meanings and relative authority
of the sources from which Muslims believe Islamic law is derived. Some
Muslims find the *sunna* ambiguous about the treatment of people who
oppose Muhammad, and do not believe the Qur'an clearly prescribes death.
In these cases Muslims may simply prefer the Qur'an and the stories in the
sunna that portray greater tolerance. Wahiduddin Khan cites a number of
passages in the Qur'an where messengers are mocked, but concludes, "nowhere does the Quran prescribe the punishment of lashes, or death, or any
other physical punishment."[65] Obaidullah Qasmi then attacks the modernist for "ignoring Hadith, the second most important source of Islamic
faith and Shariah, which prescribes death penalty" for blasphemy against
Muhammad. Qasmi claims that Islam is unanimous on this punishment
except for the "Qadianis, a community regarded infidels by Muslims across
the world."[66]

Views such as that of Wahiduddin Khan may be expressed by modernist Muslim voices, especially in the West, but is it common to find

[61]*Encyclopaedia of the Qurʾān*, ed. Jane Dammen McAuliffe (Leiden: Brill, 2001), s.v. "Barēlwīs," 1:201.
[62]*Encyclopaedia of the Qurʾān*, s.v. "Barēlwīs."
[63]Khan, "Blasphemy in Islam."
[64]Qasmi, "Blasphemy in Islam."
[65]Khan, "Blasphemy in Islam."
[66]Qasmi, "Blasphemy in Islam."

them in the preceding thousand years of Muslim tradition? And would such voices have difficulty finding a hearing even today in some majority-Muslim societies? Khan does not deny that "a negative stance towards the Prophet will be judged by God," but he does counsel believers to "observe the policy of avoidance" and speak the message of God in a way that addresses people's minds. His case is theological: God has given humanity total freedom; to this Khan approvingly adds "the modern secular concept of freedom."[67]

There is an instructive case of diversity in a Muslim-majority society in the discussion of a related topic, the Islamic punishment for apostasy. Abdullahi Ahmed An-Na'im, a professor of law who teaches at Emory University, wrote in 1986 about how new formulations of Islamic law today could be based on the parts of the Qur'an that Muslims associate with Mecca.[68] An-Na'im called these verses "texts of freedom of choice" and explained how Muslims could choose to act on these rather than on parts of the Qur'an he called "the texts of compulsion and jihad" that Muslims associate with Medina—and upon which shari'a is based. He also wrote that this technique could be used in other areas of Islamic law.[69] The potential danger of expressing this approach in Muslim-majority societies, however, is indicated in Dr. An-Na'im's report that the Sudanese advocate of the views he was describing, Mahmoud Muhammad Taha, had been convicted of apostasy and executed one year earlier.[70]

It is important to observe not only the diversity but also the reasons behind it. Mahmoud Muhammad Taha sought to reconcile Muslim belief with twentieth-century values,

> to revive ancient sacred texts in such a way that allows one to live in the modern world. . . . His vision asked Muslims to abandon fourteen hundred years of accepted dogma in favor of a radical and demanding new methodology that would set them free from the burdens of traditional jurisprudence.[71]

---

[67]Khan, "Blasphemy in Islam."

[68]Abdullahi Ahmed An-Na'im, "The Islamic Law of Apostasy and Its Modern Applicability: A Case from the Sudan," *Religion* 16 (1986): 197-224.

[69]Ibid., 216.

[70]An-Na'im, "The Islamic Law of Apostasy," 197.

[71]George Packer, "The Moderate Martyr: A Radically Peaceful Vision of Islam," *New Yorker*, September 11, 2006, www.newyorker.com/magazine/2006/09/11/the-moderate-martyr.

Taha's vision was certainly attractive to the West, but it went against orthodox Islam. As George Packer notes, Taha was the "anti-Qutb" (that is,
Sayyid Qutb, who has been very influential in the modern world).[72] The
views of modernist Muslim thinkers like Khan, An-Na'im, and Taha show
a positive response to modernity and what Muslims know are the prevailing
Western opinions about tolerance and religious freedom.[73]

A further diversity may involve differences in the Muslim regard for Muhammad, in views of what constitutes blasphemy, or in a desire for leniency
to blasphemers. If so, the expression of such differences continues to be extremely sensitive in some Muslim-majority societies. In 1990, a question was
raised in the Pakistani parliament about whether a more lenient punishment
could be considered. The Federal Shariat Court then ruled, "The penalty for
contempt of the Holy Prophet . . . is death and nothing else."[74] More recently,
in 2010 Sherry Rehman tried to suggest changes to Section 295-C and subsequently was formally charged with blasphemy.[75] In this scenario, any challenge to capital punishment for blasphemy itself becomes blasphemy.

MISSIOLOGICAL REFLECTION AND RESPONSE

The missiological response to the Islamic punishment for blasphemy provides an opportunity to address both the social and physical challenges that
Christians actually face in some Muslim societies today, and the theological
issues that accompany the Muslim veneration of Muhammad.

At the start of missiological response comes the question as to whether
Christians should declare that killing people for speaking against a religious
figure is wrong, and to oppose it. Jesus himself—who is not just a religious
figure, but the divine Son of God and Savior of the world—said, "Anyone
who speaks a word against the Son of Man will be forgiven" (Mt 12:32). Why
then should people kill to defend their claims for a merely human figure?
Should Christians consider asking their Muslim friends to oppose and stop
this punishment?

---

[72]Packer, "Moderate Martyr."
[73]See for example Peters and De Vries, "Apostasy in Islam," 21-24.
[74]Marshall and Shea, *Silenced*, 86.
[75]Agenzia Fides, "Sherry Rehman, Promoter for Amending the Blasphemy Law, Incriminated for
  Blasphemy," Pakistan Blasphemy Laws: Ending the Abuse of the Blasphemy Laws, February 18,
  2011, www.pakistanblasphemylaw.com/?p=341.

The second step would be to try to bring some precision to the terms in which Muslims describe blasphemy and to state clearly whether we accept those terms. Without this clarification, all is confusion. The concept of blasphemy often found in the Muslim legal sources is basically a denial of any of the essential dogmas of Islam,[76] following the meaning of *kafara* and *kadhdhaba* noted earlier. This includes—and arguably mainly concerns—Muslim truth claims for Muhammad. Missiologically speaking, for Christians this is exactly the point. Are Muslim claims for Muhammad and the Qur'an true? If, on the basis of the criteria of the gospel, Christians judge Islamic claims not to be true, how could this be called blasphemy? This means that the present terms of the discussion are themselves fundamentally unhelpful and need to be reformulated. Do non-Muslims really have no right to question the full range of Muslim truth claims for Muhammad? Do Muslims have no right to question these claims? If they have a right, should non-Muslims consider defending their right?

The challenges that Christians face in Pakistan because of Section 295-C are not the same as the challenges facing Christians in other Muslim societies. The Muslim world is diverse. However, missiological response needs to treat the particular diversities. What is the appropriate counsel to Christians in Pakistan when their biblical confessions of the glory and authority of the Lord Jesus seem to some Muslims to imply disrespect for the messenger of Islam? When Christians disagree with the glorification of Muhammad over all other humans? When they say that the life of Jesus in the Gospels is the model for human behavior, not the story of Muhammad? That Jesus is Lord, not another? What is the appropriate advice for Christians who are accused of blasphemy when they confess the divine Sonship of Jesus, and at the same time and in the same societies are accused of blasphemy for not affirming the full range of Muslim truth claims for Muhammad?

Section 295-C of the Pakistani Penal Code says, "by words, either spoken or written, or by visible representation, or by any imputation, innuendo, or insinuation, directly or indirectly." Is it possible that Christians in Muslim-majority societies, declaring their biblical confessions about Jesus, could be judged to "impute" or "insinuate" words about Muhammad?

---

[76]See Peters and De Vries, "Apostasy in Islam," 2-4.

What kind of missiological leadership does the church in the majority world need to help her respond biblically and faithfully to the challenges of Islam *as the church experiences Islam in her own diverse contexts*? Does it help the global church for North American Christians to say, "Such and such in our view is not the true Islam, so we needn't concern ourselves with that"? "Such and such an expression smacks of stereotyping Muslims, therefore we need to keep away from that"? The whole point of recognizing diversity should be to address the particular expressions of Islam that the church actually faces in her diverse contexts. Is it possible that the Western cultures in which many of us live have influenced us to the point that we hesitate to deal with questions that large sections of the global church face—never mind to boldly lead out in missiological response?

Happily, a number of Christians with a good knowledge of Islam and experience in Muslim societies have ventured to respond to the Muslim veneration of Muhammad in various ways. Constance Padwick, in her wonderful study *Muslim Devotions*, wrote that fully one-third of all the expressions she discovered in her survey of prayer manuals relate to the *taṣliya*— that is, the Muslim "prayer upon" the messenger of Islam commanded in Sura 33:56.[77] In contexts of concentrated Muhammad veneration, this *taṣliya* can be heard from Muslims throughout the day and seen written in Arabic on front-room walls and roadside signs. Padwick advised the church in Muslim contexts to keep this in mind and to develop its own collective expressions of praise to the Lord Jesus.[78]

Kenneth Cragg considered Muhammad veneration in a chapter of his book *Muhammad and the Christian*, at the end of which he asks,

> How should the Christian relate in both thought and community to this Muslim "possession" of and by Muhammad in the soul? *The question is the most searching of all those we have to face.* There must be careful note of the fact that Islam, even in spite of itself, finds place for categories of relationship between divine ends and human means, between the eternal and the historical, unlike and yet akin to those that are at the heart of Christian experience in Jesus as the Christ.[79]

---

[77]Padwick, *Muslim Devotions*, 152.
[78]Ibid., 165-66.
[79]Kenneth Cragg, *Muhammad and the Christian: A Question of Response* (Maryknoll, NY: Orbis, 1984), 65, emphasis mine.

As one would expect, Cragg found some possibilities in this question for mutual understanding. In spite of official pronouncements, Islam ascribes to Muhammad powers of mediation and intercession that it denies to the Messiah. Then Cragg continued,

> There remains the Christian anxiety about a pattern of religious awareness which follows, in part, the Christian elements of divine/human "association" and historical "mediation" of the eternal, but joins them to a personality so far different from the central figure of the Gospel and from that Gospel's categories of suffering and grace in which God's reconciliation of the world consists.[80]

Those who enjoy the dense Craggian prose will appreciate his point. The veneration of Muhammad joins to God's eternal purposes a figure who does not express the gospel's categories of suffering and grace and who thus cannot connect humanity to God's reconciliation.

Samuel Zwemer studied the same material as Cragg in a short book called *The Moslem Christ*, but stated his conclusion in a more straightforward expression: "The sin and the guilt of the Mohammedan world is that they give Christ's glory to another, *and that for all practical purposes Mohammed himself is the Moslem Christ.*"[81]

More recently, Mark Durie deals with Muhammad veneration in his book *Liberty to the Captives*. Durie's concern is the spiritual health and growth of both Christians living in Muslim societies and new Christians from Muslim backgrounds. In addition to isolating the problem, he suggests a series of prayers that Christians can pray in order to abjure the veneration of Muhammad and be free from its spiritual grasp.[82]

Missiological responses such as these show a realistic engagement with the phenomenon of Muhammad veneration and a responsible assessment of its social and spiritual dimensions. They recognize the diversities within societies related to Islamic beliefs and practices, as well as broad unity and consensus. These initiatives in turn help the church to think and act faithfully in the particular diverse contexts she faces within the Muslim world.

---

[80]Ibid., 65.

[81]Samuel Zwemer, *The Moslem Christ: An Essay on the Life, Character, and Teachings of Jesus Christ According to the Koran and Orthodox Tradition* (New York: American Tract Society, 1912), 157, emphasis original.

[82]Mark Durie, *Liberty to the Captives: Freedom from Islam and Dhimmitude Through the Cross* (Melbourne: Deror Books, 2010), 65-85.

7

Shari'a in a Globalized World

Historical Overview, Regional Contrasts, and the Challenge of Pluralism

David L. Johnston

The word *shari'a* conjures up indiscriminate violence, an overzealous religious police force imposing draconian laws on its population, and summary, gruesome execution scenes, particularly since the rise of the so-called Islamic State in Syria and Iraq in 2014 and a number of terror attacks that it subsequently inspired in several Western cities. Even in the late 1990s, we were reading about the Taliban in Afghanistan, who in the name of shari'a outlawed the playing of music, destroyed ancient Buddhist statues, and forbade women to work. Long before that, many Westerners knew that Saudi Arabian shari'a prohibited women from driving, banned them from going anywhere in public without a male relative as chaperone, and—if lucky enough to graduate from university—barred them from entering certain professions. Under shari'a, thieves have their hands chopped off, adulterers are stoned, and those guilty of blasphemy and apostasy are executed.

Saudi Arabia, Iran, and most Arab Gulf nations are examples of states claiming to follow shari'a as the only law of the land. By contrast, most Muslim nations, including Turkey, Algeria, and the world's most populous Muslim nation, Indonesia, have either secular or mostly secular constitutions and have signed on to the bulk of international human-rights covenants.[1] What is more, the Organisation of Islamic Cooperation (OIC), the

---

[1] There is a growing literature on Islam and human rights. See, for instance, Ann Elizabeth Mayer, *Islam and Human Rights: Tradition and Politics*, 5th ed. (Boulder, CO: Westview Press, 2013);

second-largest intergovernmental organization after the UN, has a membership of fifty-seven nations and is explicitly committed to the aims of the UN Charter: to "uphold and promote, at the national and international levels, good governance, democracy, human rights and fundamental freedoms, and the rule of law."[2]

Needless to say, each country is unique in its history, ethnic makeup, specific interpretations and practices of Islam, and sociopolitical dynamics. The spontaneous popular explosions that flared up at the end of 2010, often referred to as the "Arab Spring," effected a healthy yet fragile democratic transition in Tunisia[3] but sparked a violent counterrevolution in Egypt and ripped apart both Syria and Libya, triggering the greatest flow of refugees since World War II. Each nation must be studied on its own. Religion is just one of many factors, and any blanket statement about "Islam" would be just that—a wrong-headed generalization.

The Muslim world, then, is incredibly diverse; one could say that "pluralism" is an integral part of the ummah, the worldwide community of Muslims. A widely reported saying of the Prophet Muhammad[4] reads, "Difference of opinion in my community is a mercy." Certainly the first twelve chapters of Genesis (including the Tower of Babel story) and Pentecost are in the same spirit as this qur'anic verse[5]: "Another of his signs is the creation of the heavens and the earth, and the diversity of your languages and colours" (Q 30:22, Haleem).[6] Another verse goes even further:

Anver M. Emon, Mark Ellis, and Benjamin Glahn, *Islamic Law and International Human Rights: Searching for Common Ground?* (Oxford: Oxford University Press, 2012); Abdulaziz Sachedina, *Islam and the Challenge of Human Rights* (Oxford: Oxford University Press, 2009); David L. Johnston, "Islam and Human Rights: A Growing Rapprochement?," *American Journal of Economics and Sociology* 74, no. 1 (January 2015): 113-48.

[2]See "History," Organisation of Islamic Cooperation, http://www.oic-oci.org/page/?p_id=52&p _ref=26&lan=en (accessed March 7, 2017).

[3]See below for details.

[4]I am not taking a stand here within the Christian debates on whether Muhammad was a prophet or not. This is simply a token of respect that I show in my own writings, as many of my readers are Muslim.

[5]God promises to Abraham, "All peoples on earth will be blessed through you" (Gen 12:3). Regarding Pentecost, theologian Amos Yong makes the same connection: "And given the interconnections between language and culture, the Pentecost narrative both celebrates the divine affirmation of many tongues, and announces the divine embrace of the many cultures of the world"; *The Missiological Spirit: Christian Mission in the Third Millennium Global Context* (Eugene, OR: Cascade, 2014), 83, 113.

[6]This qur'anic verse can be read (and often is by Muslims) to say that God established the three

We have assigned a law and a path to each of you. If God had so willed, He would have made you one community, but He wanted to test you through that which He has given you, so race to do good: you will all return to God and He will make clear to you the matters you differed about. (Q 5:48, Haleem)

Scott Sunquist, in a chapter devoted to "The Holy Spirit in Mission," seeks to explicate human culture in this context. His first point is precisely the affirmation just made by the Qur'an, namely that "God loves cultural diversity."[7] I will draw out some of the implications of this truth in the last section. But the idea of pluralism is at the heart of this chapter. Yes, the Muslim world is indeed diverse, and in that sense, as a social science description, it is also pluralistic. But I also want to assert that as followers of Jesus who are serious about living out his double mission of Great Commission (making disciples of all nations) and Great Commandment (loving God and loving neighbor), the concept of "pluralism" becomes a moral imperative. This is especially so in light of the vast movement of people, including millions of Muslims, into Western lands. In the bulk of this essay I will look at shari'a and how it is interpreted and applied in various countries like Turkey, Pakistan, and Tunisia, but I will end with some missiological remarks about the growing numbers of Muslims in Britain, France, Germany, Australia, and the United States. There is a debate, understandably, about "legal pluralism," but might this not point to other areas in which, out of love for our Muslim neighbors, we should consider making room for them in our societies?

But we first need to start with a basic understanding of shari'a in its historical context. What about Islamic law and its own internal pluralism?

A PRIMER ON SHARI'A

Shari'a, which literally means "the way to the watering hole (in the desert)," is the symbolic touchstone of the Islamic faith. It includes Islam's religious rituals, the so-called five pillars, and a host of ethical teachings that enable believers to live out their faith in the world in right relationship with God and their fellow human beings, with the hope that God will receive them into his abode in the next life.[8]

---

monotheistic faiths and that on Judgment Day God will arbitrate concerning their disagreements. But it also points to cultural diversity in a general way.
[7]Scott W. Sunquist, *Understanding Christian Mission: Participation in Suffering and Glory* (Grand Rapids: Baker Academic, 2013), 247.
[8]For an authoritative and comprehensive presentation of Islamic law, see the works of McGill

In addition, the shari'a is divine, for from God's sacred texts—first the Qur'an and then the collections of the Prophet's sayings and deeds (the Sunnah)—Islamic scholars have over time derived legal rulings which cover family law and many aspects of public law, including commercial, property, contract, criminal, and judicial procedure law. This collection of jurisprudential writings has accumulated over the centuries in over a dozen different schools of law, five of which survive into the modern period. This painstaking work of "finding" God's law for human society in light of the divine revelation entrusted to the Arabian prophet Muhammad is called *fiqh*, or "understanding." It is the human attempt to capture the intent and practical import of the texts (which contain, in some fashion, God's law, or shari'a) for the purpose of setting individuals and communities on the straight path that leads to salvation in this life and the next. So in this sense, shari'a is divine, while *fiqh* is the human attempt to understand, explicate, and apply God's law in the human context.

But shari'a as God's blueprint for human society cannot be grasped outside of the vagaries of its historical embodiment. Twentieth- and twenty-first-century Islamic political activists teach that shari'a ruled supreme in every incarnation of the "Islamic state" over the last fourteen centuries. Further, they argue that all the ills of today's Muslim nations should be laid at the feet of the colonial powers and Western-leaning secularist regimes, which took over in the postcolonial period and subsequently stripped these nations of the benefit of shari'a-centered rule. Yet the historical facts belie such a simplistic view of the past.

First, Islamic states developed in a variety of directions over the centuries—from the mammoth Abbasid caliphate at its peak in the ninth and tenth centuries, to petty breakaway dynasties on the edges of societies, to the

University scholar Wael Hallaq, particularly *The Origins and Evolution of Islamic Law* (Cambridge: Cambridge University Press, 2005); *Shari'a: Theory, Practice, Transformations* (Cambridge: Cambridge University Press, 2009); *An Introduction to Islamic Law* (Cambridge: Cambridge University Press, 2009). Arguably the most influential US scholar in this field is UCLA scholar Khaled Abou El Fadl. Fadl is different from Hallaq in that he is also a practicing lawyer, specializing in human-rights issues, and a modern (I would say "postmodern") reformer of Islamic legal theory. See especially his latest work, *Reasoning with God: Reclaiming Shari'ah in the Modern Age* (Lanham, MD: Rowman & Littlefield, 2014). Another influential scholar in the same vein is Emory University scholar Abdullahi Ahmed An-Na'im: *Islam and the Secular State: Negotiating the Future of Shari'a* (Cambridge, MA: Harvard University Press, 2008); and *What Is an American Muslim? Embracing Faith and Citizenship* (Oxford: Oxford University Press, 2014).

various kingdoms and fiefdoms of West Africa and Indonesia, to the three great "Gunpowder Empires": Ottoman, Safavid (greater Persia), and Mughal (India). Second, however, what they had in common was the tremendous power of the ulama, the jurist-scholars who interpreted and applied God's law, or the shari'a. This story is about a continuous tug of war between the ulama and the political class. In Wael Hallaq's somewhat sanitized and idealized picture, the ulama were the guardians of the people, a "democratic" buffer between rulers and civilians and a bulwark against tyranny. Notice how this sociopolitical arrangement creates and guarantees the rule of law:

> Unlike other world legal cultures, however "complex," Islamic law was never a state mechanism (to use "state" anachronistically). To put it differently, Islamic law did not emerge out of a machinery of the body-politic, but rather arose as a private enterprise initiated and developed by pious men who embarked on the study and elaboration of law as a religious activity. Never could the Islamic ruling elite, the body politic, determine what the law was. This significant fact clearly means that, whereas in other legal cultures the body politic was the source of legal authority and power, in Islam this body was largely, if not totally, absent from the legal scene.[9]

Ideally, then, God was the Sovereign of the Islamic state, and on the basis of his revealed law (shari'a) jurists/scholars (ulama) in their various schools of law "determined what the law was." The ruler's role was simply to enforce that law as the chief executive. The problem with this view is that there is no constitutional law as such in the sacred texts. In fact, it was only with the eleventh-century work of al-Mawardi (d. 1058) that a new branch of Islamic jurisprudence was created—shari'a political jurisprudence, or *siyasa shar'iyya*. But this was largely in response to the invasion of the Turkic Buwayhids in the mid-tenth century, who in effect pushed the Abbasid caliph in Baghdad aside, relegating him to a ceremonial role and seizing the reins of political power. Granted, they converted to Islam, but now the state was ruled by outside forces that jeopardized the very existence of the caliphate.

---

[9]Hallaq, *Origins*, 204. Hallaq has since written an ambitious book that met with mixed reviews, mostly because he went outside of his area of expertise to argue that the nature of the modern nation-state makes it impossible to incorporate the modalities of the classical Islamic state. See *The Impossible State: Islam, Politics, and Modernity's Moral Predicament* (New York: Columbia University Press, 2013). See also Yale political scientist Andrew March's review of this book: "What Can the Islamic Past Teach Us About Secular Modernity?," *Political Theory* 43, no. 6 (2015): 838-49.

Al-Mawardi and those who followed were jurists who understood their mission to keep at bay any forces of chaos and establish new rules for this new but less-than-ideal status quo. For them the caliph remained God's deputy by virtue of his guardianship of the shari'a, and he in turn delegated political authority to the ruler (sultan). At least, the fiction of the supremacy of shari'a is maintained through such a scheme.

Rulers looked to the sacred Islamic texts for justifying all the legal and administrative regulations that they enacted. After all, it was rulers who appointed both market inspectors (*muhtasib*) to ensure that justice prevailed and all the judges, who worked not only in the shari'a courts, but also in their own more specialized courts (courts of complaints, or *mazalim*). Hallaq himself recognizes that there was some friction between rulers and ulama, though he tends to minimize it: "[The *mazalim* tribunals] were sanctioned by the powers assigned to the ruler to establish justice and equity according to the religious law. . . . They at times represented his absolutist governance and interference in the Shari'a, however marginal this may have been."[10] In the same vein, Noah Feldman, a Harvard professor of international law and adviser to the Bush administration for the drafting of the Iraqi constitution, wrote in his now-classic book *The Fall and Rise of the Islamic State* how scholars' "control over the content of the law" facilitated "the effective functioning of the classical Islamic state":[11]

> As an elite class they were able to define and administer the law "according to well-understood and well-settled rules," which "tends to produce predictability and stability across time" especially in the crucial area of the distribution of property. This is what guarantees "investment in long-term ventures and projects."

With the law in their hands, the ulama could put brakes on the executive power's confiscation of private property, thus forcing rulers "to rely on lawful taxation to raise revenues" and be more attentive to the people's needs in general. This arrangement gave "an aura of legitimacy" to that system of governance.[12]

---

[10]Ibid., 99.
[11]Noah Feldman, *The Fall and Rise of the Islamic State* (Princeton, NJ: Princeton University Press, 2008), 40.
[12]Ibid.

That said, Feldman recognizes that "no constitutional structure is immune from structural abuses." He adds, "There were sometimes corrupt or tyrannical rulers who robbed, stole, and oppressed, despite the best efforts of the scholars."[13] Still, everyone could acknowledge that this was outside the boundaries of the law. Just as in the areas of tax collection and the administrative regulations of the state, rulers had to look beyond the rules spelled out in the shari'a for the administration of criminal justice.

Why weren't the rulings of shari'a sufficient for justice to prevail? People today with little knowledge of Islam would be surprised to learn that the main obstacle was that "the standard of proof demanded by the shari'a before punishment" was too high for the kind of budget with which these states operated.[14] While the *hudud* punishments stipulated in the texts seem especially draconian today,[15] the requirement for eyewitnesses was too stringent for a court to convict such crimes in most cases (four witnesses to the actual act of penetration in the case of adultery).[16] And extreme public punishments in societies lacking police forces did serve as a deterrent to crime.

Still, because these crimes were so hard to prosecute, rulers over time came to see the need for tribunals with less rigid standards of proof and a wider spectrum of acts that could be prosecuted. Feldman argues that this more flexible system of criminal justice in past Muslim societies "could supplement the shari'a punishments so extensively that they came to constitute the bulk of what an observer would call the actual criminal law of the Islamic state."[17]

But there was another factor leading to increased tension between ulama and rulers. I am referring to the addition of local customary law[18] both in

---

[13]Ibid.

[14]Ibid., 48.

[15]*Hudud* means "limits," but here it refers more to the specific limits God has imposed on wrongful behavior or the prescribed penalties in classical Islamic law. As I mentioned earlier, most of the following punishments are still on the books in Saudi Arabia and to a lesser extent in, for example, Afghanistan, Pakistan, and Sudan: stoning of adulterers; capital punishment (beheading, crucifixion, now mostly firing squad) for murderers, "highway robbers" (armed insurgents against the state), and those who apostatize from Islam; amputation of hands for thieves; and flogging for the consumption of alcohol and false witness in an adultery trial. But just as in Islamic history, today these punishments are rarely carried out, and when they are, as in Saudi Arabia particularly, it is because the traditional rules for evidential proof have been relaxed.

[16]Feldman, *Fall and Rise*, 48.

[17]Ibid., 49.

[18]Princeton's Muhammad Qasim Zaman writes that "throughout the history of Islam, both the

the *fiqh* textbooks of various schools of law and in the administrative regulations enacted by the state. Boston University scholar Robert W. Hefner, an Indonesian specialist, uses the term "legal pluralism" in reference to these additions:

> In the premodern period, most Middle Eastern states, and some but not all Asian Muslim polities, made some variety of shari'a central to their legal systems. It must be said, however, that the understanding and practice of the shari'a varied with time and place; the shari'a was also never the only normative corpus used to adjudicate local affairs. Tribal populations applied customary law in addition to Islamic. Sultans operated non-shari'a criminal courts alongside those of Islamic judges. . . . Notwithstanding this often complex legal pluralism, in most of the central Muslim lands the popular ethical imaginary remained oriented toward the symbolism and ideals, if not the fine print, of the shari'a.[19]

We have returned to the idea of pluralistic diversity. But if anything, that diversity is even more acute today, mostly because the classical Islamic order was turned upside down by the colonial powers.

SHARI'A IN THE COLONIAL AND POSTCOLONIAL PERIODS

At the outset it is important to note that Islamic law has much more affinity with common law as opposed to civil law.[20] As in the United Kingdom and

---

shari'a and the state have had a complex relationship with local custom. While Muslim jurists did not recognize custom as a formal source of shari'a norms, it often played a significant role in their thought. Yet local customs also contravened shari'a norms, for instance in the realms of marriage, divorce, inheritance, and sexual mores. And even as the ulama have recognized that they will need to make their peace with particular customs, they—and other representatives of state authority—have long sought to curb the excesses of customary practice in their locales." See "Pakistan: Shari'a and the State," in *Shari'a Politics: Islamic Law and Society in the Modern World*, ed. Robert W. Hefner (Bloomington: Indiana University Press, 2011), 207-43, at 228. One example he gives is that of "honor killings" "in which women have been brutally murdered—sometimes by their fathers, brothers, and husbands—after being accused of sexual impropriety. Young girls have, on occasion, been given away to forestall or settle tribal vendettas" (229).

[19] Robert W. Hefner, introduction to *Shari'a Politics*, 1-54, at 2.

[20] "Most nations today follow one of two major legal traditions: common law or civil law. The common law tradition emerged in England during the Middle Ages and was applied within British colonies across continents. The civil law tradition developed in continental Europe at the same time and was applied in the colonies of European imperial powers such as Spain and Portugal. Civil law was also adopted in the nineteenth and twentieth centuries by countries formerly possessing distinctive legal traditions, such as Russia and Japan, that sought to reform their legal systems in order to gain economic and political power comparable to that of Western European nation-states." See "The Common Law and Civil Law Traditions," The Robbins

United States, for instance, judges have much more power, since the legal system is not built upon a comprehensive listing of statutes and legal regulations (a legal code) but rather on a body of legal precedents collected by courts over time. Civil law, by contrast, is codified, which substantially reduces the scope of interpretation a judge may consider. Whereas both developed during the medieval period, the common-law system originated in England, while the civil-law system emerged in continental Europe. British colonies inherited the common-law tradition (though some subsequently turned to civil law), while most independent Muslim nations after World War II chose the civil-law system. But the disruption of the traditional Islamic balance between ulama and rulers started long before that, namely under nineteenth-century Ottoman rule.

The Ottomans reasoned that one cause of European supremacy was the way they had centralized and codified their legal system. As mentioned above, "In the classical Sunni constitutional balance, the shari'a existed alongside a body of administrative regulations that governed many matters in the realms of taxation and criminal law."[21] Dubbed the "sick man of Europe," in the early 1830s the Ottoman Empire was reeling from three recent military defeats and a worrisome loss of capital. Rulers needed to borrow money from Europe, but in order to gain Europe's trust and acquire credit, the empire embarked on a series of reforms from 1839 to 1876 known as the Tanzimat. On the legal front, this involved codifying rules and statutes for state use—in other words, establishing a civil-law system. (Note here the widening scope of an already prevailing legal pluralism.) On the constitutional front, this meant institution building.

This had far-reaching consequences, as Feldman explains:

> Together, I shall argue, these legal and constitutional reforms displaced and destroyed the scholarly class, without leaving in their wake any institution or social entity capable of counter-balancing the executive as the scholarly class had done. The consequences of the displacement of the scholars were world-

Collection, School of Law (Boalt Hall), University of California at Berkeley, www.law.berkeley.edu/library/robbins/CommonLawCivilLawTraditions.html (accessed March 9, 2017). The close parallel between Islamic law and the common-law system was first argued by Lawrence Rosen, *The Anthropology of Justice: Law as Culture in Islamic Society* (Cambridge: Cambridge University Press, 1989).
[21]Feldman, *Fall and Rise*, 61.

changing. It opened the possibility of secular government; but simultaneously, the removal of the one meaningful check on executive authority cleared the way for autocratic and absolute power—which soon became, in much of the Muslim world, the dominant mode of government in the twentieth century.[22]

This was already the case in the nineteenth century. The pace only accelerated in the following century, though especially in the 1950s, when most former colonies were declaring their independence. Because the traditionally decentralized bureaucracies of Muslim lands were now in the hands of modern, power-hungry nation-states, shari'a law was demoted and relegated to at best the province of family law and religious affairs. Even one of the world's oldest universities and the most prestigious center of Islamic learning, Cairo's al-Azhar University, was nationalized in the 1960s by the secular regime of Gamal Abdel Nasser. Religious endowments, which historically were the province of the ulama and which controlled not just religious institutions but schools and clinics as well, were now taken over by most Muslim states.

Yet this decades-long policy of states encroaching on religious affairs had two other consequences, both of which can be subsumed under the rubric of "political Islam." The first is the rise of a modern mass Islamic movement, the Muslim Brotherhood, which was founded in Egypt in 1928 by Hasan al-Banna (d. 1949),[23] and its counterpart in South Asia, the Jamaat-e-Islami, which was founded in India in 1941 by Abul Ala Mawdudi (d. 1979). Then in the 1970s and 1980s, as a result of the defeat of the Arabs in the Six-Day War (1967) and the failure of the socialist pan-Arab policies of Egypt's Gamal Abdel Nasser, "Muslim lands witnessed the emergence of great social movements calling for the state to implement Islamic law once again."[24] As a result seven Muslim nations introduced amendments to their constitutions reflecting this change,[25] which is the less-understood dimension of "political Islam."

---

[22]Ibid., 60-61.

[23]The literature on this movement in Egypt and beyond is vast, but Khalil al-Anani's recent book is likely the best: *Inside the Muslim Brotherhood: Religion, Identity, and Politics* (Oxford: Oxford University Press, 2016); for a short survey, see David L. Johnston, "Muslim Brotherhood," in *Encyclopedia of Islam and the Muslim World*, ed. Richard C. Martin, 2nd ed. (London: Macmillan, 2016).

[24]Hefner, introduction, 2-3.

[25]Clark B. Lombardi, *State Law as Islamic Law in Modern Egypt: The Incorporation of the Shari'a into Egyptian Constitutional Law* (Leiden: Brill, 2006), 1.

The state manipulation of Islam since Muslim-majority nations achieved independence is brilliantly analyzed in Jocelyne Cesari's work *The Awakening of Muslim Democracy*.[26] Using primarily an institutional method[27] to measure the role of religion in democratic reforms, Cesari notes first of all that the European phenomenon of church-state separation is merely the consequence of bloody wars of religion during the sixteenth and seventeenth centuries. The various forms of secularism in the Western experience "contextualize and historicize two major principles of secularity: protection by law of all religions and equidistance of the state vis-à-vis all religions."[28] Cesari extrapolates these two principles as defining secularity more generally. Indeed, the Western experience of setting apart religion and state and privatizing religion has generally led to the marginalization of religion. In the Muslim world, by contrast, political cultures have developed quite differently.

In fact, even those nations usually considered "secular," like Turkey, Iraq under Saddam Hussein, and Syria under Hafez al-Assad and his son Bashar al-Assad, have seen no decline in religious observance—quite the contrary. Secularity, Cesari avers, is a condition whereby "states would not use religions for political purposes and would grant equality to all religions, while religious groups would refrain from capturing state institutions and politics for their specific purposes."[29] Though Western nations teeter on both sides of that balance, just about all Muslim countries fail in both respects.

Take Turkey, for example. Though France and Turkey both prohibit the display of religious symbols in public, France does not allow for religious instruction in public schools, while Turkey requires exactly that for Muslim

---

[26]Jocelyne Cesari, *The Awakening of Muslim Democracy: Religion, Modernity, and the State* (Cambridge: Cambridge University Press, 2014). Cesari directs the Islam in the West program at Harvard University and is a senior research fellow at the Berkley Center for Religion, Peace and World Affairs at Georgetown University.

[27]She explains, "Institutionalization refers to the way new sociopolitical situations are translated into the creation or adaptation of formal institutions such as constitutions, laws, administrative bodies, and agencies. The adoption of the nation-state model by Muslim majority countries after the collapse of the Ottoman Empire has been the decisive political change that led to the reshaping of values and institutions. These changes have translated into the hegemonic status of Islam" (ibid., 9).

[28]Ibid., 4.

[29]Ibid., 5.

students, though without allowing the same privilege for religious minorities like the Alevis.[30] This is true in political practice too: since the dramatic ascendancy of the Justice and Development Party (AKP) in 2002, and now especially after the failed coup of July 2016, president Recep Tayyip Erdogan has dramatically consolidated his power, ensuring that the Islamic values and objectives of his party will be implemented on a wider scale in Turkey in the years to come. Turkey, by far the most "secular" of Muslim nations until the 1990s, demonstrates that it too, under the surface, had implemented "hegemonic Islam" all along.

But as elsewhere in the Muslim world since at least the 1970s, the state has defined what is "authentic" Islam in terms of "a code of public morality," thus attempting to fuse national and religious identities—naturally, a problematic endeavor for religious minorities. "As a result of this fusion," explains Cesari, "a moral hierarchy is established in which the national government intervenes in the personal lives of its citizens on topics that range from dress to social relations and culture."[31] With the institutional tools of modernity, then, Muslim states have attempted to reconstruct religious norms, redefine Islamic law, and establish a "moderate" Islam, a politicization of religion shared often by civil society organizations in political opposition, like the Muslim Brotherhood.

Note too that both sides have used shari'a as their political weapon of choice, though this is especially true for the opposition, for whom this has been its battle cry. But this instrumentalization of religion has a long genealogy dating back to the colonial period. Further, it was always the female body that symbolized public morality sanctioned by religion.[32] Ataturk in 1920s Turkey, Bourguiba in Tunisia, and the shah in Iran all forbade (or strongly discouraged) women from wearing the veil. By contrast, Ayatollah Khomeini forced women to wear Islamic dress after the Iranian Revolution, and Islamic activism in the late 1970s launched on Egyptian university campuses what would become a

---

[30]Ibid., 7.

[31]Ibid., 111.

[32]Cesari writes, "The politicization of the female body is a general feature of Muslim societies, from the colonial to the postcolonial periods. A consistent theme throughout these different phases is that women are the symbolic embodiment of morality, and therefore are the key to securing familial, national, and religious values in an uncertain maelstrom of social change" (ibid., 112).

grassroots revolution with the hijab at its center.[33] All these are examples of how the female body has come to epitomize religious observance. However, the Qur'an only mentions modesty generally—for men as well as for women.[34] All the current debates about female Islamic dress are focused on cultural items and discourses that were invented in the 1970s.

Now back to the notion of "hegemonic religion." By this term Cesari means that a distinction must be made "between a dominant religion, an established religion, and a hegemonic religion."[35] A dominant religion is the religion of a nation's majority population, like Catholicism in Poland and Ireland and Protestantism in the United States. The Church of Denmark and the Church of England are examples of established religions. They are recognized by law as the official religion and are usually subsidized by the state. But a religion is hegemonic "when the state grants a certain religious group exclusive legal, economic, or political rights denied to other religions."[36] In practice, it means that the status of a particular religion is characterized by at least two of the following features:

1. Nationalization of institutions, clerics, and places of worship belonging to one religious tradition

2. Insertion of those doctrines into public-school curriculum (beyond the religious instruction, e.g., in history, civic education, etc.)

3. Legal discrimination against other religious adherents in education, public funding, public expression, and so forth

4. Legal restrictions of speech and expression as well as restrictions of women's rights (marriage/divorce/abortion) based on the prescription of that religion[37]

---

[33]See Leila Ahmed, *A Quiet Revolution: The Veil's Resurgence, from the Middle East to America* (New Haven, CT: Yale University Press, 2011). See also my review of this book in two parts: "The Veil, Islamism, and Spreading Religion (1)," *Human Trustees* (blog), February 14, 2014, www .humantrustees.org/blogs/current-islam/item/114-veil-islamism; and "The Veil, Islamism, and Spreading Religion (2)," *Human Trustees* (blog), February 24, 2014, www.humantrustees.org/ blogs/current-islam/item/115-veil-islamism-2.

[34]Here's the only verse with any detail at all: "And tell believing women that they should lower their eyes, guard their private parts, and not display their charms beyond what [is acceptable] to reveal; they should draw their coverings over their necklines and not reveal their charms except to their husbands, their fathers, their husband's fathers, their sons" (Q 24:31, Haleem).

[35]Cesari, *Awakening*, 9.

[36]Ibid., 9-10.

[37]Ibid., 11.

This is not unique to Islam, as Buddhism enjoys a hegemonic status in Sri Lanka and the Orthodox Church in Greece and Russia. And though Islam enjoys legal privileges in most Muslim nations, "Indonesia, Senegal, and Lebanon are the only exceptions in the Muslim world in their attempts to create regimes of legal neutrality (although discriminatory practices do exist)."[38]

Nevertheless, my statement "Islam enjoys legal privileges" must be modified in light of my previous argument. "Islam" as a religious tradition houses a vast spectrum of theologies, legal schools, and regional variations. Islamic law as such historically incorporated elements of Roman law, Persian law, and Byzantine law as well as a host of customary laws wherever it spread. Legal pluralism is inscribed into its very nature. Yet this is even more true today.

In the following two examples legal pluralism is certainly an element. However, I wish to highlight an even broader phenomenon that can be seen in all religious traditions, namely that the influence of sociopolitical dynamics and wider currents of thought is constantly transforming religious understandings of what it means to be a righteous person or society.

Two Useful Examples: Pakistan and Tunisia[39]

Pakistan is a good example of a state profoundly shaped by British colonialism (as part of India), then by a secular-leaning founding constitution, and then evolving gradually into becoming a self-proclaimed Islamic state. But all along the way, as documented by Muhammad Qasim Zaman, successive governments often contested bitterly with various factions of ulama, the modernists (mostly among the elites), and the islamists[40] about the various meanings of shari'a and how Islam should be implemented in the

---

[38]Ibid., 13.

[39]Space will not permit me to look at other cases. For a brilliant piece of comparative work, see Arskal Salim (a social anthropologist from Australia specializing in Indonesian affairs), "The Constitutionalization of Shari'a in Muslim Societies: Comparing Indonesia, Tunisia and Egypt," in *The Sociology of Shari'a: Case Studies from Around the World*, ed. Adam Possamai, James T. Richardson, and Bryan S. Turner (Berlin: Springer, 2015), 199-218. Salim opens a window for us on the issue of legal pluralism and on the variety of ways that shari'a debates are tied to democratization in three different contexts. Indonesia's constitutional revision took place in 2002, whereas such change in Tunisia and Egypt has been much more recent—in 2014 in both cases. Despite obvious parallels, each situation has evolved very differently, following the unique sociopolitical and historical developments pertaining to each nation.

[40]I write *islamists* with a lowercase *i*, thereby signaling that this kind of "political Islam" is about instrumentalizing religion for political purposes in the modern era. It is an ideological marker rather than an article of the Islamic faith.

public arena. In order to facilitate their administration of such a diverse population, the colonial authorities divided India into different religious communities and left them to judge their own affairs according to their religious laws. This, however, "created considerable and ongoing contestation on who had the authority to safeguard, interpret and administer these laws." And what is more, contends Zaman, "it also paved the way for demands that the shari'a ought to govern all facets of life and that the legitimacy of a state established as a homeland for Muslims depended on its ability to do so."[41]

Notably, with the passing of each new Pakistani constitution (1956, 1962, 1973) "the state moved further away from the secular and pluralist vision of its founders."[42] Islam became more and more hegemonic as a result. For instance, the 1973 constitution forbade Ahmadis to call themselves Muslims, the first time this had happened in Pakistani history.[43] Though the law was explicitly discriminatory only with regard to the Ahmadis, human-rights organizations regularly report that Christians, Hindus, and Sikhs face discrimination and sometimes acts of violence.[44] Still, Article 20 of the Pakistani constitution calls for freedom of religion, and Article 25 states that all citizens are equal before the law. Nevertheless, as in Egypt passports and identity cards indicate a person's religion, which is particularly difficult for Ahmadis, since they do not want to be designated as non-Muslims. In practice, of course, this leads to much discrimination either by fellow citizens or by the local authorities.[45]

---

[41]Zaman, "Pakistan," 233.

[42]Cesari, *Awakening*, 40.

[43]The Ahmadiyya, members of which are called Ahmadis, was an Islamic renewal movement founded by Mirza Ghulam Ahmad in India in 1889. One of the movement's two major factions considers Ahmad to be a prophet, but the other also gives him considerably more honor than mainstream Sunnis or Shi'ites are comfortable with. Overseas, the Ahmadiyya remains an active missionary movement in Britain, continental Europe, and the United States. See the *Encyclopedia of Islam and the Modern World*, ed. Richard C. Martin (New York: Macmillan, 2004), s.v. "Ahmadiyya."

[44]See for instance the 2015 report of the United States Commission on International Religious Freedom. Besides highlighting the continuing repression against the Ahmadis, the report states that Pakistan's "government [has] continued to enforce blasphemy laws, whose punishment ranges from life in prison to the death sentence for a range of charges, including 'defiling the Prophet Muhammad.'" Nevertheless, the Ahmadis have been by far the most numerous victims of violence. *United States Commission on International Religious Freedom: Annual Report 2015* (Washington, DC: U.S. Commission on International Religious Freedom, 2015), www.uscirf .gov/reports-briefs/annual-report/2015-annual-report.

[45]Cesari, *Awakening*, 41.

It would be unfair to leave Pakistan on such a sour note, however. It would be equally unfair to reduce Pakistan to its discouraging level of poverty.[46] The chapter devoted to Pakistan in the recent book *Islam and Democracy After the Arab Spring* offers a different perspective, as demonstrated by its title, "Pakistan: A Work in Progress."[47] First, historically one must take into account the fact that "Pakistan was established in the mid-20th century specifically to be a democracy for Muslims."[48] Its Muslim elite came together with no other platform than a vague and idealistic document adopted by the young nation's Constituent Assembly called the 1949 Objectives Resolution. Though many objectives from this document have been at least partially achieved,[49] three out of twelve have not. Here are the three "more elusive objectives":

> The second objective calls for, in addition to democracy and freedom, "equality, tolerance, and social justice, as enunciated by Islam" to be "fully observed." The fourth demands that the religious and cultural rights of minorities be protected. And the sixth objective demands that "fundamental rights including equality of status, of opportunity and before law, social, economic and political justice, and freedom of thought, expression, belief, faith, worship and association, subject to law and public morality" shall be guaranteed.[50]

That said, with all the push and pull between (and even among) military-led governments, secular-leaning parties, and Islamic parties, Pakistan has managed to further its democratic agenda over the last few years, especially after the national tragedy of Benazir Bhutto's assassination in December 2007. Esposito, Sonn, and Voll offer these steps as indications of the democratic process:

> Mostly under parliamentary pressure from the socialist Pakistan's People Party (PPP), the Public Accounts Committee found new life and the authority

---

[46]According to the 2015 United Nations *Human Development Report*, Pakistan, the second most populous Muslim nation (180 million), is ranked 147th. See the *Human Development Report 2015: Work for Human Development* (New York: United Nations Development Programme, 2015), http://hdr.undp.org /sites/default/files/2015_human_development_report.pdf.

[47]John L. Esposito, Tamara Sonn, and John O. Voll, "Pakistan: A Work in Progress," in *Islam and Democracy After the Arab Spring* (Oxford: Oxford University Press, 2014), 79-114.

[48]Ibid., 79.

[49]In this respect, the following objectives have been mostly met: the first ("government through elected representatives"), the third ("Muslims must be able to live according to the teachings of the Qur'an"), the fifth ("Pakistan shall be a federation"), the eighth ("an independent judiciary"), and the ninth ("territorial integrity"). Ibid., 113.

[50]Ibid.

in fighting corruption and pushing through federally funded development projects that had long stood dormant.

Further, the Pakistani parliament passed the 18th Amendment in 2010, transferring much federal government power to the provinces. It also repealed the 17th Amendment, which had allowed former President Musharraf to be simultaneously army chief and president, and the 8th Amendment, passed under General Zia ul-Haq's tenure, stripping the president of his power to dissolve parliament.[51]

Democracy expands through small, incremental steps such as these, all of which arguably fulfill the "objectives of Shari'a." By contrast, Tunisia's path was much simpler, yet all the more dramatic.[52] After fifty-three years of dictatorship, Tunisia, North Africa's smallest country, exploded in popular protest when in December 2010 the picture of a twenty-six-year-old street vendor setting himself aflame went viral on social media. Throughout the Arab world disenfranchised and alienated youth identified with his plight and thereby launched the "Arab Spring." By January 14, 2011, dictator Zine El Abidine Ben Ali had fled the country, and by October Tunisians were going to the polls in the first free election since independence in 1956.

The revolution itself, as in nearby Egypt, had little or nothing to do with religion and everything to do with freedom and democracy.[53] In both places the islamists had long been in the opposition with much popular support and thus gained even more admiration for their victory. But whereas the Muslim Brotherhood in Egypt, despite relentless state repression, found ways to organize its civil-society projects and run for parliament as independents, the

---

[51]Ibid., 110-11.

[52]For good surveys on the political dynamics leading up to and following the Tunisian "Jasmine Revolution," see chapter 7 ("Tunisia: From Revolution to Republic") in Esposito, Sonn, and Voll, *Islam and Democracy*, 174-201; Shadi Hamid, *Temptations of Power: Islamists and Illiberal Democracy in a New Middle East* (Oxford: Oxford University Press, 2014), especially chapter 8 ("A Tunisian Exception?"); see also my review of Hamid's book for a critique of his argument that Islamists moderate under repression and harden their illiberal positions when in power (which admittedly happened with the Egyptian Muslim Brotherhood in 2012–2013) in *Sociology of Islam* 4 (2016): 303-6. Finally, a whole issue of a German journal is dedicated to "The Tunisian Constitutional Process: Main Actors and Key Issues," ed. Mathieu Rousselin and Christopher Smith, special issue, *Global Dialogues* 7 (2015).

[53]Esposito, Sonn, and Voll cite the results of a survey conducted in Egypt and Tunisia over October and November 2012, which indicate that only 26 percent in Tunisia and 28 percent in Egypt "believe that Islam should play a governmental role" (*Islam and Democracy*, 189).

Ennahda (Renaissance) Party in Tunisia had been all but destroyed by Ben Ali. Nevertheless, the party's cofounder and leader Rached Ghannouchi returned to Tunisia after more than two decades of exile in London to great popular approval, his party winning 40 percent of the seats in parliament seven months later. Still, the Ennahda faction decided to bring into the new government the two secular parties that had won the most votes.

One cannot make sense of the dramatic evolution of political Islam and more broadly of Tunisia's relatively successful transition into democracy since 2011 without examining one of its key players, Rached Ghannouchi.[54] He has always been considered a moderate islamist[55] in that for Ghannouchi Islam at its core is a message of liberation from tyranny and of emancipation and dignity for people everywhere. Therefore it is focused on establishing justice on earth. This also means that shari'a underscores and guarantees the human rights of all, without any discrimination based on class, religion, or race.[56] In this schema, theocracy cannot exist. For Ghannouchi, an Islamic state is first and foremost a democratic state, standing as a bulwark against the authoritarian practices that have become routine in Muslim postcolonial states.

In practice, however, governing a nation in a postrevolutionary climate would prove to be a daunting task made almost impossible both by Tunisia's

---

[54]Ghannouchi is a thinker I have written about previously, and whose most famous book, *The Public Freedoms in the Islamic State*, mostly written from prison in the 1980s, I am now translating. See David L. Johnston, "*Maqasid al-Shari'a*: Epistemology and Hermeneutics of Muslim Theologies of Human Rights," *Die Welt des Islams* 47, no. 2 (2007): 149-87; and "The Fuzzy Boundaries Between Reformism and Islamism: Malik Bennabi and Rashid al-Ghannushi on Civilization," *Maghreb Review* 29, no. 12 (2004): 123-52. The translation will likely be published in late 2017 by Yale University Press. I also met Ghannouchi in person at a lecture he gave at the US Institute of Peace in October 2015. See his lecture online at "Democratizing Under Fire: Can Tunisia Show the Way? Sheikh Rachid Ghannouchi on Balancing Democracy and Security in North Africa," United States Institute of Peace, Middle East and Africa Center, October 28, 2015, www.usip.org/events/democratizing-under-fire-can-tunisia-show-the-way.

[55]See Azzam S. Tamimi, *Rachid Ghannouchi: A Democrat Within Islamism* (Oxford: Oxford University Press, 2001).

[56]Like many other contemporary Islamic scholars, Ghannouchi strongly disagrees with the traditional majority view that apostasy from Islam is punishable by death. The Qur'an, he contends, warns in several places that those who abandon their faith will suffer tragic consequences in the afterlife but does not mention punishment in this life. In fact, the words and deeds of the Prophet and the four Rightly Guided Caliphs show that apostasy was for them a political crime committed by people who posed a material threat to the young Islamic state in Medina. In modern Western culture this would be comparable to prosecuting people who had committed treason against the state.

powerful neighbor Libya, which was devolving into chaos and civil war, and by the country's economy, built largely on tourism but now shattered by the lack of tourists and years of neglect. Add to that the explosive growth of a puritanical brand of Islam called Salafism—some branches of which did call for violence—and one can understand how the fragile government coalition under Ennahda's banner stumbled along and how the rift between the staunch secularists and the fiery Salafists only continued widening, eventually spilling into violence. In 2013 two secular politicians were assassinated, presumably by Salafists, though the Ennahda party was held responsible by the secularist opposition. In response to the growing pressure, the party pulled out of Tunisian government in September 2013. An interim technocratic government then took over and began preparing the nation for new parliamentary elections after the drawing up of a new constitution.

Despite the heated debates within the Tunisian Constituent Assembly, which had remained intact, the process was successful for at least two reasons. First, the majority party in the assembly, Ennahda, had voluntarily stepped down from power—a rarity in any nation. Second, Tunisia benefitted from a very active civil-society network that came together at this point and provided the necessary glue to keep the process on track. The 2015 Nobel Peace Prize was awarded to four particular organizations recognized for their outstanding work in pulling the nation back from the brink of civil war.[57]

I have no space to recount the rest of the story, but at the time of this writing Ennahda is still involved in the current government, though as a minority party, and Ghannouchi has been reelected as the leader of his party at its tenth congress after making a revolutionary speech. Tunisia no longer needs "political Islam," he says, as the revolution and its new constitution guarantee civil liberties and human rights for all citizens. As my research shows, Ghannouchi's views have evolved. He currently holds that shari'a mandates not only a democratic state but one in which the spheres of religion and politics are "differentiated."[58]

---

[57]Esposito, Sonn, and Voll put it this way (though at the time of publication the prize had not yet been awarded): "Central to this process was the involvement of the UGTT [General Union of Tunisian Workers] and civil society groups, including the employer's union, the Tunisian Bar Association, and the country's Human Rights League" (*Islam and Democracy*, 198).
[58]For specific details on how the Islamic party Ennahda (Renaissance), which came to power after

POSSIBLE MISSIOLOGICAL DIRECTIONS

I wish to conclude this essay with three possible directions thoughtful Christians might take in response to the above exposition of shari'a as it plays out globally today and in light of what missiologist David J. Bosch calls "the two mandates." He believes that the distinction between "the commission to announce the good news of salvation through Jesus Christ" and Christ's call "to responsible participation in human society, including working for human well-being and justice," was first articulated by Jonathan Edwards (d. 1758) and that these two facets should be seen as two sides of the same coin.[59] Scott Sunquist claims that this metaphor is misleading, however. Though both are rooted in Jesus' love, evangelism and justice for Sunquist are not "partners" but spring forth simultaneously from his person:

> Jesus was a whole person, filled to overflowing with the kenotic, self-emptying love of God. Jesus's love is far deeper, wider, and more expansive than we imagine. His love is as personal as his forgiveness of those who killed him, and it is as large as his suffering love for the sins of the world.[60]

Out of Christ's love to us individually as well as collectively in the church come both proclamation and service.

Further, Sunquist notes that the Creator willed a diversity and wealth of human cultures. However, while "all cultures are marked by the image of God,"[61] according to Sunquist this cultural image has been tarnished by the fall and therefore—just like individuals—must be redeemed. The Holy Spirit is active in every cultural milieu for this specific purpose.[62]

---

the uprising, joined hands with secular parties to draft a secular constitution and officially re-
nounced its support for "political Islam" in Tunisia, see my blog posts here: *Human Trustees*
(blog), Religion and Human Rights, www.humantrustees.org/blogs/religion-and-human-rights.
[59]David J. Bosch, *Transforming Mission: Paradigm Shifts in Theology of Mission* (Maryknoll, NY:
Orbis, 1991), 403. To Bosch's trinitarian missiology of *missio Dei* Amos Yong adds the Pentecos-
tal/renewal perspective of *missio Spiritus*. This is crucial, for as the book of Acts makes abundantly
clear, the Spirit of God fell as promised on the disciples and the Jerusalem crowd at Pentecost
and empowered the early church to spread the good news throughout the Roman Empire of that
day. Moreover, this "robust pneumatological dimension" is "one that recognizes the church does
not initiate but only participates in the divine mission in the power of Christ's Spirit." As such,
the Holy Spirit enables the church to share in the divine mission to reconcile "all creation to the
Father through the Son." See Amos Yong and Jonathan A. Anderson, *Renewing Christian Theology: Systematics for a Global Christianity* (Waco, TX: Baylor University Press, 2014), 185.
[60]Sunquist, *Understanding Christian Mission*, 320-21.
[61]Ibid., 248.
[62]Ibid., 252. Besides the redemptive analogies that can be discovered as bridges to the gospel

Roughly one and a half billion Muslims are spread out among hundreds of cultures, nations, and ethnic groups. Still, Islam over the centuries has been a faith that permeates almost every cultural domain, including politics. The Arab Spring was a spontaneous explosion of protest against tyranny and oppression and a cry for freedom and human dignity. Though that animus was not sparked by religion, many sought to channel that energy in a more Islamic direction because they believed that Islam at its heart is a message about equality and freedom for all, about social justice and human rights.[63]

Therefore, if we hold that the Father who sent the Redeemer is now working through his Holy Spirit in Islamic cultural contexts to further the work of redemption, then by the same token I believe he is calling the church to at least three tasks.

First, Western Christians especially must educate themselves about the pluralistic nature of Muslim societies and about Islamic law in particular. This will provide a needed antidote to the current wave of Islamophobia that clearly contributes to the recruitment of young Muslims by terror organizations and, more importantly, dehumanizes our Muslim neighbors. Relatedly, the field of missiology would benefit from more input from the disciplines of sociology, international relations, and political theory as well as anthropology, which has long been a staple in this field.

Second, particularly relevant to the interfaith encounters between Muslims and Christians today is Yong's theology of hospitality toward people of other faiths. In *Hospitality and the Other*,[64] he develops the theme of the Hospitable God who between Pentecost and the final outpouring of the Spirit on all flesh calls us to exercise this hospitality toward our neighbors of all faiths. From the formal exchanges of interreligious academic dialogues to the warm embrace of brothers and sisters sharing meals in their various

---

within a culture's myths, stories, art, and values, Sunquist remarks that "the Holy Spirit confronts cultural sin, empowers cultures for change, and draws cultures toward the Triune God, using individuals to affect [sic] this change in particular contexts" (ibid.). I would add that even before the gospel arrives, courageous people often stand up for human rights under the pall of oppressive regimes and fight for social justice. Is that just "common grace," as some would have it, or is it the work of God's Spirit preparing the way for something greater?

[63]Cf. Mayer, *Islam and Human Rights*; Emon, Ellis, and Glahn, *Islamic Law and International Human Rights*; Sachedina, *Islam and the Challenge of Human Rights*; and Sunquist, *Understanding Christian Mission*. Also, see my essay "Islam and Human Rights: A Growing Rapprochement?"

[64]Amos Yong, *Hospitality and the Other: Pentecost, Christian Practices, and the Neighbor* (Maryknoll, NY: Orbis, 2008).

congregations, the many tongues of Pentecost point to a variety of possible practices by the power of the same Spirit. Though he uses Nigeria as a case study for Muslim-Christian relations in that book, he also mentions the situation in North America.

Practically speaking, I would add that in a context of oppressive and shameful Islamophobia,[65] Christians must do their utmost to welcome Muslims around them, particularly newly arrived refugees from the conflicts of Syria and Iraq.[66] It also means that they must go out of their way to build relationships with Muslims in their communities and find ways for churches and mosques to interact over shared meals and conversation and to cooperate on alleviating social and economic needs around them. This is what several groups are committed to doing already.[67]

Third, as the literature on shari'a in the West continues to burgeon,[68]

---

[65]Though the situation has worsened for Muslims in the United States since its publication, a good place to start is the joint report made by the Center for Race and Gender at the University of California, Berkeley, and the Council on American-Islamic Relations (CAIR) titled "Islamophobia and Its Impact in the United States (January 2009–December 2010)," available at www.cair.com/images /pdf/2010-Islamophobia-Report.pdf. The goal for the report is best stated in the section titled "Evolving Toward Ever-Greater Cultural Pluralism." This is the concluding paragraph: "Muslims have the great fortune to receive guidance, support and wisdom from the many groups who have fought bigotry before us. We also know that, by standing firm on Islamic and constitutional principles, we will contribute to evolving America toward ever greater cultural pluralism" (10). For a useful report in the United Kingdom, see the 2011 Runnymede Trust publication "Islamophobia: A Challenge for Us All," www.runnymedetrust.org/uploads/publications/pdfs/islamophobia.pdf.

[66]Yong encourages his Christian readers to think particularly about refugees displaced by war, natural disasters, and persecution—a topic that has become so much more urgent in 2017 with President Donald J. Trump's immigration ban on several Muslim nations (*Hospitality*, 154-55). Yong quotes Dana Wilbanks, who wrote these prescient words in the 1990s: "In our current nationalistic ethos, Christians are called to relativize the authority of the state and qualify the claims of the national community. Yet Christians may also participate in shaping the character of the national community. We may affirm the values of government and the existence of genuinely diverse national communities." Dana W. Wilbanks, *Re-Creating America: The Ethics of U.S. Immigration and Refugee Policy in Christian Perspective* (Nashville: Abingdon, 1996), 123.

[67]See the work of Peace Catalyst International, which currently serves in eight American urban centers (www.peacecatalyst.org/). The Abrahamic Alliance includes Jews in their leadership and outreach (www.abrahamicalliance.org/aai/).

[68]See John R. Bowen, *Blaming Islam* (Cambridge, MA: MIT Press, 2012); Rex Ahdar and Nicholas Aroney, eds., *Shari'a in the West* (Oxford: Oxford University Press, 2010); Jørgen S. Nielsen and Lisbet Christoffersen, eds., *Shari'a as Discourse: Legal Traditions and the Encounter with Europe* (Farnham, UK: Ashgate, 2010); Maurits S. Berger, *Applying Shari'a in the West: Facts, Fears and the Future of Islamic Rules on Family Relations in the West* (Leiden: Leiden University Press, 2013). For an excellent article on the use of shari'a in US courts, see Abed Awad, "The True Story of Sharia in American Courts," *The Nation*, June 14, 2012, www.thenation.com/article/true-story-sharia-american -courts. Awad writes, "As an attorney, consultant or expert witness, I have handled more than 100 cases involving components of Sharia." He argues that the movement to ban shari'a from consideration in US courts not only stokes Islamophobia but also hinders the cause of justice in many cases.

Christians should thoughtfully reflect on how our Western societies (and US culture in particular) could better "reasonably accommodate"[69] Muslims in our midst, particularly in terms of certain aspects of Islamic law. A 2008 lecture by former Archbishop of Canterbury Rowan Williams on the need to better serve Muslims with regard to the requirements of shari'a set off a firestorm of controversy in the United Kingdom.[70] Yet as anthropologist John R. Bowen writes in a useful distillation of his years of fieldwork with Muslims in Europe, the controversy about Islam ("blaming Islam"), whether in Europe or the United States, is just a new manifestation of Western phobia regarding new immigrants as "other." For instance, Jews and Catholics were the brunt of fierce discrimination in nineteenth- and early twentieth-century America.

As a Pew Trust research article from 2013 clearly demonstrates, religious courts operate daily all across the United States:

> The Roman Catholic Church alone has nearly 200 diocesan tribunals that handle a variety of cases, including an estimated 15,000 to 20,000 marriage annulments each year. In addition, many Orthodox Jews use rabbinical courts to obtain religious divorces, resolve business conflicts and settle other disputes with fellow Jews. Similarly, many Muslims appeal to Islamic clerics to resolve marital disputes and other disagreements with fellow Muslims.[71]

Though there are a variety of informal means imams can use to counsel married couples and resolve family disputes according to their understanding of shari'a, perhaps the most organized effort to date has been the Islamic Tribunal in the Dallas-Fort Worth area.[72] Like its counterparts in

---

[69]"Reasonable accommodation" was the byword of Western European nations that welcomed millions of guest workers after World War II in order to fill gaps in their labor forces. As John Bowen shows, this accommodation to the African and Asian immigrants included such pragmatic measures as building mosques, allowing Arabic or Turkish instruction in schools, and conducting job training and instruction in native languages. This came to be labeled "multiculturalism" in the course of time, a term that has seen much backlash recently, starting with German Chancellor Angela Merkel's 2010 quip that multiculturalism has "failed and failed utterly" (Bowen, *Blaming Islam*, 17).

[70]Several of the essays in the volume edited by Ahdar and Aroney (*Shari'a in the West*) look at various aspects of this debate, including a theophilosophical contribution by John Milbank ("The Archbishop of Canterbury: The Man and the Theology Behind the Lecture," 43-58).

[71]Pew Research Center, "Applying God's Law: Religious Courts and Mediation in the U.S.," April 8, 2013, www.pewforum.org/2013/04/08/applying-gods-law-religious-courts-and-mediation-in -the-us/.

[72]For more information on the Islamic Tribunal, see "About Us," www.islamictribunal.org/. See also a Politifact.com article refuting a chain email claiming that this represented the nation's first

Britain, this tribunal has power only in voluntary and nonbinding arbitrations in conformity with the laws of the land. My contention is that we could go further to accommodate Muslim needs in the United States, which are varied and at times a source of tension among Muslims themselves.[73] We have done this for Christians and especially for Jews, since (just like Muslims) these groups rely heavily on their religious law for righteous living.

In this regard, we can learn a great deal from the United Kingdom, and in particular from the debates being carried out there. Two government-initiated inquiries into shari'a courts were launched in June 2016. The House of Commons's home affairs committee initiated the first and the Home Office launched the second, which is being led by Mona Siddiqi, a professor of Islamic and interreligious studies at Edinburgh University.[74] In particular, the Commons's committee is seeking to examine "the range of services offered by sharia councils, reasons for their use, and how sharia law deals with family, divorce, domestic violence and child custody cases,"[75] and how they compare to other religious courts operating in the United Kingdom. The Siddiqi-led inquiry, for its part, is interested in similar questions, but because they have greater expertise in Islamic law, they would be able to ascertain to what extent some courts could be influenced by ultra-conservative ideologies (like Salafism), which are more likely to abuse women's rights as defined in international and UK law.

Those concerns are shared by a number of outside observers and by many Muslim women themselves. The *Guardian* carried two very different opinion pieces on the subject written by these women. The first represents over three hundred Muslim women who together with women of other faiths issued a statement published by Open Democracy strongly opposing all religious courts and calling for one civil law for all. Some of these women had witnessed

---

shari'a court: W. Gardner Selby, "Chain Email: Muslims Tried to Open Nation's First Sharia Court in Irving, Texas," July 16, 2015, www.politifact.com/texas/statements/2015/jul/16/chain -email/chain-email-muslims-tried-open-nations-first-shari/.

[73] Again, take into account our findings in this chapter. Muslims themselves display a spectrum of views on these issues. Bowen mentions a 2009 Gallup poll showing that "Muslims in Germany and Britain had more confidence in the courts and the national governments than did the German and British publics. . . . In France, half of all Muslims supported the law most often cited there as anti-Islamic: the 2004 ban of Islamic headscarves from public schools" (*Blaming Islam*, 61).

[74] Owen Bowcott, "MPs Launch Inquiry into Sharia Courts in UK," *The Guardian*, June 27, 2016, https://www.theguardian.com/law/2016/jun/27/mps-launch-inquiry-sharia-law-courts-uk.

[75] Ibid.

or experienced in their families honor killings, forced marriage, domestic violence, polygamy, sexual assaults, and rape.[76] The other article was by Shaista Gohir, who, while admitting that abuses do occur, argued that women of faith should have the freedom to consult with specialists of their own community on matters of divorce and child custody issues.[77] Gohir represents the Muslim Women's Network UK and contends that the only way for these courts to be improved is for women to speak up. At the same time, she seems to imply that down the road, as these communities integrate more fully into British life, the role of shari'a councils might become obsolete.

Keeping in mind the healthy nature of such debates, as Christians standing by the Muslim communities around us, we should do all we can to support their right to fully practice their faith as they understand it—and all the more in this climate of growing Islamophobia. Yet when it comes to religious courts dealing with family law, we would also want to encourage as much transparency and government supervision as deemed necessary, only to ensure that no ruling would ever transgress the US Constitution or any state, federal, or international (human rights) laws. Followers of Jesus, out of their love for God and neighbor, should be in the forefront of such advocacy.[78]

[76]Pragna Patel, "Sharia Courts Have No Place in UK Family Law. Listen to Women Who Know," *The Guardian*, December 14, 2016, www.theguardian.com/commentisfree/2016/dec/14/sharia-courts-family-law-women?CMP=share_btn_tw.

[77]Shaista Gohir, "Listening to Women on Sharia Divorce Could Change It for the Better," *The Guardian*, November 1, 2016, www.theguardian.com/commentisfree/2016/nov/01/muslim-women-sharia-divorce.

[78]I am aware of the complexity of these issues and debates on multiculturalism, legal pluralism, and citizenship. They are debated with several sides represented in the books cited in note 63. For a useful essay providing some pushback against my view (though not in its entirety), see Bryan S. Turner and James T. Richardson, "America: Islam and the Problems of Liberal Democracy," in *Applying Shari'a in the West*, 47-64.

PART III

Missiological Assessments

8

Diversity and Change in Contemporary Muslim Societies

Missional Emphases and Implications

John Jay Travis

W hen friends hear that my wife and I have spent most of our adult lives living and working in Muslim-majority countries, they often ask, "What are Muslims like?" I usually respond by asking, "Which *Muslims* are you referring to? Traditional rice farmers from the island of Java? Gulf businessmen? South Asian Sufis? Guitar-playing Turkish youth?" No simple answer adequately describes the rich diversity of languages, cultures, political systems, worldviews, and spirituality found throughout the Muslim world.[1]

Lately, when I am asked this question by friends in the West, the real, unstated question seems to be, "Are all Muslims like the Taliban or ISIS as depicted in the media?" I explain that we lived many years in Muslim neighborhoods and that, instead of being threatened or harassed, we were respected and cared for. I tell stories of hospitality and friendship with Muslims and of Muslim neighbors who were like uncles and aunties for our children as they grew up. The more we share, the more they can begin to feel that Muslims are people just like us, experiencing joys and struggles, successes and failures, hopes and shattered dreams. Yes, the social and cultural contexts for these common human experiences are indeed different for the

---

[1] I realize that the expression "Muslim world" can itself be problematic, adding to the misconception that Muslims are a monolithic bloc. I use the term only because it is so commonly used to refer to countries and regions where Muslims are a clear majority.

Indonesian farmer, Gulf businessman, South Asian Sufi, and Turkish teenager. But with us they share a common humanity, with its full range of emotions and longings.

I concur with what other contributors to this volume are saying: the Muslim world is neither an unchanging monolith nor a united international movement promoting violence and the destruction of the West. For my contribution to this volume on contemporary Muslim societies and missiological implications, I begin by highlighting some of the diversity and recent changes observed in Muslim societies. I next present research showing that a small but significant spiritual shift has been happening in recent decades across the Muslim world in which there is an increased openness to following Jesus. I close with five new emphases I see occurring in missional engagement among Muslims. Missiological implications are noted throughout the chapter.

DIVERSITY AND CHANGE IN CONTEMPORARY MUSLIM SOCIETIES

Diversity and change have characterized the whole history of Islam as it spread from the Arabian Peninsula in the seventh century to other peoples and places. Today there are 1.6 billion Muslims encompassing hundreds of distinct language and ethnic groups across Africa, the Middle East, and South and Southeast Asia. Diversity in Muslim societies has never been greater. In the section below I offer a brief overview of four types of diversity among Muslims and some key changes occurring in contemporary Muslim societies.

Ethnic, linguistic, and socioreligious diversity and change. Hundreds of ethnic and linguistic groups are majority Muslim, speaking many different dialects and languages, most of which have been influenced by Arabic terminology.[2] The world's largest population of Muslims lives in South and Southeast Asia. In Indonesia alone, over one hundred distinct Muslim people groups speak their own language or dialect. While Arabic has remained the language of qur'anic recitation and ritual prayer, most are

---

[2]Although hundreds of smaller languages exist, the major languages spoken by Muslims are Arabic (about 20 percent of the Muslim world), Malay/Indonesian (about 20 percent of the Muslim world), Urdu, Bengali, Swahili, Farsi, and Turkish. Farsi (the language of Iran) and Turkish form the basis for a number of other central Asian languages. Each of these languages contains numerous Arabic religious and legal terms.

surprised to learn that it is only spoken as a mother tongue by approximately 20 percent of the world's Muslims. As various groups have become Muslim, they have adapted Islamic practice to reflect their own cultural norms in areas such as dress (particularly for women[3]), religious celebrations, life-cycle rituals, folk traditions, cosmology, and religious architecture and artwork.

In terms of socioreligious[4] distinctions, Islam is quite diverse (much like Christianity with its many different denominations). Within its first century, Islam had split into two major streams (Shi'ite and Sunni), and within those streams today are dozens of smaller sects and religious orders, some even pushing the boundaries of what it means to be Muslim.[5] One source of this socioreligious diversity is the presence of Sufism, a mystical stream sometimes condemned yet very influential and found in many parts of the Muslim world, encompassing both Sunnis and Shi'ites. Another layer of diversity is added by the presence of folk or popular Islamic practices, in which Muslims engage in esoteric or folk-spiritual practices in search of healing, deliverance from jinn,[6] success in business, or protection from enemies.

Missionally, this broad ethnic, cultural, linguistic, and socioreligious diversity means that multiple approaches are needed to make the message of Jesus relevant and meaningful across the Muslim world. Some of these approaches will emphasize a particular language and culture, while others a specific socioreligious orientation.

Political and national diversity and change. Today approximately fifty countries are majority Muslim. Each of these countries is unique in some way, struggling to find the best balance between religion and state, an issue Muslims have dealt with from Islam's inception. In the words of John Esposito,

---

[3]In some parts of the Muslim world, most women wear some type of head covering in public (some wear a loose scarf, others a closely wrapped head covering, others a veil that covers all but the eyes). Still others wear nothing on their heads and dress in Western clothing.

[4]I use the term *socioreligious* to highlight the fact that social, cultural, and religious factors for most of the world's populations are highly interrelated. In addition, many people are part of particular religious communities primarily due to their ethnicity, nationality, and/or family of origin.

[5]Some examples would be Druze, Alevis of Turkey, and Ahmadis.

[6]Jinn are a type of spiritual being mentioned in the Qur'an and other Muslim writings. Jinn are generally feared and often seen as the invading entities in cases of spirit possession.

The history of Islam has often been linked to the existence of an Islamic state or empire. From its beginning, Islam existed and spread as a community-state; it was both a faith and a political order.[7]

What is different today, however, is the existence of so many Muslim countries with their own governments and seats at the United Nations. This is unlike earlier centuries, in which most Muslims were part of an Islamic empire or kingdom.

The last great Sunni Islamic empire (or caliphate) was the Ottoman Empire, which collapsed in 1924. Modern-day Turkey was birthed in its wake, and other former Ottoman areas (representing most of the Middle East) were placed under British and French administration. This meant that at the onset of World War II almost every traditional Muslim homeland was in some way under European ("Christian") domination.[8] This domination ceased, however, following World War II and the end of the European colonial era.[9] The demise of colonialism led to the establishing of Muslim-majority nations from Morocco to Indonesia. The birth of dozens of independent Muslim-majority nations has brought great change to the Muslim world, with some of these newly formed nations becoming Islamic kingdoms, others being led by prime ministers, and others being governed through popularly elected presidents. In a number of countries, women have had leading roles in government, even serving as heads of state in three of the world's largest Muslim-majority countries: Indonesia, Pakistan, and Bangladesh.[10]

Damage has been done to many Muslims' sense of honor because of the fact that only sixty or seventy years ago most Muslims were in some way living under foreign European control. While bitter wounds of war and colonialism must be healed, in Muslim societies today Muslims are no longer under direct European ("Christian") administration. The hope is that over

---

[7]John Esposito, *Islam: The Straight Path*, 3rd ed. (New York: Oxford University Press, 1998), 37.

[8]At the onset of World War II, England, France, Holland, and Russia ruled over most of today's independent Muslim-majority nations, either through colonial or some other political arrangement.

[9]While aspirations for independence existed in most of these Muslim areas prior to the war, it was the Second World War and the subsequent destruction of European empires (or in the case of Russia, of Soviet control), either through wars of independence, economic and political pressures, or both, that finally opened the door for full nationhood for these various groups.

[10]Indonesia was led by Megawati Sukarnoputri, Pakistan by Benazir Bhutto, and Bangladesh by Khaleda Zia and Sheikh Hasina.

time Muslims will differentiate the message and person of Jesus from the empires that are commonly associated with the religion that bears his name.

Educational and socioeconomic diversity and change. Access to modern liberal-arts education and the socioeconomic advantages that education brings have resulted in more diversity. Traditional forms of Islamic education (e.g., the madrasa system of South Asia or *pesantren* system of Indonesia) are still common and preferred by many, especially in rural settings. But in recent years, great efforts have been made to provide both private and government-sponsored liberal-arts education at both the high school and university level. In certain areas of the Muslim world, the majority of people now have access to such education.[11] For some students, a good education in their home country can lead to study abroad and international work opportunities.

Social media and the proliferation of TED Talks, online educational programs, and electronic books and journals are significant causes of change in Muslim societies, leading to a more globalized worldview. With only a digital device and Internet access, Muslims are able to take advantage of these virtually limitless online resources. Especially in rural Muslim areas (such as the town where I lived in the 1970s as a university student), access to books and educational opportunities had historically been limited, and conservative Islamic teachers were charged with the task of keeping the philosophies of other peoples and religions away. Today, however, from street vendors to affluent business people, from rural farmers to urban students, outside ideas have entered the mix.

Since many Muslims have easy access to the Internet and are often more than willing to interact over religious and spiritual issues online, Bible studies and gospel discussions can occur where it was nearly impossible decades before. At the same time, the Internet can also be used to reinforce traditional Islamic thinking and can equip Muslims to resist any competing spiritual or religious ideas.[12]

---

[11]These areas include Saudi Arabia, South Asia, and Southeast Asia. In Saudi Arabia, for example, 50 percent of all women qualified to enter university are now receiving college educations.

[12]In *Islam: The Straight Path*, John Esposito explains that in the early twentieth century some Muslims felt that liberal-arts education and ideas of globalization would lead Muslims away from Islam. He points out that often just the opposite has occurred, with some Muslim scholars successfully using the Internet and education to reinforce traditional Islamic teaching.

Spiritual and individual diversity and change. Spiritual and individual diversity exists in Muslim societies as it does among all peoples everywhere. Most Christians who become friends with Muslims are struck immediately by how much their newfound friends do not match some real or imagined Islamic stereotype.[13] Every Muslim, like every person, is unique. I have known Muslims longing to know and please God with all their heart and soul. I have known others who seem to have little or no interest in spiritual matters.

From a missional point of view, it is important to be aware of the elements of Muslim societies I have described above. As Jesus ministered, he was aware of culture and context but also of the spiritual needs of each person he encountered. Jesus demonstrated this in his interaction with the woman at the well as recorded in John 4. The context makes clear he knew the implications of the woman's gender, ethnicity, and religion for their interaction. Yet the story also shows that he looked beyond these external factors and addressed the deeper spiritual needs in her life, even breaking certain social norms to do so. I now turn to some research describing the beginning of a spiritual shift occurring in parts of the Muslim world.

A SMALL BUT SIGNIFICANT SPIRITUAL SHIFT IN THE MUSLIM WORLD

In spite of diversity and constant change, one historically unifying factor among Muslims has been an almost universal rejection of following Jesus. The reasons behind this rejection are many. However, in recent decades another change in the Muslim world has begun to take place. For the first time in history, significant numbers of Muslims in multiple locations worldwide are voluntarily choosing to follow and obey Jesus as the risen Savior of the world.[14] Before discussing this spiritual shift and some of the numbers involved, I share these thoughtful words of Father Jean-Marie Gaudeul, who has written much on how Muslims individually have come to follow Jesus:

---

[13]We and many we have worked with have chosen to rent space in a Muslim household for a period of time. Consistently, these experiences serve to break down our Muslim stereotypes, leading to a more realistic understanding of Muslims and a deeper love for them as well.

[14]This is not to say that Muslims have never before become followers of Jesus. For instance, during a time of great social and political upheaval in 1960s Indonesia it is estimated that two million Muslims became Christians. However, now is the first time Muslims are choosing to follow Jesus both in significant numbers and in numerous locations around the world.

My first thought is a sense of wonder at God's ways of leading people toward a real, live encounter with Himself. We are treading on holy ground as we examine the extraordinary variety of personal experiences through which God revealed His tenderness and love to so many millions of human beings. Each human conscience is a holy temple where the Lord meets His children as He draws them to Himself.[15]

While a number of books and articles have addressed this spiritual shift, I will look at only two: *From Seed to Fruit* and *A Wind in the House of Islam*.

From Seed to Fruit, edited by Dudley Woodberry,[16] is a compilation of articles inspired by research and writings surrounding a four-day gathering in 2007 known as the Global Trends and Fruitful Practices (GTFP) Consultation. At this consultation, scholars, mission leaders, and 280 field workers gathered in an effort to better understand recent missional developments in Muslim societies and how fellowships or churches are being planted among people who were born Muslim. The 280 field workers, who came from 37 different countries of origin and 56 different ministries, had served on teams that planted 738 fellowships throughout the Muslim world.[17] The field workers shared their experiences and analyzed compiled data from more than 5,800 surveys filled out by other workers in the Muslim world.

Two key findings from this empirical data emerged during the consultation. First, there were indications from some of the fellowships planted that potential existed for movements to take place. The second was that these 700+ fellowships mirrored the diversity in language, culture, religious forms, and socioreligious identity that is reflected in the C1-C6 Spectrum,[18] a heuristic tool developed to show diversity in the types of fellowships that Muslims either join or form as they follow Jesus.[19] The following shows the

---

[15]Jean-Marie Gaudeul, "Learning From God's Ways," in *From the Straight Path to the Narrow Way: Journeys of Faith,* ed. David H. Greenlee (Waynesboro, GA: Authentic Media, 2006), 81.
[16]J. Dudley Woodberry, ed., *From Seed to Fruit: Global Trends, Fruitful Practices and Emerging Movements Among Muslims* (Pasadena, CA: William Carey Library, 2007).
[17]Ibid., viii.
[18]See John Travis, "The C1 to C6 Spectrum: A Practical Tool for Defining Six Types of 'Christ-centered Communities' ('C') Found in the Muslim Context," *Evangelical Missions Quarterly* 34, no. 4 (1998): 407-8; and "Must All Muslims Leave 'Islam' to Follow Jesus?," *Evangelical Missions Quarterly* 34, no. 4 (1998): 411-15. See also John Travis, "The C1-C6 Spectrum After Fifteen Years: Misunderstandings, Limitations and Recommendations," *Evangelical Missions Quarterly* 51, no. 4 (2015): 358-65.
[19]The C1-C6 Spectrum presents six types of fellowships. On the spectrum, C1, C2, and C3 fellowships,

breakdown of these 700 or more fellowships in terms of the C-Spectrum categories:[20]

C1 fellowships—1 percent of the total number of fellowships reported

C2 fellowships—5 percent of the total number of fellowships reported

C3 fellowships—28 percent of the total number of fellowships reported

C4 fellowships—37 percent of the total number of fellowships reported

C5 fellowships—21 percent of the total number of fellowships reported

C6 fellowships—8 percent of the total number of fellowships reported

In a sense, David Garrison's work picks up where GTFP research left off. Garrison, whose doctoral work is in church history, has spent much time in the Muslim world. He refers to reports not only of fellowships being planted but of movements taking place where Muslims are being baptized and following Jesus as their Savior. He defines a movement as either 1,000 baptized believers or 100 fellowships planted within a twenty-year period.[21] In his research, he sets out to investigate these movements, attempting to understand the historical, cultural, and spiritual dynamics surrounding them.

For the purposes of his study, he divides the Muslim world into nine cultural-linguistic regions.[22] At the end of his multiyear analysis, he identifies eighty-two movements occurring among Muslims today, with at least one such movement in each of the nine regions he observes. (This does not mean that there are only eighty-two movements, but that these are the ones he was able to identify and study.) One of the most striking aspects of these eighty-

although differing in form, have clearly stated "Christian" religious identities, with some C1 and C2 churches in the Middle East even predating Islam. C4 groups no longer refer to themselves as "Muslims," but alternatively as "Isa followers," "followers of God through Isa," or some other such label to avoid the often-negative stereotypes of the term "Christian" in Muslim contexts. C5 fellowships represent Muslims who follow Jesus as the risen Savior. C6 refers to individuals or very small groups of Muslims who follow Jesus underground, often in very hostile environments; these would be recognized simply as Muslims in the eyes of the surrounding population.

[20]The higher the number on the C-Spectrum, the more the fellowship reflects biblically permissible aspects of Islamic culture, worship forms, and/or identity. The distribution of C-Spectrum categories shown in the data indicates a variety of ways that Muslims coming to Christ either embrace or reject different facets of Muslim life.

[21]In his book, Garrison estimates that the number of Muslims who have recently decided to follow Jesus is between two and seven million. David Garrison, *A Wind in the House of Islam* (Monument, CO: WIGTake Resources, 2014), 5.

[22]His nine regions or "rooms" consist of the following: West Africa, East Africa, North Africa, Turkestan, Arab World, Persian World, Western South Asia, Eastern South Asia, and Indo/Malaysia.

two movements is that sixty-nine of them began after the year 2000. In addition, in the preceding 1,400 years of church history Garrison identifies only a handful of movements. It is also significant that these movements are occurring among numerous Muslim ethnic groups and locations. Although he does not use the C1-C6 categories to classify these movements, Garrison's findings do reflect the types of diversity the spectrum describes. We now turn to five missional emphases I see as important in witness among Muslims.

FIVE EMPHASES AND MISSIONAL IMPLICATIONS

In recent decades, as these movements have started and grown, much has changed in the way Christians reach out to Muslims. No single missional approach can account for the growing numbers of followers of Jesus from Muslim backgrounds. In addition, the high degree of diversity and change occurring in the Muslim world would indicate that a number of different approaches to witness are essential. There are, however, five key elements of witness I see being emphasized that are important in most contexts. I will refer to these five elements as *missional emphases* since they are not new approaches, but rather ones that at times have been neglected or seen as unnecessary.

An emphasis on proximate witness. When Jesus sent out the twelve apostles, he empowered them to heal the sick, drive out demons, and "proclaim the kingdom of God" (Lk 9:2). He also instructed them to live in local households as they carried out this ministry (Lk 9:4). He gave almost identical instructions to seventy-two other disciples, telling them to live in homes with people who would accept them, eating and drinking what was offered (Lk 10:5-8). This model of disciples living in close proximity to those they are called to serve is one that has not always received the emphasis it should.

After the colonial period, and with the rise of newly independent Muslim countries, obtaining an official missionary visa became more and more difficult over time. In addition, because of globalization and increasing access to the Internet, any educational or technological superiority that missionaries may have had in previous decades has now ended. When Christians today cross cultural barriers to bear witness to Jesus, they must arrive as guests and live in nonoffensive, honoring, and culturally appropriate ways. We are indebted to the writings and training of Tom and Betty Sue Brewster, who encouraged crosscultural workers to live with families among the people with whom they share the gospel.[23] In addition, the writings of Christian anthropologists such as Dan Shaw, Paul Hiebert, Charles Kraft, and Darrell Whiteman stress the importance of engaging deeply with a people to understand their worldview and faith from an insider or emic point of view.

This renewed emphasis on proximate witness has been especially important for fruitful mission, since most Muslims have never personally known a true follower of Jesus. Radio broadcasts, satellite TV, online communication, and other media speak of Jesus, but life-on-life human interaction is still crucial. Survey research conducted by Dudley Woodberry and others confirms this. In response to an extensive questionnaire, approximately 750 Muslims who became followers of Jesus ranked the lifestyle of followers of Jesus as the number one influence in their decision to follow Christ.[24]

Living in close proximity with Muslims, or even renting a room from or living with a Muslim family (something my wife and I and others we know have done), is not only an effective way to engage in spiritual conversations with Muslims, but also an opportunity for God to do something in our own hearts. Where it is impractical to live with a Muslim family or in a Muslim neighborhood, close relationships can also be formed in the workplace. Over months and years of living and working among Muslims, walls come down, and Christians and Muslims begin to look at each other with new eyes. Once this level of meaningful relationship has been formed, cultural and religious barriers start to diminish and heart-to-heart communication about spiritual matters can begin. I have seen this type of proximate witness both in Muslim countries and also in Western nations with large immigrant populations. Several missional implications arise from this renewed emphasis on proximate witness.

First, proximate witnesses of Jesus need much humility. It can be difficult to place ourselves in a position of needing to be helped—living among others, on their turf, and relying on them as friends, guides, and teachers.

---

[23]See Tom and Betty Sue Brewster, "Bonding and the Missionary Task," in *Perspectives on the World Christian Movement: A Reader*, ed. Ralph D. Winter and Stephen C. Hawthorne, rev. ed. (Pasadena, CA: William Carey Library, 1992).

[24]J. Dudley Woodberry, Russell G. Shubin, and G. Marks, "Why Muslims Follow Jesus: The Results of a Recent Survey of Converts from Islam," *Christianity Today*, October 24, 2007, www .christianitytoday.com/ct/2007/october/42.80.html.

Second, we need to overcome fear and prejudice. Many Christians, often due to the influence of the media, have become afraid of Muslims or hold them in disdain or suspicion. Third, disciples of Jesus committed to proximate witness must be very intentional about bonding relationally with Muslims—it usually takes time and effort to find the right living or working situation and to maintain regular, genuine interaction with Muslims.

An emphasis on prayer and miracles. In one of the earliest recorded Christian prayer gatherings, the believers, under great pressure, prayed for miracles and boldness.

> "Now, Lord, consider their threats and enable your servants to speak your word with great boldness. Stretch out your hand to heal and perform signs and wonders through the name of your holy servant Jesus." After they prayed, the place where they were meeting was shaken. And they were all filled with the Holy Spirit and spoke the word of God boldly. (Acts 4:29-31)

This passage underscores the relationship between prayer, miracles, and a bold proclamation of the word of God. Prayer in its various forms has always been part of church life. In the past few decades, however, what could only be called prayer movements have been launched and sustained to intercede for the Muslim world. Focused prayer is occurring in large meetings with thousands in attendance over several days, in smaller gatherings of teams living in Muslim societies who devote significant portions of their week to intercessory prayer, in virtual gatherings using the Internet, and in individual efforts guided by prayer booklets and current field communications. A diversity of up-to-date field realities informs these prayer endeavors.

This emphasis on prayer has affected the Muslim world in at least four ways. First, the names of distinct Muslim people groups are being continually mentioned in prayer. Second, prayer is changing the hearts and lives of those who are praying, often giving them both greater love and greater boldness to reach out to those they are praying for. Third, the international nature of these prayer movements has encouraged thousands from Asia, Africa, and Latin America, in addition to those still being sent from Western countries, to work among Muslims. Fourth, prayers asking God to do miracles "through the name of [his] holy servant Jesus" (Acts 4:30) are being answered with increased signs, wonders, divine dreams, and healings.

The Qur'an speaks of the miracles and healing power of Isa (Jesus): his miraculous feeding of crowds, healing of those with blindness and leprosy, and raising of the dead.[25] Muslims often seek out Christians to pray for them with the power of Jesus for healing and deliverance from jinn. My wife and I have often been asked by Muslims to pray for their physical healing or their inner heart healing. Many of our colleagues throughout the Muslim world report similar experiences.[26]

Dreams from God also figure largely in Muslim spiritual life. It is believed that Muhammad, shortly before his death, told his followers that after he died there would be no further source of divine revelation except through true dreams given by God.[27] This means that Muslims are very alert to spiritual dreams and will seek answers from others concerning the meaning of them.

These prayer movements among Christians and the openness to receiving prayer and experiencing miracles by Muslims invite a number of missional implications. First, in sharing the gospel and our life in Jesus with Muslims, it is essential that followers of Jesus make the time to pray. Attending to the various tasks of crosscultural living and witness are important, but so is focused and intentional prayer.

Second, it is important to recapture the spiritual importance of dreams from God. Dreams play an integral role in key biblical narratives, and as Morton Kelsey convincingly demonstrates, dreams were considered important by Christians in the West until the Age of Enlightenment in the mid-1700s. At that time, regrettably, the Western church relegated spiritual dreams and dream interpretation to a place of superstition.[28] Christians, particularly those from the West, should reexamine the role of dreams in the Bible and in church history, asking God to send dreams and to help them pay attention to what he is saying to them and to Muslims through dreams.[29]

---

[25]"I [Isa] heal him who is born blind and the leper and I raise the dead by Allah's leave" (Q 3:49, Pickthall).

[26]At the moment I am working with three teams who regularly pray with Muslims for physical healing, inner healing, and/or freedom from demonic oppression.

[27]See the introduction to John C. Lamoreaux, *The Early Muslim Tradition of Dream Interpretation* (Albany: SUNY Press, 2002).

[28]See Morton T. Kelsey's excellent book on the topic of dreams throughout church history, *God, Dreams, and Revelation: A Christian Interpretation of Dreams*, rev. and expanded ed. (Minneapolis: Augsburg Fortress, 1991).

[29]Some of my colleagues in the Muslim world, knowing how important dreams are to Muslims, begin their witness by asking the question, "Have you had any significant dreams lately?" Recent

Third, a renewed focus on expecting and training for miracles and healing should be encouraged. Just as the Western church has largely ignored the significance of dreams, so too it has deemphasized (or even rejected) the place of signs, wonders, and miracles, in spite of the fact that miracles are expected and experienced regularly by many believers in the non-Western church. Is this because God only allows miracles to happen in certain types of churches? Or is it because of the prayers and expectations of those in such churches? I am convinced training can be an important part in seeing miracles happen as they did when Jesus sent out the Twelve and the seventy-two.[30]

An emphasis on Jesus, not religion. The life, death, and resurrection of Jesus figure largely in fruitful discussions with Muslims about matters of faith. This is in keeping with what Paul called "the gospel I preached to you," which leads to salvation (1 Cor 15:1-8). In interaction with Muslims, however, the simple message of the life, death, and resurrection of Jesus are frequently co-opted by arguments over religion. These arguments often mirror the religious debates on ontology and Christology (e.g., the Trinity) in the earliest years of Christian-Muslim interaction. They also often center on negative actions, both past and present, of those who bear the name "Christian" (e.g., the Crusades, colonialism, current political policies of the "Christian" West). In both cases it is the religion of Christianity that often becomes the focus of attention rather than the life and message of Jesus of Nazareth.

Whether Muslims drawn to Jesus officially end up changing religions or finding some way to remain Muslims culturally, socially, and legally while loving and following Christ, our witness needs to be centered on Jesus alone and a transforming encounter with him.[31] Thankfully, this focus on Jesus has become an increasing part of deeply impactful witness to Muslims. For many Muslims the word *Christianity* is often strongly associated with a bitter history.

---

research indicates that dreams of Jesus have been extremely important in the lives of Muslims who have decided to follow Jesus.

[30]The dialogue between Jesus and the seventy (or the seventy-two) disciples recorded in Luke 10:17-19 would indicate he was getting feedback from them on their field experience. I think this practice of getting feedback suggests that we should be training witnesses to ask for and expect miracles.

[31]For a very helpful discussion on a Jesus-centered versus religion-centered approach to witness, see the kerygma model developed by Martin Accad in "Christian Attitudes Toward Islam and Muslims: A Kerygmatic Approach," in *Toward Respectful Understanding and Witness Among Muslims: Essays in Honor of J. Dudley Woodberry*, ed. Evelyne A. Reisacher (Pasadena, CA: William Carey Library, 2012).

Or for some it leads to polite resistance and a "that's your religion" response. Yet speaking of Jesus the Messiah (Isa al-Masih) allows conversations to move more readily from war, politics, and doctrine to the one who heals, comforts, and saves the spiritually hungry who commit their lives to him.

Several missional implications arise at this point. First, we must reexamine biblically what is the core message of the gospel that we present. Is it the type of preaching we see on the lips of Paul and Peter in Acts? Or is it that message plus later third-, fourth-, and fifth-century theological discussions that resulted in the formation of early church creeds? Or is it all of the above, plus a focus on certain present-day denominational beliefs and practices? Those bearing witness among Muslims must answer these questions for themselves so as not to put unnecessary stumbling blocks in the way of those moving toward Jesus.

When religion is deemphasized and Jesus' life and teaching are placed front and center, the question arises: "What am I becoming a part of if I choose to follow Jesus?" The most direct answer seems to be the one Jesus himself gave: the kingdom of God. The kingdom of God (or kingdom of heaven) is mentioned over one hundred times in the Gospels. Jesus made it abundantly clear that salvation and entering the kingdom come through following him, not through following a particular religious affiliation. In fact, some refer to the early church as a Jesus movement or a kingdom-of-God community.[32] While following Jesus also means entering into fellowship with other Jesus followers, the notion of entering the kingdom of God rather than that of a changing religion is an important missiological paradigm.[33]

An emphasis on allowing the Bible to speak for itself. In the New Testament the Bereans were commended for receiving the word with great eagerness and examining the Scriptures daily to see if what Paul was saying was true (Acts 17:11). It is interesting that one of the six major articles of faith in Islam is the acknowledgment of different scriptures or books (*kutub*) sent by God to different prophets at different times. The four books Muslims emphasize are the

---

[32]For example, see the discussion toward the end of chapter one, "Reflections on the New Testament as a Missionary Document," in David Bosch, *Transforming Mission: Paradigm Shifts in Theology of Mission* (Maryknoll, NY: Orbis, 2011), 15-56.

[33]For a very insightful discussion, see Anthony Taylor, "The Kingdom of God: A Biblical Paradigm for Mission," in *Understanding Insider Movements: Disciples of Jesus Within Diverse Religious Communities*, ed. Harley Talman and John Travis (Pasadena, CA: William Carey Library, 2015).

Taurat (Torah or Old Testament[34]), *Zabur* (the Psalms), *Injil* (the Gospel or New Testament[35]), and the Qur'an. Muslims know of these four books, but they seldom read or study any but the Qur'an. This is due to the common teaching by local Muslim leaders and teachers that the former holy books, the *Taurat, Zabur,* and *Injil* (the books of the Jews and the Christians), have been corrupted over time and are no longer reliable. The Qur'an, however, does not support this accusation of corruption and only alludes several times to Jews who "corrupted" their scriptures when they verbally taught their contents to others. In fact, well over one hundred verses in the Qur'an validate or encourage looking to the previous holy books, or what we know as the Bible.

Inductive Bible study (often referred to as IBS) or the related Discovery Bible Study (DBS) method are designed to allow the Bible to speak for itself. These methods of reading and reflecting on Scripture did not originate in outreach to Muslims but have had great impact in the Muslim world.[36] Muslims have been suspicious of Christian attempts to convert them, as can be the case when a Christian leads a Bible study by formally teaching those present, explaining what the verses mean. But an openhanded method of study, where the Christian simply reads the Bible with Muslim friends, only asking prompting questions from time to time, completely changes this dynamic. My wife and I have invited Muslims to read the Bible with us, and then we simply ask what they see in the passage and in what ways they feel God is giving them guidance through it. It is amazing how God brings truth and insight to the reader or hearer. When Muslims have experienced some form of miracle or dream followed by an inductive reading of Scripture, the impact is usually profound and life changing.

---

[34]Muslims understand Musa (Moses) to be the prophet to whom was revealed the *Taurat.* Thus, the *Taurat* is normally associated with the Jewish Torah or the first five books of the Old Testament. However, the *Taurat* is also viewed by many Muslims as the comprehensive name given to the Jewish scriptures as a whole, which would widen the definition to include most of what Christians today call the Old Testament.

[35]Muslims understand Isa (Jesus) to be the prophet to whom was revealed the *Injil.* Some Muslims would contend that the *Injil* is only the words and teaching of Jesus, the parts of the New Testament sometimes printed in red ink. On the other hand, Muslim tradition considers the *Injil* to be the book of Christians at the time of Muhammad (the seventh century CE). Looked at from this perspective, the *Injil* would consist of the entire New Testament.

[36]The modified forms of inductive Bible study and the DBS approach emphasized by David Watson in his Disciple Making Movements training have been used in outreach to Muslims in many locations not only as a means of sharing Christ, but also as a means of ongoing spiritual formation and discipleship.

We know, for example, a Muslim woman who decided to follow Jesus after reading the Bible inductively on her own and seeing her son healed of a serious disease after being prayed for in Jesus' name. She had Christian friends, and she sometimes read the Bible and prayed with them. But she never joined an existing church or saw herself as anything other than a Muslim woman who felt called by God to follow Jesus. Over a three-year period, this woman shared with her family and social network what Jesus had done in her life and encouraged them to read the *Injil* (New Testament) as she had done. In time over twenty Muslim households were reading the *Injil*, and dozens professed faith in Isa the Messiah as their risen Lord and Savior.[37] One of the keys to this growth was that those studying Scripture believed that as they read God's Word as a community, the Holy Spirit would guide them both in understanding it properly and in knowing how to communicate these truths to others.

One important missional implication of allowing the Bible to speak for itself is the need for culturally and linguistically appropriate Bible translations for Muslim readers. Remembering the diversity throughout the Muslim world, many different translations and styles of translations will be needed. Ideally, translations that are accessible to Muslims should use vocabulary, layouts, title pages, and artwork that encourage Muslims to feel that the words they are reading are indeed the *Taurat, Zabur*, and *Injil* that the Qur'an commends. To produce such translations or revisions of existing translations requires a deep understanding of how particular groups of Muslims express spiritual concepts and what they understand a holy book to look like. It takes a committed team, working with Muslim readers for field-testing and input, to produce such a contextually appropriate translation. Elsewhere I have described a number of features such a translation should contain.[38] One hope would be that Muslims would read such a translation in their own dialect or language and feel comfortable enough to read it and discuss it with family and friends in the simple inductive style modeled for them.

---

[37]Examples like this of Muslims following Jesus but remaining culturally and socioreligiously Muslim are often referred to as insider movements. For a thorough explanation of the subject, see Talman and Travis, *Understanding Insider Movements*.
[38]See John Travis, "Producing and Using Meaningful Translations of the Taurat, Zabur and Injil," in *International Journal of Frontier Missiology* 23, no. 2 (2006): 73-77.

A second missional implication involves not only reading Scripture but interpreting it as well. No one reads the Bible, even inductively, in a completely unbiased or neutral way. We instinctively interpret and filter what we read through own cultural lens and worldview. Western readers, for instance, are likely to miss key elements of the parables of Jesus that Middle Eastern readers would naturally perceive. As the record of church history shows, various passages of Scripture can be interpreted in various ways, often resulting in church splits and the formation of different denominations. So how then do we view Muslims (like the woman in the example mentioned above) who, along with their community, go straight to Scripture, relying on the Spirit of God to instruct them as they read the Word under the lordship of Jesus? Can we trust that the Holy Spirit will guide them? Can we believe that through enough inductive Bible study these new followers of Jesus will be able to discern over time what God wants them to do and be in Christ? Those who work among Muslims give different answers to that question. Some emphasize the role of teaching on the part of those bringing the gospel to Muslims. Others emphasize the role of self-theologizing or indigenous theologizing,[39] saying that the "apostles' teaching" mentioned in the book of Acts (e.g., Acts 2:42) is contained within the New Testament and that, therefore, the need for a teacher is not the same as it was before the New Testament was written.

An emphasis on new expressions of following Jesus. The book of Acts describes how the good news of Jesus spread from Jerusalem to Judea and then from Samaria to the then-known ends of the earth. Acts 15 records the tensions that resulted when church leaders discussed how much of Jewish custom would be required of Gentile followers of Jesus. Circumcision, a reviled and often illegal act for Gentiles, was the most pressing issue, but the Jerusalem leaders' decision to allow Gentiles to follow Jesus as Gentiles had many other far-reaching ramifications. In short, their decision meant that Gentiles did not have to obey most Jewish laws and were free to follow Jesus, making obedience to God through him the only requirement for salvation (Acts 15:11).

---

[39]William A. Dyrness has written extensively on the topic of indigenous theology. His most recent book examines how theology develops in insider movements. See William Dyrness, *Insider Jesus: Theological Reflections on New Christian Movements* (Downers Grove, IL: InterVarsity Press, 2016).

Over the ensuing centuries, much of mission history became the story of messengers bringing the good news of Jesus to thousands of the world's animistic and tribal peoples, those of the so-called minor religious traditions. Since then, Bible translators have done the painstaking work of putting Scripture into many different mother tongues. Tens of thousands of churches have been planted, each attempting, with varying degrees of success, to reflect elements of the culture and customs of church members. But until recent years, precious few from today's major world religions—Islam, Hinduism, and Buddhism—have decided to become disciples of Jesus.

From the 1970s onward, crosscultural workers have been vigorously discussing not only evangelism but also what appropriate expressions of church might look like among Muslims. Some have looked to the experience of Messianic Jews,[40] thinking there might be applicable parallels. The main questions being asked were what elements of Islamic heritage could or should be retained, what elements could be modified, and what beliefs or practices must be discarded entirely in order to follow Jesus. As might be expected, different scholars and field practitioners came to different conclusions. Phil Parshall framed much of this discussion on contextualization at that time.[41] As mentioned earlier in this chapter, in 1998 a tool I had developed (the C1-C6 Spectrum) was published that described six basic types of expressions of following Jesus observed in Muslim contexts. Bearing in mind the ethnic and socioreligious diversity among Muslims, I used language, culture, religious forms, and religious identity as the parameters that framed the spectrum, with traditional Christian churches on one end and fellowships of Muslim followers of Jesus on the other.

As the research presented earlier in this chapter indicated, the data from the Global Trends and Fruitful Practices conference showed that in the more than seven hundred fellowships studied, all six types or expressions of Christ-centered communities in Muslim contexts were observed, with the majority being C3 to C5. Elsewhere I have discussed possible reasons why different groups of Muslims choose different ways of following Jesus.[42]

---

[40]Messianic Jews are those who follow *Yeshua* (Jesus) as Messiah and Savior while retaining their Jewish heritage, culture, and socioreligious identity.

[41]See Phil Parshall, *New Paths in Muslim Evangelism: Evangelical Approaches to Contextualization* (Grand Rapids: Baker Books, 1980).

[42]See John Travis and Anna Travis, "Social Factors Impacting Socioreligious Identities of Muslims

At least two missional implications arise related to new expressions of following Jesus among Muslims.

First, we may have a role in helping Muslims who have turned to Jesus to think through some of the different types of expressions of following Christ, bearing in mind the great diversity that exists in the Muslim world. Ultimately, however, how they as a community decide to follow Jesus will be up to them and to the leading of the Spirit. What they choose may look like something we have imagined, but it may be quite different, especially for those Muslims who prefer to remain part of their original Muslim communities as they follow Jesus.

The second missional implication is that we must determine before God who is part of God's family, or in other words, who is our brother and sister in Christ. We need to develop sensitivities to look beyond forms and labels to people's hearts. This will be challenging, to be sure, but it is an important aspect of loving and accepting the whole body of Christ, even those who are quite different from us in the ways that they worship, gather, and express faith in Jesus.

Who Follow Jesus," in Talman and Travis, *Understanding Insider Movements*, 599-607.

9
. . . .

Peacemaking Initiatives
Among Muslims

Rick Love

Evangelicals understand the importance of Christ's mandate to "make disciples of all nations." There have been valiant efforts to reach Muslims, and some have even experienced significant breakthroughs. I rejoice in what God is doing around the world through my brothers and sisters. But overall, evangelicals haven't done well in loving their Muslim neighbors or fulfilling Christ's peacemaking mandate among Muslims. Some may even doubt the validity of a peacemaking mandate.[1] The upsurge in violent extremism, the brutal persecution of the church in the Middle East, and the worst migration crisis of our generation underscore the urgency of peacemaking between two global faith communities: Islam and Christianity.[2]

In this chapter we will analyze peacemaking initiatives among Muslims from three perspectives. We will examine the biblical mandate for peacemaking, the strategic urgency of peacemaking between Christians and Muslims, and some practical peacemaking initiatives taking place in the twenty-first century.

PEACEMAKING: THE BIBLICAL MANDATE

Peacemaking is a central part of God's mission. The call to "seek peace and pursue it" (Ps 34:14; 1 Pet 3:11) pervades Scripture and provides both motivation

---

[1]For more on this, see "FAQ: How Does Peacemaking Relate to Evangelism?," Peace Catalyst International, accessed September 30, 2016, www.peacecatalyst.org/faq.

[2]Christians and Muslims comprise over half of the world's population. Thus, relationships between Christians and Muslims are vital for global peace.

and guidelines for making peace with Muslims.[3] We begin with one of the most concise and comprehensive peacemaking passages in the Bible: "If it is possible, as far as it depends on you, live at peace with everyone" (Rom 12:18).

Notice how realistic Paul was about peacemaking. The condition "if it is possible" acknowledges that it is not always possible to make peace. Scripture is realistic about conflict and discord. Biblical peacemaking is neither sentimental nor naive. It addresses the harsh realities of brokenness and evil (the broader context of Romans 12 makes this clear). Even our most sincere efforts may fail. *Peacemakers aren't always peace achievers.*

This verse also affirms proactive peacemaking: "If it is possible, *as far as it depends on you,* live at peace with everyone." Since it involves at least two parties, reconciliation isn't always possible. But the responsibility for taking steps toward peace always rests on us as Christians. "As far as it depends on you!" We can't ignore it, and we can't wait for the other party to come to us. We are repeatedly commanded to take the initiative in pursuing peace ourselves (Mt 5:23-26; 18:15; Lk 17:3; Heb 12:14).

Finally, notice the last clause of Romans 12:18: "If it is possible, as far as it depends on you, *live at peace with everyone.*" The scope of biblical peacemaking is comprehensive—without borders or barriers. It challenges us to live out the peaceable ways of Jesus with our neighbors and our enemies. As the author of Hebrews says, "Make every effort to live in peace with everyone" (Heb 12:14).

Romans 12:18 provides an excellent starting point and summary of biblical peacemaking. But to build a more robust understanding of this mandate, we turn our attention to Jesus. We outline a Jesus-centered approach to peacemaking by examining the person, teaching, example, death, and second coming of Christ.

The person of Christ. In two of the Bible's best-known prophecies of the future Messiah, Jesus is called the Prince of Peace (Is 9:6-7) and is described as the one who is our peace (Mic 5:2-5). Paul's letter to the Ephesians also makes this affirmation: "But now in Christ Jesus you who once were far off

---

[3]For a comprehensive look at the biblical basis for peacemaking, see Rick Love, *Peace Catalysts: Resolving Conflict in Our Families, Organizations and Communities* (Downers Grove, IL: InterVarsity Press, 2014), and Emmanuel Katongole and Chris Rice, *Reconciling All Things: A Christian Vision for Justice, Peace and Healing* (Downers Grove, IL: InterVarsity Press, 2008).

have been brought near by the blood of Christ. For he is our peace" (Eph 2:13-14 NRSV).

Thus, peace "is not merely a concept nor even a new state of affairs, it is bound up with a person."[4] The phrase "he is our peace" is emphatic in the original Greek language and should be translated "he himself is our peace." Jesus is the embodiment of peace according to Paul. He is the source of peace and the one who brings peace.[5]

The teaching of Christ.[6] Jesus' teaching about peacemaking begins with the famous Beatitude: "Blessed are the peacemakers, for they will be called children of God" (Mt 5:9).[7] In the original language, the term *peacemaker* combines two Greek words: "peace" (*eirēnē*) and "to make, do or produce" (*poieō*), implying that peacemakers not only resolve their personal conflicts, but also take the initiative in helping others resolve conflict. Thus, the very term *peacemaker* implies some form of mediation.[8]

Finally, it is noteworthy that these blessed peacemakers are described as God's children. One of the defining characteristics of God's children is that they make peace.[9]

Jesus also teaches that this blessed work of peacemaking is an urgent priority:

> Therefore, if you are offering your gift at the altar and there remember that your brother or sister has something against you, leave your gift there in front

---

[4]Andrew T. Lincoln, *Ephesians*, Word Biblical Commentary 42 (Dallas: Word, 1990), 140.

[5]"It does not say that he gives peace but rather that he is our peace, probably echoing Mic. 5:5 (cf. Isa. 9:6)." Ben Witherington III, *The Letters to Philemon, the Colossians, and the Ephesians: A Socio-Rhetorical Commentary on the Captivity Epistles* (Grand Rapids: Eerdmans, 2007), 259.

[6]It is beyond the scope of this chapter to give a detailed summary of all that Jesus taught about peacemaking, so I will focus on Jesus' teaching that is most relevant to peacemaking with Muslims.

[7]The context of Jesus' ministry provides an important insight into the meaning of peacemaking. Jesus lived under Roman rule and as such ministered in occupied territory. In the original context of the Beatitudes, this emphasis on peacemaking was most likely directed against the Zealots, Jewish revolutionaries who hoped to throw off the yoke of Roman oppression and establish the kingdom of God through violence. In contrast to the Zealots, Jesus speaks of a peaceable kingdom and a nonviolent extension of that kingdom.

[8]Mediation refers to third-party peacemaking. The ideal of Scripture is that the two parties in conflict work it out between themselves—in cooperative resolution. But often people in conflict need help. So they turn to a trusted third party to aid them in resolving their dispute. See Mt 18:16; 1 Cor 6:1-8; Phil 4:2-3; and the letter to Philemon.

[9]"Peacemaking is a divine activity. God has made peace with us and between us through Christ. We cannot claim to be his authentic children unless we engage in peacemaking too." John Stott, *Issues Facing Christians Today*, 4th ed. (Grand Rapids: Zondervan, 2006), 128.

of the altar. *First* go and be reconciled to them; *then* come and offer your gift. (Mt 5:23-24, emphasis added)

Jesus commands us to stop worship and seek reconciliation. In other words, reconciling with our brother or sister even trumps worship![10] "First go and be reconciled" teaches that we must take responsibility for broken relationships. Even if I don't have anything against my brother or sister, if he or she has something against me, I must take the initiative. This passage also indicates that the Great Commandments—love of God and love of neighbor— are inseparable. One cannot truly love God without loving one's neighbor— which is demonstrated by our commitment to pursue reconciliation.[11]

Peacemaking also begins with humility according to Jesus.

Why do you look at the speck of sawdust in your brother's eye and pay no attention to the plank in your own eye? How can you say to your brother, "Let me take the speck out of your eye," when all the time there is a plank in your own eye? You hypocrite, *first* take the plank out of your own eye, and *then* you will see clearly to remove the speck from your brother's eye. (Mt 7:3-5, emphasis added)

With a sense of humor, Jesus the carpenter exhorts us to *first* get the metaphorical log out of our own eye, for only *then* can we take the speck out of our neighbor's eye. Again, Jesus gives us clear steps in the peacemaking process—"first . . . then."

Sadly, it is human nature to find specks in others and be blind to our own issues. If there were an organization called "SpeckFinders.org," we would all automatically be members. But instead of being speck finders, Jesus calls us to be log removers! He calls those in conflict to begin with humble introspection.

This is especially important in Christian-Muslim relations. Christians tend to compare the best interpretation and practice of their faith with the

---

[10]This particular passage focuses on peacemaking among God's people. However, Jesus' use of the terms *opponent* (Mt 5:42), *Gentiles* (Mt 5:47; 6:7, 32), *enemies* (Mt 5:43-44), *unrighteous* (Mt 5:45), and *persecution* (Mt 5:10, 11, 12, 44) in the Sermon on the Mount indicates that peacemaking is not restricted to believers only. It takes place in an unbelieving world, beyond the boundaries of the church. Thus, it relates to broader social and global challenges such as racism, terrorism, poverty, and war.

[11]It is noteworthy that the first mention of the command to love one's neighbor in the Bible is linked to peacemaking. "Do not seek revenge or bear a grudge against anyone among your people, but love your neighbor as yourself. I am the LORD" (Lev 19:18). Love is contrasted with taking revenge and bearing a grudge. In other words, when we overcome vengeance and grudges (i.e., peacemaking), we are truly loving our neighbor.

worst interpretation and practice of Islamic faith. This natural tendency fosters a sense of superiority, blinds Christians to the darkness in their own community, and hinders them from seeing any light or beauty in Islam. Moreover, it is the opposite of what Jesus taught.[12]

During a Vineyard Great Lakes Regional Conference in Columbus, Ohio,[13] Yale theologian and peacemaker Miroslav Volf shared with the pastors in attendance a story about the Common Word dialogue between Christians and Muslims at Yale:[14] "Prior to the dialogue, we inserted a brief apology in the Yale response to the Common Word, asking for forgiveness. People got so upset! They said you should not ask for forgiveness until Muslims ask for forgiveness first!" Volf paused and, with a big smile on his face, asked, "Since when is my moral behavior predicated on the moral behavior of another?"[15]

Jesus' teaching on love of neighbor and love of enemy also pushes us toward peace. If we truly love others, we will want to be at peace with them. Making peace or working toward reconciliation is an act of love.

Immediately after teaching about the Great Commandments (love of God and neighbor), Jesus told the famous parable of the Good Samaritan in response to a religious expert's question, "Who is my neighbor?" This religious leader wanted to limit the definition of *neighbor* so that the demand of neighborly love could be confined to his comfort zone (Lk 10:29-37). Like most people of his day, he believed that a neighbor referred

---

[12]Point three of "Seven Resolutions Against Prejudice, Hatred and Discrimination" says it well: "We seek to be accurate when we speak about one another's faith. Overstatement, exaggeration and words taken out of context should not be the case among people of faith. The Torah teaches us 'not to bear false witness against our neighbor' (Exodus 20:16). The Gospel teaches us to 'do unto others as you would have them do unto you' (Matthew 7:12). The Qur'an teaches us to 'stand out firmly for justice as witnesses to God, even though it be against ourselves or our parents' (Qur'an 4:135). Thus we strive to speak truthfully about one another's faith, to respect each faith community's own interpretation of itself, and not to compare the best interpretation and practice of our faith with the worst interpretation and practice of others. We encourage every person to be discerning regarding how media and literature portray the 'other.'" See "Seven Resolutions Against Prejudice, Hatred and Discrimination," World Interfaith Harmony Week, worldinterfaithharmonyweek.com/wp-content/uploads/2011/03/Seven-Resolutions-final2.pdf (accessed May 16, 2017).

[13]The conference was held at the Columbus Vineyard, May 15-17, 2012.

[14]"'A Common Word' Christian Response," Yale Center for Faith & Culture, accessed August 24, 2016, http://faith.yale.edu/common-word/common-word-christian-response.

[15]Miroslav Volf, "Making Room," Vineyard Great Lakes Regional Conference, Columbus, Ohio (May 15-17, 2012), www.vineyardcolumbus.org/celebrating/blog/making-room-conference-photos.

to someone of his race or faith. *Neighbor* meant someone "like me" or a person "I like."

But Jesus' revolutionary parable shattered the religious leader's relational categories. Jesus showed that love for one's neighbor reaches beyond race or religion, color, or creed. The hero of the story was a Samaritan! At the time, Jews viewed Samaritans as despised heretics—syncretistic in faith, ethnically inferior, and excluded from the true worship of God (Jn 4:9). In other words, a "good Samaritan" would have been an oxymoron for a Jew. Yet this Samaritan showed compassion toward his enemy the Jew, demonstrating that love of neighbor includes the people we find most difficult to love. An accurate understanding of love of neighbor means we love even our enemies.

But in case this wasn't clear, Jesus made it explicit: "You have heard that it was said, 'Love your neighbor and hate your enemy.' But I tell you, love your enemies and pray for those who persecute you, that you may be children of your Father in heaven" (Mt 5:43-45). According to Jesus, we demonstrate that we are God's children when we love our enemies.

The example of Christ. Jesus' hospitality reverberates with peacemaking implications.[16] Jesus freely and habitually ate with people regarded as "sinners," to the extent that he had the reputation for being "a glutton and a drunkard, a friend of tax collectors and sinners" (Lk 7:34 NRSV). The stories of Jesus with the tax collectors Levi (Lk 5:27-32) and Zacchaeus (Lk 19:1-10), the "sinful" woman at Simon the Pharisee's house (Lk 7:36-50), the adulterous woman (Jn 8:1-11), and the Samaritan woman at Jacob's well (Jn 4:1-43) are perhaps the best illustrations of Jesus' practice. What I find amazing is that Jesus also ate with his greatest critics—the Pharisees. He accepted their hospitality while at the same time boldly confronting them about their hypocritical traditions of ritualistic washing (Lk 11:37-42) and Sabbath observance (Lk 14:1-6).

Jesus' hospitality reflected inclusive love. Unlike the Pharisees and many evangelicals, Jesus engaged the "other" without fear of compromise or contamination. Jesus taught and modeled both exclusive truth claims and inclusive love aims.[17] Jesus made exclusive truth claims: "I am the way and the

---

[16]"Hospitality is at the heart of the gospel and practice of the early church; its themes and language pervade the NT." Christine D. Pohl, "Hospitality," in *New Dictionary of Biblical Theology*, ed. Brian S. Rosner et al. (Downers Grove, IL: InterVarsity Press, 2000), 561.

[17]In a personal email to me, my friend Andres Duncan exclaimed, "Jesus shatters our theological

truth and the life. No one comes to the Father except through me" (Jn 14:6). At the same time, he made inclusive love aims. He commanded his followers to love their neighbors as themselves and even love their enemies (Mt 22:39; 5:44).

Jesus was also a nonviolent activist. When I speak about Jesus' call to be a peacemaker (Mt 5:9), people often counter with this question, "Yes, but Jesus also said he did not come to bring peace but a sword (Mt 10:34). So how do you reconcile these two verses?" Walter Kaiser gives wise guidance: "When Jesus said that he had come to bring 'not peace but a sword,' he meant that this would be the *effect* of his coming, not that it was the *purpose* of his coming."[18] As children of God, our purpose is to represent the Prince of Peace, regardless of what effect this might have.

Jesus said: "My kingdom is not of this world. If My kingdom were of this world, then My servants would be fighting so that I would not be handed over to the Jews; but as it is, My kingdom is not of this realm" (Jn 18:36 NASB). Jesus also said to Peter, "Put your sword back in its place; for all who take up the sword shall perish by the sword" (Mt 26:52 NASB).

However, being nonviolent did not mean that Jesus was passive. He was also a peace disturber! Perhaps the most striking example is when he cleansed the temple.

> Then they came to Jerusalem. And he entered the temple and began to drive out those who were selling and those who were buying in the temple, and he overturned the tables of the money changers and the seats of those who sold doves; and he would not allow anyone to carry anything through the temple. He was teaching and saying, "Is it not written, 'My house shall be called a house of prayer for all the nations'? But you have made it a den of robbers.'" And when the chief priests and the scribes heard it, they kept looking for a way to kill him; for they were afraid of him, because the whole crowd was spellbound by his teaching. (Mk 11:15-18 NRSV)[19]

---

and political categories. Exclusive truth challenges the liberal, while inclusive love challenges the conservative. Jesus is so exclusive in His truth claims as to shame the most exclusive conservative. And he is so inclusive in His love aims as to shame the most inclusive liberal."

[18]Walter C. Kaiser Jr. et al., *Hard Sayings of the Bible* (Downers Grove, IL: InterVarsity Press, 1996), 378.

[19]In the parallel passage in John it says he made a whip of cords and "drove all of them out of the temple, both the sheep and the cattle. He also poured out the coins of the money changers and overturned their tables" (Jn 2:15 NRSV).

This is the one place in the Gospels where Jesus appears to be violent. It is true that Jesus was forceful and angry, but he did not physically attack people. Despite a reference to his making a whip of cords, there is no mention of him whipping people. As Ben Witherington notes, "Jesus did not burn anything, nor did he lead any troops or bandits into the temple; he simply interrupted the economic activities there temporarily."[20]

Religious leaders allowed merchants to sell animals in the outer courts of the temple. Instead of being the "house of prayer for all the nations" (Mk 11:17 NRSV) that God had intended, the temple had become an ingrown religious club. So Jesus confronted this religious corruption. As Donald English notes,

> The point of Jesus' complaint . . . seems to be that it all took place in the Court of the Gentiles. Hence (17) quoting Isaiah 56:7, the bone of contention is that the place intended for Gentiles ("all nations") to pray was being misused by the Jews for trade (and profit). "Den of robbers" (17) is very strong language, and may have its origin in Jeremiah 7:11. The anger of Jesus is clear.[21]

The cleansing of the temple was a passionate prophetic act against the discrimination of Jewish religious leaders toward Gentiles. It was an act of radical reform intended to shake up the status quo. Perhaps the best modern example of a peace disturber is Martin Luther King Jr. He confronted white hypocrisy, racism, and injustice. But his goal was not to defeat white people in America; rather he sought to reconcile with white America.

The cross of Christ. The death of Christ on the cross is a central tenet of the Christian faith and the ultimate peacemaking event in history. Through his death, Jesus ushered in peace to a broken, alienated world (Col 1:19-20; Eph 2:13-17). In fact, the gospel (the story of the life, teaching, death, and resurrection of Jesus) is described in terms of peace twice in Old Testament prophecies (Isaiah 52:7; 53:5) and five times in the New Testament (Acts 10:36; Rom 5:1; Eph 2:13-17; 6:15; Col 1:20).

At the cross Jesus cried out, "Father, forgive them, for they do not know what they are doing" (Lk 23:34). "In the midst of this dreadful experience,

---

[20]Ben Witherington III, *The Gospel of Mark: A Socio-Rhetorical Commentary* (Grand Rapids: Eerdmans, 2001), 315.
[21]Donald English, *The Message of Mark: The Mystery of Faith* (Downers Grove, IL: InterVarsity Press, 1992), 190.

Jesus remains true to his own vision: God is still his Father, and love for his enemies is still his practice, even in this extreme situation."[22] In other words, Jesus' death on the cross not only procures peace but also demonstrates love for enemies—a key to making peace and an important part of the gospel (Rom 5:10; Col 1:21-22).

Jesus' final moments on the cross also demonstrate my previous assertion about Jesus' exclusive truth claims and inclusive love aims. He prayed that his Roman oppressors, his Jewish opponents, and even the thieves crucified with him would be forgiven (inclusive love aims).[23] Yet only the thief who responded to him entered into paradise (exclusive truth claims).

My brother-in-law once asked, "Rick, your peacemaking work with Muslims seems to ignore the stumbling block of the cross (1 Cor 1:23), and this is the heart of our faith. How do you respond to that?" I said, "In our peacemaking efforts we primarily demonstrate the cross. We seek peace and model love. And if we model it well they will be much more receptive to hearing the message of the cross." He liked my answer!

The second coming of Christ. According to the Hebrew Scriptures, the end times will include both a day of judgment and the ushering in of a universal reign of peace (Mic 4:1-4; Is 2:2-4; 11:1-9; Ezek 37:24-27).

The New Testament teaches that Jesus is the promised Messiah who ushers in this age of peace in two stages—at his first coming and ultimately at his second coming (Mt 1:1; 16:16; Eph 1:10; Rev 21–22).

Jesus-centered peacemakers follow the person of Christ. They obey the teaching of Christ. They imitate the example of Christ. They believe and share the message of the cross of Christ, and they long for the return of Christ.

THE STRATEGIC PRIORITY OF PEACEMAKING WITH MUSLIMS

The primary reason we work for peace between Muslims and Christians has been outlined above. We work for peace because that's what God's children do. We work for peace because that's what the Bible teaches. Clearly this is all the motivation we need! We follow the Prince of Peace into a world of conflict.

---

[22]John Nolland, *Luke 18:35–24:53*, Word Biblical Commentary 35C (Dallas: Word, 1998), 1148.
[23]It appears that Jesus is praying primarily for the Roman oppressors and Jewish opponents, but the very fact that one of the thieves receives the promise of paradise indicates that it was an inclusive prayer.

But there is also a unique strategic urgency to this task. The upsurge in violent extremism, embodied in ISIS, and the number of Muslim refugees flooding Western countries make peacemaking initiatives with Muslims imperative. Making peace with Muslims has important implications for national and international peace and security, though many evangelicals are hesitant to initiate peacemaking with Muslims.

My interaction with the following group of Christians captures something of the angst and anger many people feel about Islamist extremists. One dinner guest asked the rest of us sitting around the table, "What do you think followers of Jesus should do about ISIS?" After a moment of silence, one woman responded, "To be honest with you, I feel like we should respond to ISIS like we did to Japan after Pearl Harbor in World War II. We should completely destroy them. I am not saying this is what I should do as a follower of Jesus, but that's how I feel." Others responded in similar fashion, sharing raw emotions while at the same time confessing that what they were saying was not necessarily how a follower of Jesus should respond. I let the conversation continue for a while before I spoke up. "We cannot bomb our way to peace," I said. "Let's say we drop a nuclear bomb on them and kill all of ISIS. What will happen then?" The man who initiated the conversation shook his head, acknowledging that many more terrorists would rise up and that many innocents would suffer.

The original question was, "What do you think followers of Jesus should do about ISIS?" But the answers were *not* about what Christians should do but rather what the government or military should do. This confusion over the role of the church and the role of the state, especially as they relate to countering violent extremism, is common in the United States.

I acknowledge the important role of the state in countering terrorism, but my primary focus is on what followers of Jesus should actually do.[24] How followers of Jesus relate to Muslims and how we tackle terrorism evoke great passion and controversy. What follows is my attempt to be faithful to Jesus, loving toward Muslims, and practical about how Christians can undermine violent extremism.

---

[24]Rick Love, "Loving Muslims and Dealing with Terrorists," personal website, December 22, 2010, http://ricklove.net/?p=726.

Here's my proposal for a long-term solution. Imagine what could happen if even a small percentage of the 2.2 billion Christians in the world did *the heart work and the hard work* of waging peace. A preemptive love initiative by those who take Jesus' commands seriously would help undermine and thwart violent extremism in at least two ways: first, such an initiative would counter the Islamists' narrative that the West is at war with Islam, and second, it would greatly reduce the number of Muslim prospects receptive to being recruited to violent groups.

According to Ed Stetzer, 59 percent of evangelical pastors say Islam is dangerous and promotes violence. They agree with Franklin Graham's characterization of Islam as "a very evil and a very wicked religion."[25] Yes, there is a minuscule number of violent extremists who want to do us harm. But the vast majority of Muslims are just like you and me. They want to be faithful to God, love their family, and be productive members of society. They want to be treated with dignity and respect. And contrary to what most people think, prominent Muslim leaders around the world have taken a strong and public stand against ISIS and terrorism.[26]

Many Christians aren't aware of this because of the media's bombardment of sound bites and stereotypes. How do we discern between media hype and actual reality? How do we distinguish between the majority of Muslims and the radical extremists?

We begin waging peace by loving God with our minds. We need to learn about Islam and actually meet Muslims. We get the facts. We practice the art of evaluation. We don't believe everything that comes across our computer screens or fills our inboxes. We critically assess what we read or watch.

The Muslim world is radically diverse and pluralistic. There are over 1.5 billion Muslims in the world representing over two thousand different ethnic groups. There are two major sects (Sunni and Shi'a) and eight legal schools of Islam. In addition, there is a strong mystical movement within Islam called Sufism, which influences a large percentage of Muslims. There are Muslim secularists, modernists, traditionalists, fundamentalists, and terrorists.[27]

---

[25]Lisa Cannon Green, "Pastors Grow More Polarized on Islam," LifeWay Research, October 22, 2015, http://lifewayresearch.com/2015/10/22/pastors-grow-more-polarized-on-islam/.

[26]See articles on terrorism at the Peace Catalyst International website, www.peacecatalyst.org /articles.

[27]For more on this, see Rick Love, *Grace and Truth: Toward Christlike Relationships with Muslims* (Arvada, CO: Peace Catalyst International Publications, 2013).

So when someone makes a comment that Muslims believe this, or that Islam is like such and such, you need to ask, "Which Islam?" Another common question is, "Does Islam oppress women?" Women are oppressed in Afghanistan. But Pakistan, just next door, once had a female head of state—Benazir Bhutto. With all of its problems, the country of Pakistan has, in some ways, been more progressive on women's issues than the United States.

The overwhelming majority of Muslims are not our enemies. ISIS and violent extremists are. Yet Jesus commanded us to love our enemies. So how can we love violent extremists? Certainly we should pray for them (this is one of the commands related to enemy love). And while I don't think a Christian love campaign will stop the brutal regime of ISIS at this point,[28] I do believe a Christian love campaign can prevent future terrorists from being raised up.

The call to love Muslims—whether they are our enemies or our neighbors—is undeniable. We may disagree on our assessment of Islam (and in fact Christians do), but Jesus' teaching about love is straightforward and indisputable. What if followers of Jesus around the world demonstrated pre-emptive love toward Muslims everywhere? Our love could and would undermine the recruiting efforts of radical extremists who say the West is at war with Islam.[29] Enemies and potential enemies could become friends and partners. This could be a game-changer!

Nevertheless, we need to be realistic about the evil intentions of *some* Muslims. The command to love our enemies must be balanced by the command to be as wise as serpents: "See, I am sending you out like sheep into the midst of wolves; so be wise as serpents and innocent as doves" (Mt 10:16 NRSV).

Jesus says we are sent like defenseless sheep among ravenous wolves. Because we are vulnerable, Jesus urges us first of all to be as wise as snakes.

---

[28]I believe we thwart ISIS through military might (partnering with our Arab allies) and diplomatic muscle, through the use of hard power and soft power. For more on this see "Jeremy Courtney on ISIS: A Perspective from Iraq," Rick Love's personal website, October 8, 2014, http://ricklove .net/?p=2939.

[29]It is beyond the scope of this chapter to address the causes of Islamist extremism. Many reasons are given: Islam is inherently violent, the West is at war with Islam, Islam needs to reestablish a global caliphate, and Islamic rulers are oppressive, unjust dictators. In addition there are ethnic, political, sectarian, and economic factors that lead to violent extremism. See Ed Hussain, *The Islamist: Why I Became an Islamic Fundamentalist, What I Saw Inside, and Why I Left* (New York: Penguin, 2009), and Tass Saada and Dean Merrill, *The Mind of Terror* (Carol Stream, IL: Tyndale House, 2016).

Snakes use camouflage, fit in with their environment, and maintain a low profile. In this way they avoid predators. In other words, loving our enemies does not mean we should be naive or gullible. We love *and* we ask questions. We trust *and* we verify. We talk *and* we ask God for discernment.

This doesn't mean, however, that we live in suspicion of all Muslims, because Jesus also calls us to be as innocent as doves. This refers to the innocence of integrity or the purity of intention.[30] He expects us to be both shrewd and innocent in our relationships. We should maintain a low profile yet remain guileless—be wary but wear no masks. Snake-like behavior alone can become devious. Dove-like behavior alone can become gullible.

Colin Chapman, a well-respected British evangelical scholar of Islam, encourages us to find a middle path between demonization of Islam and naive political correctness:

> A middle way between these two extremes would mean (a) being realistic about the real intentions of *some* Muslims, (b) recognising the diversity among Muslims and relating to them as individuals and groups with openness and honesty, (c) taking a firm stand on issues of human rights, (d) working for the common good of the whole society, (e) demonstrating a fundamental respect for Islam (without agreeing with all its teaching), and (f) unapologetically commending the Christian faith through word and deed.[31]

When followers of Jesus say, "What should we do about ISIS or violent extremism?" it must be clear that the "we" does not include the state. The state is going to do what the state is going to do. While we can at times influence the decisions governments make, we are responsible to obey the commands of Jesus—which leads to my last major point.

I believe that how the church responds to Muslims is one of the most important challenges of our generation. Loving our Muslim neighbors fulfills the Great Commandment, which pleases God. In light of present realities, it also provides a strategic way to undermine violent extremism.

The majority of people killed by ISIS and other terrorist groups are Muslim. They face the brutal brunt of violent extremism more than anyone else.

---

[30]"[The Twelve] must be as . . . harmless or 'innocent' (*akeraios* means 'unmixed,' thus here 'with purity of intention') 'as doves.'" Robert H. Mounce, *Matthew* (Grand Rapids: Baker Books, 2001), 94.

[31]Colin Chapman, "Christian Responses to Islam, Islamism and 'Islamic terrorism' by Colin Chapman," *Jubilee Centre* (blog), May 16, 2017, www.jubilee-centre.org/christian-responses-to-islam-islamism-and-islamic-terrorism-by-colin-chapman.

Because of this, they want to see the end of violent extremism. And if we love our Muslim neighbors as ourselves, we will want what is best for them.

Mainstream Muslims are some of the most important voices for undermining and thwarting violent extremism. We need to amplify their ideas and support their efforts. We need to partner with them in any way we can to stop the spread of violent extremism. Thus, interfaith dialogue and various peacemaking efforts between Christians and Muslims are not just "feel good" efforts. While they often result in warm relationships, they also address real issues in a violent world. The long-term impact of these efforts has the potential to radically reduce terrorism.

EVANGELICAL PEACEMAKING INITIATIVES WITH MUSLIMS

Jer Swigart and Jon Huckins founded the Global Immersion Project with the goal of raising up everyday peacemakers. While they do not focus exclusively on Christian-Muslim peacemaking, they do train peacemakers in Israel and the West Bank and are thus engaging Muslims.[32] Huckins's article "Why You Need More Muslim Friends: 5 Reasons We Need to Form True (Not Agenda Driven) Friendships with People of Other Faiths" is a brilliant example of their orientation and the work they do.[33]

Southern Baptist megachurch pastor Bob Roberts Jr. is a high-profile ambassador for peace—"relentlessly pursuing peace and reconciliation among all people in all places for all things."[34] He spends much of his time working with Muslims both in the United States and around the world.[35] His partnership with imam Mohamed Magid is particularly noteworthy.[36] These two faith leaders bring pastors and imams together for retreats to break down barriers of prejudice and foster authentic friendships.

---

[32]See the home page of the Global Immersion Project, accessed September 30, 2016, www .globalimmerse.org.

[33]Jon Huckins, "Why You Need More Muslim Friends: 5 Reasons We Need to Form True (Not Agenda Driven) Friendships with People of Other Faiths," *Relevant*, October 1, 2014, www .relevantmagazine.com/god/worldview/why-you-need-more-muslim-friends.

[34]See the home page of Glocal.net, accessed September 30, 2016, www.glocal.net.

[35]Ed Stetzer, "A Muslim Declaration on Religious Minorities: An Interview w/ Pastor Bob Roberts in Marrakesh, Morocco," *The Exchange* (blog), *Christianity Today*, January 28, 2016, www .christianitytoday.com/edstetzer/2016/january/marrakesh-morocco-interview-w-pastor.html; and Diane Smith, "Keller Pastor Keeps Fighting 'Islamophobia,'" *Star-Telegram*, August 7, 2015, www.star-telegram.com/news/local/community/northeast-tarrant/article30393678.html.

[36]Rick Love, "Evangelicals, Muslims Commit to Mutual Peace," EthicsDaily.com, November 6, 2015, www.ethicsdaily.com/evangelicals-muslims-commit-to-mutual-peace-cms-23055.

Douglas Johnston, described by *Christianity Today* as the "father of faith-based diplomacy,"[37] is another brilliant example of Christian-Muslim peacemaking. While Johnston may not self-identify as an evangelical, he works closely with evangelicals like Bob Roberts and myself.[38] The development of the International Interfaith Network and the conference on Islamophobia and Religious Freedom at Temple University are two examples of his recent peacemaking efforts.[39]

Jim Mullins, Michael Ly, and I founded Peace Catalyst International (PCI) in 2010.[40] Our mission is to "catalyze Christian-Muslim peacemaking in the way of Jesus."[41] We organize loving initiatives that create safe spaces and foster authentic relationships between Christians and Muslims. And we do this as Jesus-centered peacemakers. We strive to imitate Jesus, follow his teachings, and demonstrate his love.

Hospitality radically shapes our peacemaking practices. PCI's most well-known and frequent peacemaking event is the "peace feast": a meal that includes a culturally related presentation or experience, hosted in a home or at a Muslim-associated restaurant. In fact, most of our programs center around a meal. We have learned that breaking bread brings down barriers and builds friendships.

We presently work in fourteen cities in the United States and one in Indonesia. A number of times each week in these two countries Christians and Muslims gather to make peace. Every week, US Christians are being trained in Jesus-centered peacemaking. Jesus' peace mandate is changing Christian-Muslim relations and undermining violent extremism. It is equipping Christians to love and serve suffering refugees. Christians are learning how to unleash peace in a polarized, violent world.

---

[37]Rob Moll, "The Father of Faith-Based Diplomacy: Doug Johnston Is Going Where Few Foreign Policy Experts Have Gone Before," *Christianity Today*, September 19, 2008, www.christianitytoday.com/ct/2008/september/29.54.html.

[38]Rick Love, "Peacemaking in Pakistan: Promoting Religious Freedom," personal website, November 6, 2013, http://ricklove.net/?p=2639.

[39]"Interfaith Leadership Network," International Center for Religion & Diplomacy, accessed September 30, 2016, http://icrd.org/interfaith-leaders-network/; and Rev. Dr. Mae Elise Cannon, "Evangelicals Reject Anti-Muslim Hatred," *Huffington Post*, October 19, 2015, www.huffingtonpost.com/rev-mae-elise-cannon/evangelicals-reject-anti_b_8330088.html.

[40]See the home page of Peace Catalyst International, www.peacecatalyst.org.

[41]"Mission," Peace Catalyst International, accessed September 30, 2016, www.peacecatalyst.org/about/.

10

Defining Islam and Muslim Societies in Missiological Discourse

Evelyne A. Reisacher

Some time ago I received this request from a journal that was publishing one of my articles: "To illustrate your article, can you please send a picture of you with a Muslim woman?" As I browsed through scores of pictures of Muslim friends stored on my computer, I realized the awkwardness of the question. How would readers identify someone from my photos as "Muslim"? Would it be by a headscarf? But sometimes I wear headscarves, and I am not Muslim. Would it be by a full-body veil? But what about my other pictures of Muslim friends wearing shorts at the beach? Why choose one over the other? Why would a veiled woman better represent Islam than a woman in shorts at the beach? I then realized the subjectivity involved in trying to visually communicate Muslim identity.

If I were to ask readers for a definition of Islam, I anticipate that the responses would be very diverse. Some may say that Islam is a religion, others a faith, others a culture, while others may question the validity of using religion as a category. Some may talk about a monolithic Islam, while others—more aware of the diversity of Muslim societies—may dispute such a definition. Scholars and missiologists from various academic disciplines have long debated the definition of Islam and identity of Muslims.

Why is it crucial to raise this question in missiological circles? First, Christians often seem confused when confronted with various manifestations of Islam. They cannot neatly connect definitions succinctly packaged in seminars or books with what they observe in Muslim societies. I am currently teaching a class on Muslim societies. When students read socio-logical and anthropological articles on prayer rituals (*ṣalāt*) in various Muslim communities, their first reaction is often astonishment over the diversity of ways that Muslims pray.

Second, debates over the nature of Islam and of Muslim societies have often divided missiologists and mission practitioners. I have personally ob-served disputes in mission circles between mission practitioners supporting a uniform definition of Islam and those recognizing more diverse manifes-tations in Islam. The former leaned toward a "one approach fits all" expla-nation, while the latter advocated for greater diversity in mission practices. Third, the Christian community is regularly critiqued for not representing Muslims accurately, especially in regards to their diversity.

In this chapter, I offer a review of various definitions of Islam and of Muslim societies by theologians, anthropologists, and sociologists of Islam and how these definitions have influenced Christian theological and mis-siological discussions. I also suggest categorical concepts that will help theo-logians and missiologists better express what they observe in Islam and Muslim societies.

UNITY

Let me start with the claim that Islam is monolithic, universal, uninfluenced by culture, and uniform in its message. I call this view of Islam the cookie-cutter approach. I remember my first workshop on Islam in a church context. The instructor said, "Islam can be summarized in a nutshell as having five rituals and six core beliefs. It is divided into two branches (Sunnism and Shi'ism)." He added that most Muslims would agree with this definition. To him this short list of beliefs and practices represented "Islam." Consequently, I assumed that I could use this cookie-cutter approach to define all Muslim societies.

Like me, many Christians who receive this kind of training are surprised when they move to another cultural context and encounter an "Islam" that is quite different from the one they studied in the classroom. We as Chris-tians today don't need to travel overseas to face this. Through the news, social media, and conversations with friends, we are flooded with diverse expressions of Islam, to the point that we are often left in total confusion when these expressions do not match up with what we understand as the basic tenets of Islam.

Theologically, it may be tempting to define Islam in a monolithic way since there is so much emphasis on unity (*tawḥīd*)—the oneness of God, the one language (Arabic) used in the Qur'an, and common practices and beliefs almost universally shared by Muslims. After defining common Islamic beliefs, however, most scholars of Islam, even theologians, acknowledge differences between Islamic branches, trends, schools, interpretations, and so on. Furthermore, although Muslims believe in one eternal God, they have debated his nature and identity since the founding of Islam. It takes only a cursory glance at the shelves of commentaries in libraries specializing in Islamic studies to realize that Muslims have not yet solved their internal doctrinal differences. We have to live with the fact that those debates will probably go on as long as the world does. Scholars and practitioners will always have to face the question of what fits in the Islam and Muslim "box" and what does not.

Anthropological and sociological studies of Muslim societies have further highlighted Islamic diversity. In the fourteenth century, Muslim historian and sociologist Ibn Khaldūn found that social forces influenced the development of Muslim societies.[1] Later, in the twentieth century, anthropologist Clifford Geertz found striking differences in comparing Muslim societies in Morocco and Indonesia.[2] The link between diversity and unity in Islam and Muslim societies is therefore an issue that every scholar of Islam needs to wrestle with. For example, anthropologist Ahmed Akbar claims, as reported by Clinton Bennett, that there is "one Islam but many Muslim societies."[3] Other authors talk about "unity and diversity"[4] or "diversity within unity"[5] when they describe Muslim societies.

---

[1] Ibn Khaldūn, *The Muqaddimah: An Introduction to History*, trans. Franz Rosenthal (Princeton, NJ: Princeton University Press, 1967).

[2] Clifford Geertz, *Islam Observed: Religious Development in Morocco and Indonesia* (Chicago: University of Chicago Press, 1971).

[3] Clinton Bennett, *Studying Islam: The Critical Issues* (New York: Continuum, 2010), 67.

[4] Muzzamil Siddiqi, "Unity and Diversity: Islamic Perspective," *American Muslim*, October 26, 2005, http://theamericanmuslim.org/tam.php/features/articles/unity_and_diversity_islamic_perspective.

[5] Herbert L. Bodman and Nayereh Tohidi, eds., *Women in Muslim Societies: Diversity Within Unity* (London: Lynne Rienner Publishers, 1998).

But many Christians continue to promote the idea that Islam is monolithic and that it ultimately shapes uniform Muslim societies. Instead of exploring new ways to engage with Muslims, they view Islam as static and unchanging. To them, one approach fits all. Their view of Islam as one and not reducible to different parts, manifestations, or interpretations easily leads to reductionist judgments. They leave no room for gray areas or nuances. They don't believe it is important to spend time exploring the various manifestations of Islam, because they presuppose that all the other views besides theirs do not characterize Islam. When others state that there are different voices in Islam, they don't believe them. They don't trust them. With the cookie-cutter approach there is no possible nuance. This methodology involves boiling down a faith fourteen centuries old into something that the whole Muslim world can identify with—in other words, a few beliefs. But can the category "religion" be equated to "a few beliefs"? I do not think so.[6]

A number of Christians have used this reductionist and essentialist view to evaluate Islam. Some of us may remember the statements of certain evangelical leaders after 9/11 who described Islam as evil. Laurie Goodstein reported their view in an article titled "Seeing Islam as 'Evil' Faith, Evangelicals Seek Converts."[7] On what basis did they claim Islam is evil? Only the adoption of a reductionist view of Islam allowed them to make such a statement. They completely disregarded the various manifestations and interpretations of Islam. They often based their positions on a rapid and shallow review of qur'anic verses on killing and war. Those views still have proponents today. A survey conducted in 2015 revealed that "most self-identified evangelical ministers view [Islam] as a violent and dangerous faith."[8] The same danger lies in believing that Islam is only "peace, love, and compassion" and denying any evil perpetrated in the name of Islam.[9] This too is a cookie-cutter approach.

---

[6]Isn't viewing Christianity in the same way also problematic?

[7]Laurie Goodstein, "Seeing Islam as 'Evil' Faith, Evangelicals Seek Converts," New York Times, May 27, 2003, www.nytimes.com/2003/05/27/us/seeing-islam-as-evil-faith-evangelicals-seek -converts.html.

[8]Lisa Cannon Green, "Pastors Grow More Polarized on Islam," LifeWay Research, October 22, 2015, http://lifewayresearch.com/2015/10/22/pastors-grow-more-polarized-on-islam/.

[9]According to the same LifeWay study, "Most self-identified mainline pastors associate [Islam] with peace, love, and compassion" (Green, "Pastors Grow More Polarized").

Although I believe it is important to highlight the common denominators in Islam, if we don't mention the observable differences in Islam and Muslim societies, we run the risk of reductionism, essentialism, and a distortion of a religion that spans centuries and the globe. In claiming that Islam is either bad with nothing good in it or good with nothing bad in it, we become blind to the many manifestations and interpretations of Islam. We also face the danger of becoming monolithic in our models of engagement and stifling new initiatives that may be more relevant to the contemporary needs of Muslim societies.

DIVERSITY

Though some scholars reduce Islam to a set of common beliefs and practices, there are others who believe Islam is much more complex. Anyone studying the development of Islam would agree that there are different manifestations of Islam. According to anthropologist Ronald A. Lukens-Bull, in the early 1900s Ignaz Goldziher, a prominent theologian of Islam, "demonstrated the dynamics of diversity evident in Islam from early in its history to the time of his writing."[10] Likewise, J. Dudley Woodberry has recently said,

> The media has bombarded us with generalizations about the peacefulness or militancy of Islam, and fundamentalists (Islamists) and militants have been frequently equated. Such generalizations fail to grasp the diversity within Islam, both in its contemporary expressions and in its roots.[11]

Woodberry, like Goldziher, claims that diversity existed since the founding of Islam. But what does this diversity look like, and how does it intersect with the oneness also advocated by those scholars?

Binary view of Islam. Some observers of Islam, dissatisfied with the view that Islam is one, have described Islam as two. According to them, Islam can be divided into good and bad Islam. This is different from the previous cookie-cutter approach, which sees Islam as either good or bad. A recent book by Elizabeth Shakman Hurd titled *Beyond Religious Freedom: The New Global Politics of Religion*[12] describes governments that are using the rhetoric

---

[10]Ronald A. Lukens-Bull, "Between Text and Practice: Considerations in the Anthropological Study of Islam," in *Defining Islam: A Reader*, ed. Andrew Rippin (New York: Routledge, 2014), 43.

[11]J. Dudley Woodberry, "Terrorism, Islam, and Mission: Reflections of a Guest in Muslim Lands," *International Bulletin of Missionary Research* 26, no. 1 (2002): 2.

[12]Elizabeth Shakman Hurd, *Beyond Religious Freedom: The New Global Politics of Religion* (Princeton, NJ: Princeton University Press, 2015).

of a good and bad Islam to engage with Islam locally and internationally. In a nutshell, they support the "good Islam" to fight the "bad Islam." Contenders of such a view hold a binary position regarding Islam. The binary elements do not have to be the "good" or "bad." It can be Islam for or against modernity or democratic Islam versus antidemocratic Islam.

Some mission practitioners seem to adopt a binary view. For example, Georges Houssney in his book *Engaging Islam* believes that "a healthy attitude recognizes both the good and bad in Islam and Muslims." He adds, "We need to face the fact that Islam has two elements: one peaceful and one at war with the world."[13] This is different from the approach presented in the previous section by those who claim that Islam is only evil or only good. But the binary view of Islam runs the risk of being as reductionist as the previous one. Reducing Islam to good and bad means ignoring so many other factors that shape Islam, such as qur'anic interpretations, culture, social factors, economics, and politics. If Islam is two, why can it not be three, four, or five? Houssney understands this: after describing the bad and good in Islam, he moves away from the binary view and talks about the misconception he encountered that "Islam is a monolithic religion." He explains, "Actually, Islam is as diverse as Christianity. There are ethnic, national, tribal, linguistic, and sectarian differences between Muslims. . . . Muslims can be as different from each other as a Russian Orthodox Ukrainian is from a Texas Pentecostal."[14]

A common core. To avoid a binary view and acknowledge diversity many scholars have attempted to identify a core, an essence, an authentic Islam that does not negate diversity but that unites all Muslims under the single category "Islam." Such scholars often describe this as the common denominator or the DNA of all Muslims. In other words, if Islam would be stripped of all its diverse cultural and social features, the remaining fundamentals would represent the core or essence of Islam.

Theologically, it seems to make sense to talk about a core. We have seen above that some common beliefs and practices unite Muslims universally. One of the obvious practices shared by all Muslims is the pilgrimage to Mecca (hajj). Muslims performing the hajj circumambulate the Kaaba seven

[13]Georges Houssney, *Engaging Islam* (Boulder, CO: Treeline, 2010), 46-47.
[14]Ibid., 28.

times. One pilgrim explained, "The Kaaba is the heart and as pilgrims we flow around it like blood flows through the veins and arteries and through motion our own hearts are strengthened and purified."[15] In this sense, we may have found a core. But a closer study of the Islamic pilgrimage will reveal that it also comprises variances: historical divergences over what branch of Islam presides over the pilgrimage, diverse experiences of Muslims who perform the pilgrimage, and different interpretations of the salvific function of the hajj.

Moreover, there has rarely been universal agreement on what is normative in Islam. Anthropologist Dale F. Eickelman states, "If current debates over what are 'correct' or 'normative' interpretations of Islam are particularly intense, they are hardly unique to the present or to the recent past."[16] Both historically and today, then, there have been diverse official representations of Islam. The question that this argument raises is who decides what is the core, the normative, or the official Islam. Thus, if Muslims decide to go on a virtual hajj, who decides whether this practice is Islamic or not? Aaron W. Hughes explains,

> There is always a danger in defining an "authentic" (or, alternatively, "real" or "essential") Islam at the expense of various "inauthentic" (or "fake") representations. In any such attempt, we must always ask ourselves: Who decides what criteria to use, and what gets to count as a true (or false) expression of faith?[17]

Defining the core of Islam seems impossible without defining human agency.

Despite this difficulty, missiologists have often attempted to define *the* core of Islam. Michael W. Goheen talks about an "orienting core." He explains, "This central religious impulse throbs in every aspect of a religion and binds it together in organic unity." He believes the "orienting core of Islam is to proclaim one transcendent God and to found a community ruled by God and his prophet."[18] But identifying a core means ruling out certain elements that other Muslims would include. Different scholars will perceive

---

[15]Jasmin Zine, "A 'Thank You Letter' to God," in *Women Writing Letters: Celebrating the Art Season 2*, ed. Tara Goldstein and Amanda Greer (Toronto: Galey Road Productions, 2014), 22.

[16]Dale F. Eickelman, "The Study of Islam in Local Contexts," in Rippin, *Defining Islam*, 69.

[17]Aaron W. Hughes, *Muslim Identities: An Introduction to Islam* (New York: Columbia University Press, 2013), 2.

[18]Michael W. Goheen, *Introducing Christian Mission Today: Scripture, History and Issues* (Downers Grove, IL: InterVarsity Press, 2014), 355.

different factors that shape the core. Daniel W. Brown, an Islamic theologian, expresses well this challenge when he writes,

> The student who sets out to learn about Islam will soon face a problem something like this. If we were to draw a circle and designate the contents of that circle as the complete set of phenomena that fall under the rubric of Islam, how would we decide what would be included within the circle and what must be excluded?[19]

Great and little traditions. Instead of simply talking about a core or essence, scholars of Islam sometimes talk about "great tradition" and "little tradition."[20] The great tradition is also called orthodox Islam and refers to the religion of theologians and religious leaders.[21] The little tradition is also called popular or folk Islam. Lukens-Bull says,

> The little tradition is the heterodox form of the cultural/religious periphery. The little tradition incorporates many elements of local tradition and practice. . . . [It] is the religion as it is practiced in daily life by ordinary people.[22]

Although not every scholar would agree with this division, a number of prominent missiologists have adopted this way of thinking. Samuel M. Zwemer was one of the first missiologists in the modern mission era to distinguish between ideal or high Islam and popular Islam.[23] To him, popular Islam is influenced by animism. He writes,

> Islam sprang up in Pagan soil and retained many old Arabian beliefs in spite of its vigorous monotheism. Wherever Mohammedanism went it introduced old or adopted new superstitions. . . . The religion of the common people from Tangier to Teheran is mixed with hundreds of superstitions many of which have lost their original significance but still bind mind and heart with constant fear of demons, with witchcraft and sorcery and the call to creature-worship.[24]

---

[19]Daniel W. Brown, *A New Introduction to Islam*, 2nd ed. (Oxford: Wiley-Blackwell, 2009), 3.
[20]See, for example, Robert Redfield, *Peasant Society and Culture* (Chicago: University of Chicago Press, 1956).
[21]Lukens-Bull lists several terms used to describe orthodox Islam: "textual traditions," "orthodoxy," "philosophical religions," "high traditions," and "universal traditions" ("Between Text and Practice," 40).
[22]Ibid.
[23]Samuel M. Zwemer, *Studies in Popular Islam* (London: Sheldon Press, 1939).
[24]Samuel M. Zwemer, *The Influence of Animism on Islam: An Account of Popular Superstitions* (New York: Macmillan, 1920), vii.

Zwemer adds, "Popular Islam is altogether different from the religion as recorded in its sacred Book."[25]

Several missiologists, such as Dudley Woodberry[26] and Phil Parshall,[27] have followed in Zwemer's footsteps by exploring further the theme of popular Islam. Missiologist Bill Musk explains the reasons he wrote on popular Islam: "The 'Islam' my Turkish friends told me about seemed far removed from the religion I had studied while at university in England." He explains,

> I wanted to help others, especially Christian missionaries, realise the signifi-
> cance of the folk-Islamic world for the lives of many of the Muslims with
> whom they dealt. My goal was to provide an anthropological and missio-
> logical framework for coming to terms with the realities of popular Islam.[28]

What are the missiological implications of distinguishing between high and low Islam? Such a differentiation has encouraged the development of models of encounter adapted to the worldview of popular Islam. For example, those who work among "folk Muslims" often talk about nurturing mission practices such as healing and praying for miracles rather than witnessing through theological debates.[29] They also promote "power encounter" with the spirit world.[30]

One of the downsides of the division between high and low Islam is the difficulty of defining what is purely "low" and purely "high" Islam. Another problem is that supernatural manifestations become automatically ascribed to

---

[25]Ibid.

[26]A recent blog on J. Dudley Woodberry's life and scholarship reports that "folk Islam was a dominant form of practice in places where Dudley ministered. . . . Academic resources on these phenomena were few and far between, so Dudley set about recording the facets of what is now called
'Muslim popular piety.' He collected talismans, books, and prayers, and in the meantime discovered a world outside the mosque that believed in and feared magic, spirits, demons, and curses."
"The Extraordinary Life and Work of Dudley Woodberry," *Fuller Studio*, https://fullerstudio.fuller
.edu/extraordinary-life-work-dudley-woodberry (accessed May 11, 2017).

[27]Phil Parshall, *Bridges to Islam: A Christian Perspective on Folk Islam* (Atlanta: Authentic Media,
2007).

[28]Bill Musk, *The Unseen Face of Islam: Sharing the Gospel with Ordinary Muslims at Street Level*, 2nd
ed. (Oxford: Monarch, 2003), 7-8.

[29]See, for example, J. Dudley Woodberry, "Power Ministry in Folk Islam," in *Encountering the
World of Islam*, ed. Keith E. Swartley (Downers Grove, IL: InterVarsity Press, 2005), 201-8; and
Vivienne Stacey, "The Practice of Exorcism and Healing," in *Muslims and Christians on the Em-
maus Road: Crucial Issues in Witness Among Muslims*, ed. J. Dudley Woodberry (Monrovia, CA:
Missions Advanced Research and Communication Center, 1988), 317-31.

[30]Rick Love, "Power Encounter Among Folk Muslims: An Essential Key of the Kingdom," *International Journal of Frontier Missions* 13, no. 4 (1996): 193-95.

low Islam. This gives the faulty impression that high Islam does not address the supernatural. Additionally, scholars do not always draw clearly the line between Sufism and popular Islam. Are they the same? If we adopt the definition of popular Islam proposed by Zwemer, then they are certainly not the same. Sufis do not claim to follow animistic practices, although Muslim leaders sometimes accuse them of doing so. Missionaries are not always equipped to distinguish between the spiritual dynamics of Sufism and popular Islam.

That said, I believe the concept of low and high Islam has allowed missiologists to understand religious practices that they would have been unable to analyze otherwise. However, a better definition of these two divisions in Islam needs to exist in order to avoid misinterpretation. I believe that anthropologist Redfield provides a helpful suggestion when he concludes his study of primitive and peasant societies by saying, "Great and little tradition can be thought of as two currents of thought and action, distinguishable, yet ever flowing into and out of each other."[31] Likewise Lukens-Bull proposes that "the question to be explored is how the two aspects are interconnected. Implicit is the notion that in order for any great tradition to spread and be commonly practiced it must have mass appeal, that is to say, it must become a little tradition."[32] The same author also quotes anthropologist Eickelman, who warns "that when scholars mention great and little traditions they tend merely to juxtapose them and not explore their complex interrelationships."[33]

I therefore encourage missiologists and anthropologists not to look at these two manifestations of Islam as completely separate from each other. Those who have taught high and low Islam in separate courses should look more carefully at the intersection between the two, because their boundaries are not always as clear as we think.

ISLAMS OR NO ISLAM

A few scholars have ventured to say that there is not just one Islam, nor an Islam with diverse manifestations, but rather several islams. Anthropologist Abdul Hamid el-Zein, for example, wonders "if a single true Islam exists at

---

[31]Robert Redfield, *The Little Community and Peasant Society and Culture* (1960; repr., Chicago: University of Chicago Press, 1989), 42-43.
[32]Lukens-Bull, "Between Text and Practice," 41.
[33]Ibid., 42.

all."[34] Daniel Martin Varisco summarizes el-Zein's argument this way: "We are better off . . . [focusing] our skills on the many 'islams' we can approach anthropologically."[35] Like him, Varisco has played with the notion of several islams.[36] He writes, "Observing Muslims in particular 'islams' is one of the few things that anthropologists have been able to contribute to the broader academic interest in how Islam is continually defined and redefined and, indeed, how religion itself is conceptualized."[37] He believes "'Islam,' 'economy,' 'history,' 'religion' and so on do not exist as things or entities with meaning inherent in them, but rather as articulations of structural relations, and are the outcome of these relations and not simply a set of positive terms from which we start our studies."[38] Consequently, according to him,

> This logic of relations implies that neither Islam nor the notion of religion exists as a fixed and autonomous form referring to positive content which can be reduced to universal and unchanging characteristics. Religion becomes an arbitrary category which as a unified and bounded form has no necessary existence. "Islam" as an analytical category dissolves as well.[39]

Very few missiologists have embraced the view of several islams, probably because this view is more easily supported by anthropologists than theologians of Islam. However, the idea of revisiting the definition of religion seems attractive to some missiologists and mission practitioners who believe that the notion of religion is complex, cumbersome, and misleading when witnessing among Muslims. They would like to share the gospel without adding the weight of centuries of tradition and manifold expressions of Christianity that sometimes have inaccurately portrayed the gospel.

Although I find this thesis attractive, I am hesitant to embrace it completely. Since the beginning of this chapter, we have seen how much faith

---

[34]Abdul Hamid el-Zein, "Beyond Ideology and Theology: The Search for the Anthropology of Islam," in *The Anthropology of Islam Reader*, ed. Jens Kreinath (New York: Routledge, 2012), 78.

[35]Daniel Martin Varisco, *Islam Obscured: The Rhetoric of Anthropological Representation* (New York: Palgrave Macmillan, 2005), 111.

[36]See, for example, Aziz Al-Azmeh, *Islams and Modernities*, 3rd ed. (London: Verso, 2009). Likewise, Earl H. Waugh talks about "several Islams in the West." "Islam in the West," in *The SAGE Handbook of Islamic Studies*, ed. Akbar S. Ahmed and Tamara Sonn (Thousand Oaks, CA: SAGE Publications, 2010), 263.

[37]Varisco, *Islam Obscured*, 160.

[38]Abdul Hamid el-Zein, "Beyond Ideology and Theology: The Search for the Anthropology of Islam," *Annual Review of Anthropology* 6 (1977): 251.

[39]Ibid., 252.

needs context. To me, completely eliminating the notion of religion means getting rid of the social and cultural contexts necessary for the transcendent to interact with the mundane. Focusing only on the relationship between believer and God and discarding all references to history, culture, and society feels as reductionist and essentialist as the notion of "one Islam" or "one Islamic culture." It reflects a representation of God disconnected from the world in which we live and from its history. But I agree with el-Zein that the notion of religion should be revisited. The way mission practitioners use a static definition of religion to define Islam does not allow them to address the diversity that they observe in the Muslim world.

ISLAMIC CULTURE OR CULTURES?

Our attempt to define the nature of Islam cannot ignore the important debates that take place among social scientists who study the influence of culture on Islam and the influence of Islam on culture. It is probably easier for anthropologists and sociologists than for theologians of Islam to claim that Islam is shaped by culture since they explore Islam by studying cultures and societies. Eickelman explains that

> the study of a world religion in local contexts implies what from some perspectives is obvious—any religion's ideology and practice are elaborated, understood and subsequently reproduced in particular places and at particular moments. Even eternal truths are necessarily revealed in a specific language and setting.[40]

But Eickelman also states,

> The main challenge for the study of Islam in local contexts is to describe and analyze how the universalistic principles of Islam have been realized in various social and historical contexts without representing Islam as a seamless essence on the one hand or as a plastic congeries of beliefs and practices on the other.[41]

Given its influence on culture, anthropologists have been tempted to define Islam according to its geographical location. Akbar Ahmed shows how anthropologists have categorized Islam as Pakistani Islam, Moroccan

[40]Eickelman, "Study of Islam," 58.
[41]Ibid.

Islam, Malay Islam, and so on. He believes this is a distortion of the reality and thus "is no answer." He acknowledges that culture influences Islam, but adds, "The demarcation of Muslim societies is therefore not a division between white ideal and black non-ideal but an ongoing relationship between the two marked by areas of grey."[42] Thus, scholars show that despite its universalistic principles, cultural and social factors are shaping diverse manifestations of Islam.

Not everyone agrees, however. Some scholars believe that there is only one Islamic culture that all Muslims should embrace. In other words, they argue for a single system of values, norms, behaviors, attitudes, and beliefs that would be similar across the Muslim world. But given the diverse manifestations of Islam in various cultures, they must develop theoretical concepts that allow for the integration of diversity within unity. Seyyed Hossein Nasr, for example, says that "there is a single Islamic culture with distinct 'zones' or worlds contained within it, 'worlds' which are united by the spirit and sacred form of the tradition and separated by local ethnic, linguistic, geographical and other factors."[43]

On the other hand, some Islamic groups promote the one Islamic culture that they want to apply to every geographical context. They believe that the Qur'an and the hadith give us a snapshot of the life and customs adopted by Muhammad that every Muslim after him should imitate. This position is problematic, however, because the Qur'an is sometimes silent about what Muhammad said, did, and believed. Furthermore, manifold interpretations of the Sunnah or tradition of Muhammad have been offered throughout the centuries. It is not possible to talk about one Islamic culture without contesting all the other Islamic cultures recognized throughout Muslim history. Another strong argument against the thesis of one Islamic culture is that even an "ideal culture" morphs when exported to other contexts. One example of this is the diversity of behaviors and practices among ISIS followers, which can be witnessed around the world by simply watching the news. Another is the different faces of political Islam today.[44]

---

[42]Akbar S. Ahmed, *Discovering Islam: Making Sense of Muslim History and Society*, rev. ed. (New York: Routledge, 2002), 5.

[43]Seyyed Hossein Nasr, *Islamic Life and Thought* (London: George Allen & Unwin, 1981), 39.

[44]For the various manifestations of Islamism, see for example Asef Bayat, ed., *Post-Islamism: The Changing Faces of Political Islam* (Oxford: Oxford University Press, 2013). See also Mohammed

Although it seems almost impossible to defend the concept of a universal Islamic culture, I still meet Christians who state, "Converts from Islam should entirely give up their Islamic culture." They say this as if converts could take off their Islamic culture like a coat. One cannot simply separate cultural elements from religious ones, for they have been interwoven for years in the lives of believers. Anthropologist Samuli Schielke gives an example of this interdependence in a study of Ramadan, the month of Islamic fasting. He noticed that for young Egyptians in Cairo, playing soccer is an integral part of the experience of Ramadan. It would be almost impossible to separate it from other practices, such as praying or breaking the fast, that usually fall under the category of "religious" activities. Schielke explains, "Ramadān football is an ambivalent exercise. It is one of the gatherings so characteristic of the sense of community that prevails in the month of fasting, and a way to kill time that is not deemed immoral or un-Islamic."[45]

Thus, during Ramadan playing soccer almost morphs into a religious practice, because it allows young Muslims to be involved in a social activity that relieves the stress of fasting and prevents them from engaging in other activities that could be immoral. This example demonstrates that isolating cultural practices from religious practices is much more complex than we imagine.

Debates about the relationship between faith and culture have fostered a wide variety of models, which range from Islam being a cultural system, on one side of the spectrum, to Islam being a-cultural, on the other side.[46] According to Patrick J. Ryan, SJ, the relationship between faith and culture in Islam can be analyzed using Richard Niebuhr's categories.[47] If we were to apply these categories, we could easily identify examples in Islam of each

Ayoob, *The Many Faces of Political Islam: Religion and Politics in the Muslim World* (Ann Arbor: University of Michigan Press, 2007).

[45]Samuli Schielke, "Being Good in Ramadān: Ambivalence, Fragmentation, and the Moral Self in the Lives of Young Egyptians," in Kreinath, *Anthropology of Islam Reader*, 175.

[46]See, for example, the work of Clifford Geertz, especially his chapter on "Religion as a Cultural System," in *The Interpretation of Cultures* (New York: Basic Books, 1973), 87–125.

[47]Patrick J. Ryan, SJ, with responses by Daniel Polish and Amir Hussain, "Faith and Culture: Jewish, Christian and Muslim Perspectives" (lecture, Laurence J. McGinley Chair Lecture Series, Fordham University, April 8, 2010). See also H. Richard Niebuhr, *Christ and Culture* (1951; repr., New York: Harper & Row, 1975).

dimension, as Ryan did.[48] This shows again that we cannot simply differentiate between religion and culture but must ask how they relate.

Instead of assuming a binary division between faith and culture, I would propose therefore to explore how they intersect in any given context and at any given time. I have shown above that several anthropologists have already attempted this exercise. The following statement by Eickelman best expresses how to integrate the oneness and diversity of Islam when looking at Muslim societies. Eickelman argues for a middle ground between the local and universal. He explains,

> The "middle ground" between these two extremes[49] appears to be the most productive for comprehending world religious traditions. Exploration of this middle ground also facilitates an understanding of how the universalistic elements of Islam are practically communicated and of how modes of communication affect religious "universals."[50]

Today, Muslim populations exist on every continent. Their behaviors, attitudes, feelings, and thoughts are influenced by their cultural and social contexts. Missiologists have long been interested in the contextual expressions of Islam. In the early 1900s, Constance E. Padwick, for example, looked at Muslim piety by collecting devotional materials throughout the Muslim world.[51] In today's world, we have access to a wealth of data collected by anthropologists and sociologists that can help us understand Muslims much better than by relying on theology alone. Although there are still fierce missiological debates about how much weight should be given to context in the study of Islam, I believe that an anthropology and sociology of Islam offers a much "thicker description"[52] (to borrow an expression of Clifford Geertz) of Muslim societies than the study of Islam limited to the sacred texts. Given that theology only offers a partial view of what individual Muslims and societies believe and think, every student enrolled in Islamic studies at Fuller Theological Seminary is required to take a class on the theology of Islam and

---

[48]Ryan, "Faith and Culture."
[49]To Eickelman the two extremes are "the specific village locales" and "the Islam of all times and places" ("Study of Islam," 69).
[50]Ibid.
[51]Constance E. Padwick, *Muslim Devotions: A Study of Prayer-Manuals in Common Use* (Oxford: Oneworld Publications, 1996).
[52]Geertz, *Interpretation of Cultures*, 3.

another on the anthropology and sociology of Islam. Studying Islam through the lens of "locality" (as anthropologists would say) has allowed Christians to get closer to their Muslim neighbors by understanding not just what they believe and practice but also how the tenets of their faith shape their daily living. They have gained better tools for learning languages, understanding social networks, comprehending social practices (such as gift exchange), and so on. This in turn has created more opportunities for interfaith dialogue.

MUSLIM OR MUSLIMS?

The study of Islam from an anthropological perspective also raises the question of whether Islam should be defined by the actual experience of Muslims rather than by an idealized form of Islam. Why do I raise this question? Remember the story I told in the introduction to this chapter about the request for a picture of me with a Muslim woman. There are probably as many experiences of being a Muslim woman as there are women who self-identify as Muslims.

Anthropology, sociology, and I would add psychology provide valuable insight into the phenomenology of Islam, or in other words how Muslims experience being Muslims. This way of examining Islam puts a human face on what otherwise could be a very abstract notion. When an anthropologist like Lila Abu-Lughod conducts her study of the oral poetry of a Bedouin community in the Western Desert of Egypt, she highlights specific features of Islam in that context.[53] Through her study, Islam becomes a living faith.

But this raises the question of whether there is a specific identity marker that all Muslims display. It is common practice in Christian circles (and elsewhere) to use the term *Muslim* as the primary identity marker of people who were born in a Muslim context. I sometimes do it inadvertently and have probably done it in this chapter. But by calling someone a Muslim, have I not adopted the same cookie-cutter definition for Islam discussed above? What is "a Muslim"? Hughes claims, "There exist many types of Muslim groups or communities, all of whom have constructed identities for themselves based on their particular understanding of the tradition, which they subsequently

---

[53]Lila Abu-Lughod, *Veiled Sentiments: Honor and Poetry in a Bedouin Society* (Oakland: University of California Press, 1986).

deem as the best or the most authentic."[54] He then cautions readers against holding "one particular Muslim identity as the most authoritative."[55]

Another significant issue in this discussion is whether religion should be used as the primary marker of a person's identity. In casual conversations with people, I occasionally hear someone refer to another person as "a Muslim." This person, however, though labeled a Muslim, may not pray five times a day or recite the Muslim confession of faith. Their only tie to Islam may come through Muslim grandparents. Should they really be called a Muslim? What complicates the matter is that in Islam people are often identified first by their religion. Riaz Hassan, for example, writes, "Religion is the essence of Muslim identity."[56] Is it really? I know people who want to be called Muslims, but according to Muslim standards they would not qualify. They may bear a Muslim name, enjoy fasting during Ramadan, and desire to be called a Muslim, but they do not practice any other rituals. Should they be refused the title "Muslim" because they do not pass the test of piety? I often remind my students that they will encounter Muslims not just at the local mosque. Rather, they will meet lots of Muslims outside the mosque who still feel they belong to the Muslim community. Thus, the question of religion being the essence of Muslim identity is more complex than often thought.

Should we then continue to use such statements as "Muslims believe" or "Muslims do"? I argue that by using the term *Muslim* as the sole identity marker for people, we run the risk of misrepresenting them. There are many Muslim identities. Christian sociologist Kathryn Kraft relates her encounter with a Muslim professor. She writes, "He was proud to call himself a heretical Muslim who refused to follow the religion he inherited from his family, but he was a Muslim even so."[57] Even among Muslims who self-identify as Muslims there is great diversity. It is crucial when exploring Muslim identities to measure the vitality of faith, religious patterns, and religious symbols. But we also need to ask, as anthropologist Gabriele Marranci does today, how a person self-identifies and feels about being Muslim:

[54]Hughes, *Muslim Identities*, 9.
[55]Ibid.
[56]Riaz Hassan, "On Being Religious: Patterns of Religious Commitment in Muslim Societies," *Muslim World* 97, no. 3 (2007): 437-49.
[57]Kathryn Ann Kraft, *Searching for Heaven in the Real World: A Sociological Discussion of Conversion in the Arab World* (Eugene, OR: Wipf and Stock, 2012), 2.

My explanation of personal identity suggests that to the question "what is a Muslim?" we cannot answer merely by highlighting cultural symbolic elements of reference to Islam as codified religion (a very common practice even in recent anthropological studies). Rather, to the question "what is a Muslim?" we need to answer "a human being." In other words, "I'm Muslim" means "I feel to be Muslim."

I conclude that it is by focusing on that "feel to be" more than on the symbolic "Muslim" that we can understand how Muslims express, form and develop their identity beyond the imposed stereotypes.[58]

Through this approach, Marranci suggests "that we may understand Islam as a *map* of discourses on how to 'feel Muslim.'"[59]

Missiology must wrestle with these questions if it wants to accurately represent Muslims and genuinely connect with them. When someone in a church says, "I love Muslims," what does it actually mean? What does the church mantra "I love Muslims" really mean? It does not mean anything until one talks to a Muslim person, visits a Muslim person, and eats with a Muslim person, after which one can say, "I love one Muslim person." And after an encounter with a second Muslim, one can say, "I love two Muslims." Christian anthropologist Miriam Adeney highlights the importance of looking at Muslims not in general terms but as unique individuals. In her research on Muslim women who have become followers of Christ, she writes, "Politically active women, religious fundamentalists, professional women, settled village and town women, and nomads—the world of Arab women is a rich mosaic. But in the end, every woman is an exception."[60]

Should we therefore consider all Muslims as exceptions in order to better relate to them? John L. Esposito and Dalia Mogahed, in their research on what one billion Muslims think, want to "understand Muslims holistically."[61] Instead of looking at Islam through "sensational headlines and violent images," they seek to understand Islam through "the actual views of everyday

[58]Gabriele Marranci, *The Anthropology of Islam* (Oxford: Berg, 2008), 11.
[59]Ibid., 8.
[60]Miriam Adeney, *Daughters of Islam: Building Bridges with Muslim Women* (Downers Grove, IL: InterVarsity Press, 2002), 43.
[61]John L. Esposito and Dalia Mogahed, *Who Speaks for Islam? What a Billion Muslims Really Think* (New York: Gallup, 2007), 1.

Muslims."[62] In their view, every individual Muslim voice contributes to an understanding of Islam and Muslims.

What should we say in conclusion? Is there one Muslim identity that represents all people who recite the Islamic confession of faith? There are certainly beliefs and practices that people share, but no two Muslims are exactly alike—unless someone cloned one, and even then their education would shape them differently. Nonetheless, is there a sign that would identify all Muslims? The confession of faith probably functions in this capacity, but apart from some basic tenets of faith and particular practices that identify members of the same Islamic denomination or branch, Muslims are as diverse as the rest of humanity. What does this mean for mission? We should look at Muslims not only through the lens of their religious beliefs and practices but also through the way they define themselves.

Discursive Tradition

Another important approach to defining Islam and Muslim societies has been offered by Muslim anthropologist Talal Asad. I believe his work may provide some valuable insight into this discussion. Asad offers the "notion of Islam as a discursive tradition."[63] He defines this term as follows: "An Islamic discursive tradition is simply a tradition of Muslim discourse that addresses itself to conceptions of the Islamic past and future, with reference to a particular Islamic practice in the present." Asad believes one cannot understand Islam without this ongoing conversation between the past and the present, the universal and the local. To him, the discursive tradition "includes and relates itself to the founding texts of the Qur'an and the hadith. Islam is neither a distinctive social structure nor a heterogeneous collection of beliefs, artifacts, customs and morals. It is a tradition."[64] Some anthropologists have critiqued Asad for putting too much emphasis on theology and the sacred texts. The problem with the discursive tradition, according to Samuli Schielke, is that "there is too much Islam in the anthropology of Islam."[65] But Asad offers nevertheless a model that acknowledges

---

[62]Ibid., x.

[63]As quoted in Lukens-Bull, "Between Text and Practice," 44.

[64]Ibid.

[65]Samuli Schielke, "Second Thoughts About the Anthropology of Islam, or How to Make Sense of Grand Schemes in Everyday Life," *Zentrum Moderner Orient Working Papers*, no. 2 (2010): 1.

a heterogeneity of religious practices while at the same time an aspiration for coherence within Islam.

Lukens-Bull comments, "As a discursive tradition, Islam is constantly being reshaped to fit with an ever-changing world."[66] Discursive tradition thus becomes a useful model for describing the continuity of Islam in various cultural contexts. This notion seems closely related to the one elaborated by Wilfred Cantwell Smith in his book *The Meaning and End of Religion*.[67] In this book Smith prefers to talk about cumulative tradition rather than religion as a closed system. He writes,

> By "cumulative tradition," I mean the entire mass of overt objective data that constitute the historical deposit, as it were, of the past religious life of the community in question: temples, scriptures, theological systems, dance, patterns, legal and other social institutions, conventions, moral codes, myths, and so on; anything that can be and is transmitted from one person, one generation, to another, and that an historian can observe.[68]

But to Smith, the cumulative tradition is not enough. Faith, or "the inner religious experience or involvement of a particular person," is also important. The link between faith and cumulative tradition to him is "the living person."[69]

Along the same lines, Hughes proposes the concepts of inheritance and creation and calls attention to the "complexity of Islam as a social formation and the ways in which inheritance and creation contribute to this process of imagining different Islams."[70] Bowen identifies concepts such as selection and creativity to explain this process. He writes,

> Even as Muslims align globally around their major obligations—to pray, to sacrifice, to carry out the pilgrimage to Mecca—they also exercise choice and creativity in how they understand and carry out those rituals. From these opportunities for selection and creativity comes the observable diversity of religious lives within and across Muslim social worlds.[71]

---

[66]Lukens-Bull, "Between Text and Practice," 46.
[67]Wilfred Cantwell Smith, *The Meaning and End of Religion* (Minneapolis: Fortress, 1991).
[68]Ibid., 156.
[69]Ibid.
[70]Hughes, *Muslim Identities*, 11.
[71]John R. Bowen, *A New Anthropology of Islam* (Cambridge: Cambridge University Press, 2012), 42.

Other scholars take this reasoning even further. They don't just underline heterogeneity. To them, ambivalence and fragmentation are an integral part of traditions. Schielke, for example, writes,

> To find ways to account for both the ambivalence of people's everyday lives and the often perfectionist ideals of good life, society and self they articulate, I argue that we may have to talk a little less about traditions, discourses and powers and a little more about the existential and pragmatic sensibilities of living a life in a complex and often troubling world. By broadening our focus to include the concerns, practice and experience of everyday life in its various moments and directions, we may eventually also be better able to make sense of the significance of a grand scheme like Islam in it.[72]

Even el-Zein, quoted earlier on the concept of several islams, believes that we cannot reduce Islam to an entity, but rather that we should look at the various categories of culture, economy, and religion as "articulations of structural relations." He suggests listening to Muslims themselves talk about "Islam" and their analyses of "the relations which produce its meaning." He continues,

> Beginning from this assumption, the system can be entered and explored in depth from any point, for there are no absolute discontinuities anywhere within it—there are no autonomous entities and each point within the system is ultimately accessible from every other point.[73]

Looking at Islam as a discursive tradition renders the task of defining Islam even more complex, requiring careful and sophisticated exploration. Varisco contends, "Searching for the idea of an anthropology of Islam, I argue, should not lead us beyond ideology and theology but rather probe these very powerful discursive traditions through thick description of ethnographic contexts."[74]

Conclusion

In this brief presentation I have examined the numerous ways scholars have proposed to respond to the question of whether there is one Islam or several

---

[72]Schielke, "Second Thoughts," 1.
[73]el-Zein, "Beyond Ideology" (1977), 251-52.
[74]Varisco, *Islam Obscured*, 160.

islams. I have described how missiologists and missionaries have also adopted different views on this question. We should not be afraid to address this diversity (and its implications for current debates on the insider movement, forms of dialogue, Islamic violence, etc.) in our current missiological discussions.

Let me conclude by making a few recommendations. First, I suggest that theologians and human and social scientists conduct an ongoing dialogue on this issue. Missiologist Phil Parshall states that "sociology and theology are inseparable components of Islam."[75] We cannot study the texts without looking at individuals, societies, and context.

Second, I believe it is important to revisit missiological terminology. Scholars outside the field of missiology have devised varied expressions to explain diversity. Hughes talks about "versions of Islam,"[76] "various constructions of Muslim belief and practice,"[77] and "an overlapping set of Islams."[78] Professor of international politics Raymond William Baker talks about the "many incarnations of Islam."[79] Scholar Vartan Gregorian talks about Islam as "a mosaic, not a monolith."[80] Esposito and Mogahed claim that "religiously, culturally, economically, and politically, there are multiple images and realities of Islam and of Muslims."[81] We definitely need to abandon the view of one monolithic and static view of Islam and of Muslim societies.

Similar attempts should be made in missiological circles to create analytical categories that allow Christians to make sense of the diverse manifestations of Islam. John Azumah, for example, talks about the various faces of Islam (he identifies four,[82] and then later five[83]). Nabeel Jabbour also

---

[75]Phil Parshall, *Beyond the Mosque: Christians Within Muslim Community* (Grand Rapids: Baker, 1985), 177.

[76]Hughes, *Muslim Identities*, 274.

[77]Ibid., 2.

[78]Ibid., 10.

[79]Raymond William Baker, *One Islam, Many Muslim Worlds: Spirituality, Identity, and Resistance Across Islamic Lands* (New York: Oxford University Press, 2015), 3.

[80]Vartan Gregorian, *Islam: A Mosaic, Not a Monolith* (Washington, DC: Brookings Institution Press, 2003).

[81]Esposito and Mogahed, *Who Speaks for Islam?*, 2.

[82]John Azumah, "Christian Responses to Islam: A Struggle for the Soul of Christianity," *Church & Society in Asia Today* 13, no. 2 (August 2010): 83-94.

[83]John Azumah, "The Five Faces of Islam," *ScholarLeader Insights*, www.scholarleaders.org/wp -content/uploads/2016/10/Five-Faces-of-Islam-Azumah.pdf, accessed March 17, 2017.

discusses "the many faces of Islam."[84] I particularly like the category Cliff Geertz uses when he references "family resemblances."[85] According to Dale Eickelman, Geertz

> suggests a strategy of comparison based upon "family resemblances" rather than upon typological classifications which presume in advance the essential features of phenomena being compared. The result is to depict in concrete instances how Islam can remain catholic to "an extraordinary variety of mentalities . . . and still remain a specific and persuasive force with a shape and identity of its own."[86]

Have we answered the question of whether there is one Islam or many islams? I believe the answer cannot be simply yes or no. This might be disappointing, but I believe this ambivalence cannot be avoided. We could perhaps look at Islam as an open system (instead of defining it as one static and monolithic entity or as a binary tension between two entities, which is far too essentialist). Islam could also be conceived as a web or as several webs that intersect without one single center. Whoever is defining Islam, then, could decide which hub they choose for their analysis. Perhaps we could also do more adjectivizing of Islam or Muslims. In other words, we could avoid using these terms in a standalone manner, without a qualifier. Thus we could talk about the Islam of a particular group. Or if we believe there is a core (for example, a shared belief), we would define how wide we want to draw the circles around the core. I suggest that we take this conversation into every church and mission organization so that Christians learn to engage with what sometimes looks like dissonance or ambivalence in the definition of Islam. Let's not be afraid of these dissonances. We may be surprised by the variety of Islamic representations, just as Muslims may be surprised by the great diversity within Christianity. Finally, if there is one lesson that we can take away from the discussion of one or several islams, it is that Islam cannot be defined in one sentence. I believe that our task as missiologists is to expand the definition of Islam to make it reflect the realities of the people we encounter in mission.

---

[84]Nabeel Jabbour, *The Many Faces of Islam* (Oasis Audio, 2001), compact disc.
[85]Eickelman, "Study of Islam," 61.
[86]Ibid.

List of Contributors

Martin Accad is based at the Arab Baptist Theological Seminary in Lebanon, where he founded and directs the Institute of Middle East Studies. With his PhD from the University of Oxford, he teaches on Islam, Middle Eastern Christianity, and Christian-Muslim relations both at ABTS and Fuller. He is also cofounder and senior fellow on the Middle East program of the recently launched Centre on Religion and Global Affairs. Dr. Accad has contributed many articles and chapters to international academic publications and is currently working on a book on Christian-Muslim relations.

Cathy Hine earned her PhD from Australian National University and has pursued ongoing research in Islam, women, change, and mission, with experience working in Pakistan and the Middle East. She was part of the International Leadership Team of Interserve until November 2014. In September 2015, Dr. Hine launched When Women Speak, a network creating space for women to share and debate their work on mission, women, and Islam.

Philip Jenkins is Distinguished Professor of History at Baylor University and serves as codirector for the program on historical studies of religion in Baylor's Institute for Studies of Religion. Dr. Jenkins's major current interests include the study of global Christianity, new and emerging religious movements, and twentieth-century US history (chiefly post-1970s). He has published twenty-four books, and his works have been translated into ten languages.

David L. Johnston came back to the United States after sixteen years as a pastor and teacher in Algeria, Egypt, and the West Bank. He earned a PhD from Fuller's School of Intercultural Studies with a specialty in Islamics. Since then he has pursued his research in Islamics and has taught as an adjunct lecturer at Yale University, the University of Pennsylvania, and St. Joseph's University. Besides a number of articles on contemporary Islam published in leading academic journals, Dr. Johnston is the author of *Earth, Empire and Sacred Text: Muslims and Christians as Trustees of Creation* (2010). He blogs on his website HumanTrustees.org.

Rick Love is a global citizen who has lived in Indonesia and England. He has worked for over thirty-five years with Muslims and has enjoyed their hospitality in every major region of the world. Currently the president of Peace Catalyst International, Dr. Love has a DMin in urban studies from Westminster Theological Seminary as well as a PhD in intercultural studies from Fuller Theological Seminary. He has published four books, including *Grace and Truth: Toward Christlike Relationships with Muslims* (2013) and *Peace Catalysts: Resolving Conflict in Our Families, Organizations and Communities* (2014).

Gordon Nickel researches the interaction between Islam and the gospel. In addition to a recent monograph on early commentaries on the Qur'an, he has been published widely in scholarly journals, collections, and encyclopedias. After earning his PhD from the University of Alberta, Dr. Nickel taught in Pakistan and India for ten years. More recently he has taught on Islam and the Qur'an at Associated Canadian Theological Schools and several universities, including the University of Calgary, where he is adjunct professor of Islamic studies.

Evelyne A. Reisacher is associate professor of Islamic studies and intercultural relations at Fuller's School of Intercultural Studies, where she also received her PhD. She has published articles on gender issues in Islam, Muslim-Christian relations, and intercultural relations in mission. Dr. Reisacher is the general editor of *Toward Respectful Understanding and Witness Among Muslims: Essays in Honor of J. Dudley Woodberry* (2012) and the author of *Joyful Witness in the Muslim World: Sharing the Gospel in Everyday Encounter* (2016).

David Emmanuel Singh is research tutor at the Oxford Centre for Mission Studies in the United Kingdom, where he also did his PhD. He currently serves as editor for *Transformation*, a SAGE journal. Originally from India, he has been researching and supervising postgraduates since 2003. His areas of interest are Islam and interfaith relations in South Asia. Dr. Singh is the author of numerous articles, edited volumes, and research monographs.

John Jay Travis received his PhD from the Fuller Theological Seminary School of Intercultural Studies, where he is now an affiliate assistant professor. He is coeditor of *Understanding Insider Movements: Disciples of Jesus Within Diverse Religious Communities* (2015) as well as the author of numerous chapters and journal articles on ministry in Muslim contexts, contextualization, and healing prayer. Dr. Travis has lived most of his adult life in Asian Muslim communities and presently resides in South Asia.

Nimi Wariboko is the Walter G. Muelder Professor of Social Ethics at Boston University School of Theology. In his scholarship he employs African social traditions that are common to both Christians and Muslims as a foundation for interreligious dialogue in Nigeria. Dr. Wariboko has advised the Nigerian government on the economic dimensions of peace building and conflict resolution with regard to Christian-Muslim relations. He is the author and editor of over fifteen books.

Author Index

Abdel-Samad, Hamed, 51
Abdolah, Kader, 43
Abduh, Muhammad, 18, 20
Abu-bin-Almaz, 93
Abū-Ḥanīfa, 86, 149
Abu Lughod, Lila, 113, 234
Abū Yūsuf, 149
Abu Zaid, Nasr Hamid, 43
Adeney, Miriam, 236
Afghani, Jamal ad-Din al-, 18, 20
Ahdar, Rex, 177, 178
Ahmad, Mirza Ghulam, 96, 97, 170
Ahmad, Sadaf, 117, 118
Ahmed, Akbar S., 221, 229, 230, 231
Ahmed, Leila, 168
Ahmed, Sara, 104
Ake, Claude, 66, 67, 74
Akhtar, Shabbir, 148
Akinade, Akintude E., 57
Ali, Imran Anwar, 129
'Ali, Safdar, 99
Alsoswa, Amat Al-Alim, 127
Ambros, Arne A., 141
Anani, Khalil al-, 165
Anderson, Jonathan A., 175
Andrae, Tor, 146
An-Na'im, Abdullahi Ahmed, 151, 152, 159
Aristotle, 50
Aroney, Nicholas, 177, 178
Arskal, Salim, 169
Asad, Talal, 237
Assad, Bashar al-, 166
Assad, Hafez al-, 22, 23, 29, 166
Ataturk, 167
Atif, Laiq Ahmed, 143, 148
Attahiru, Shehu Muhammad, II, 68
Augustine, 27
Awad, Abed, 177

Awad, Najib George, 28, 29
Ayaz-bin-Mahmood, 94
Ayoob, Mohammed, 232
Azmeh, Aziz al-, 229
Azumah, John, 26, 64, 240
Bailey, Kenneth, 120
Baker, Raymond William, 240
Banna, Hassan al-, 46, 165
Barēlwī, Aḥmad Riḍa Khān, 150
Barnes, Andrew E., 68
Barlas, Asma, 122, 123, 124
Bass, Jonathan, 107
Bayat, Asef, 19, 21, 22, 231
Bearman, P. J., 141, 145
Ben Ali, Zine El Abidine, 172, 173
Bencheikh, Soheib, 52
Beglinger, Martin, 47
Bell, David, 104
Bennett, Clinton, 221
Bennett, Linda Rae, 114
Berger, Maurits S., 177
Bhadmus, Muhammed, 92
Bhutto, Benazir, 171, 186, 214
Bibi, Asia, 136
Bidar, Abdennour, 51, 52, 53
Bin-Almaz, Abu, 88
Bin Mahmood, Ajaz, 106
Bodman, Herbert L., 221
Bosch, David J., 175, 196
Bosworth, C. E., 144
Bourguiba, 167
Bowcott, Owen, 179
Bowen, John R., 177, 178, 179, 238
Brewster, Tom and Betty Sue, 191, 192
Brinner, William, 100
Brotherton, Bob, 104
Brown, Daniel W., 226
Browner, J., 104
Brueggemann, Walter, 35

Buehler, Arthur F., 101
Buergener, Elisabeth, 114, 118
Bukhārī, al-, 142
Burgoyne, S. R., 97, 98, 103
Bustros, Evelyne, 127
Calder, Norman, 138, 143
Cannon, Mae Elise, 217
Carr, Jimmy, 92
Cerić, Mustafa, 45
Cesari, Jocelyne, 166, 167, 168, 170
Chandapilla, Christian P. T., 120
Chapman, Colin, 215
Chattopadhyay, Bankim Chandra, 93
Chishti, Moinuddin, 101
Chodkiewicz, Michel, 101
Choudary, Anjem, 41
Chrisman, Laura, 113
Christoffersen, Lisbet, 177
Cohen, Nick, 44
Cooper, Dale, 82
Courtney, Jeremy, 214
Cragg, Kenneth, 154, 155
Creighton, Louise, 97
Daftary, Farhad, 138
Dale, Moyra, 117, 119
Deleuze, Gilles, 28
De Vries, Gert J. J., 141, 152, 153
Diakhou, Maba, 63
Dodd, Vikram, 42
Doğan, Mehmet A., 107
Donohue, John, 18
Dovlo, Elom, 68
Dowie, John Alexander, 96, 97
Duncan, Andres, 208
Durie, Mark, 155
Dyrness, William A., 199
Edwards, Jonathan, 175
Eickelman, Dale F., 225, 228, 230, 233, 241

Ekeh, Peter, 67
Ellis, Mark, 157, 176
Elmore, Gerald T., 101
Emon, Anver M., 157, 176
English, Donald, 210
Erdogan, Recep Tayyip, 167
Escobar, Samuel, 31
Esposito, John L., 18, 82, 85,
   171, 172, 174, 185, 186, 187,
   236, 240
Evans, Edward, 113
Fadl, Khaled Abou el-, 159
Fakirbhai, Dhanjibhai, 102
Falola, Toyin, 76
Feldman, Noah, 161, 162, 164
Fides, Agenzia, 152
Flood, Gavin, 93
Fodio, Usman dan, 68
Fouadgirgis, Hany, 104
Francis, Alexander, 88
Friedmann, Yohanan, 140,
   142, 144, 147, 149
Fukuyama, Francis, 14
Gairdner, William Temple, 98,
   105
Gall, Carlotta, 135
Gardezi, Fauzia, 128
Garrison, David, 190, 191
Gaudeul, Jean-Marie, 188
Gbadamasi, T. G. O., 62
Geertz, Clifford, 221, 232, 233,
   241
Ghannouchi, Rached, 173-74
Ghazali, Zainab al-, 127
Ghazzawi, Razan, 126
Gibb, H. A. R., 142
Glahn, Benjamin, 157, 176
Goffman, Carolyn, 107
Goheen, Michael W., 225
Gohir, Shaista, 180
Goldstein, Tara, 225
Goldziher, Ignaz, 223
Goodstein, Laurie, 222
Gort, Jerald, 93
Graham, Franklin, 213
Green, Lisa Cannon, 213, 222
Greenlee, David, 113, 189
Greer, Amanda, 225
Gregorian, Vartan, 240
Grierson, Jamie, 42
Griswold, Wendy, 92
Guattari, Félix, 28

Hackett, Conrad, 38
Haddad, Yvonne, 18
Hajja Faiza, 116
Hallaq, Wael, 159, 160, 161
Hamid, Shadi, 172
Hasina, Sheikh, 186
Hassan, Riaz, 235
Hawthorne, Stephen C., 192
Hazelton, Claire Kodah, 43
Hefner, Robert W., 163, 165
Heldke, Lisa, 114
Hertig, Young Lee, 133
Hidayatullah, Aysha A., 121,
   123, 124
Hiebert, Paul, 192
hooks, bell, 114, 131
Hoover, Jon, 142, 144
Horton, Robin, 64, 66
Houssney, Georges, 224
Huckins, Jon, 216
Huda, Anisah, 117
Hughes, Aaron W., 225, 234,
   238, 240
Hughes, Alicia, 103
Hughes, Arnold, 63
Huntington, Samuel, 12, 14, 15,
   16, 17, 28, 31
Hurd, Elizabeth Shakman, 223
Hussain, Amir, 232
Hussain, Ed, 214
Hussain, Neelum, 128
Hussain, Zakir, 143
Hussein, Saddam, 166
Hyderabadi, Shaykh Fasih, 86
Ibn ʿĀbidīn, 149
Ibn al-Bazzāz, 147, 149
Ibn-Anas, Mālik, 149
Ibn-ʿArabi, 90, 101
Ibn Ḥanbal, Aḥmad, 149
Ibn Hishām, 142
Ibn Isḥaq, 142
Ibn Khaldūn, 221
Ibn-Rushd, 50
Ibn Saʿd, 142
Ibn Taymiyya, 144, 147, 148, 149
Ikramullah, Shaista
   Suhrawardy, 127
Imaduddin, Mawlawi, 96, 98,
   99
Iwuchukwu, Marinus C., 57,
   68, 69, 72
ʿIyāḍ, Qāḍī, 142, 146, 147

Jabbour, Nabeel, 240, 241
Jaffrelot, Christophe, 83
Jahangir, Asma, 126
Jamal, Tazim, 104
Jamous, Raymond, 104
Jansen, Henry, 93
Jeffery, Arthur, 101
Jilani, Hina, 126, 129
Johanns, Pierre, 102
Johnston, Douglas, 217
Jones, Kenneth W., 85, 96
Jones, Lindsay, 141
Joye, Afrie Songco, 120
Kaba, Fode, 63
Kaiser, Walter C., Jr., 208
Kamil, Maqsood, 96
Karimi, Ahmad Milad, 50
Karman, Tawakkol, 126
Kartini, Raden Adjeng, 127
Katongole, Emmanuel, 204
Kelsey, Morton T., 194
Kendhammer, Brandon, 73
Khaled, Amr, 53
Khan, Ahmed Raza, 85
Khan, Nighat Said, 129
Khan, Nizam Osman Ali, 83, 89
Khan, Sadiq, 54
Khan, Wahiduddin, 148, 150,
   152
Khizruddin, 90, 91, 100
Khomeini, Ayatollah, 167
Khorchide, Mouhanad, 48,
   49, 50
Khwaza-Gharib-Nawaz, 89, 90
Kindi, al-, 50
King, Martin Luther, Jr., 107,
   210
Kings, Graham, 103
Klauck, Hans-Joseph, 141
Kraft, Charles, 192
Kraft, Kathryn Ann, 97, 99, 235
Kreinath, Jens, 229, 232
Kukah, Matthew Hassan, 57
Kumar, Sanjay, 83
Kwame, Osei, 65
Lamoreaux, John C., 194
Lashley, C., 104
Laude, Patrick, 105
Layth, al-, 149
Lee, Matthew T., 103
Leibniz, Gottfried Wilhelm, 50
Lekhramj, Pundit, 96

Lienemann-Perrin, Christine, 120
Lincoln, Andrew T., 205
Lindhal, Victoria, 133
Lipner, J. J., 93
Lombardi, Clark B., 165
Longkumer, Atola, 120
Lot, 102, 104
Lugard, Frederick, 68, 69
Lukens-Bull, Ronald A., 223, 226, 228, 237, 238
Ly, Michael, 217
Ma, Wonsuk, 102
Maalouf, Amin, 17
McAuliffe, Jane Dammen, 141, 146, 150
McCaskie, T. C., 66
McDonald, M. V., 143
McGarvey, Kathleen, 57
Magid, Mohamed, 216
Mahmood, Saba, 116-20
Makiya, Kanan, 44
Mallett, Alex, 142, 146
Manderson, Lenore, 114
March, Andrew, 160
Marks, G., 192
Marranci, Gabriele, 235, 236
Marshall, Paul, 135, 139, 152
Martin, Richard C., 165, 170
Martyn, Henry, 103
Mary, 103, 106
Masih, Abdul, 103
Massignon, Louis, 104
Maturidi, al-, 50
Mawardi, al-, 160, 161
Mawdudi, Abul al-, 165
Mayer, Ann Elizabeth, 156, 176
Meddeb, Abdelwahab, 51
Meral, Ziya, 26
Merrill, Dean, 214
Michel, Thomas F., 144
Milbank, John, 178
Miller, Duane, 99, 100
Minda Yimene, Ababu, 89
Mogahed, Dalia, 236, 240
Moll, Rob, 217
Momodou-Lamin, 63
Monchanin, Jules, 102
Morrison, A., 104
Mounce, Robert H., 215
Mullins, Jim, 217
Mumtaz, Khawar, 128

Mumtaz, Samiya, 128
Mumtaz, Sofia, 129
Musharraf, Pervez, 172
Musk, Bill, 227
Muslim, 142
Nasr, Sayyid Husain, 101, 231
Nasser, Gamal Abdel, 19, 165
Nawawī, al-, 140
Nawaz, Maajid, 54
Netton, Ian Richard, 101
Niebuhr, Richard, 232
Nielsen, Jørgen S., 177
Niles, David T., 120
Nolland, John, 211
Noorani, A. G., 83
Novriantoni, 53
Obadare, Ebenezer, 70
Obasanjo, Olusegun, 74
O'Connor, Peg, 114
O'Gorman, K., 104
Ojo, Matthews A., 67, 76, 77
Olupona, Jacob Kehinde, 62
Packer, George, 151, 152
Padwick, Constance E., 145, 154, 233
Page, Meg, 133
Parekh, Manilal, 102
Parshall, Phil, 113, 133, 200, 227, 240
Patel, Pragna, 180
Peel, John D. Y., 60, 61, 62, 65, 66, 69, 70
Perfect, David, 63
Peters, Rudolph, 141, 152, 153
Pierce, Steven, 67
Pierret, Thomas, 22
Pinch, William, 93
Polh, Christine D., 208
Polish, Daniel, 232
Poloma, Margaret M., 103
Possamai, Adam, 169
Post, Stephen G., 103
Powell, Avril, 96
Presler, Henry Hughes, 87, 100
Procházka, Stephan, 141
Pruzan-Jørgensen, Julie Elisabeth, 127
Puente, Christina de la, 145
Qadri, Mumtaz, 135, 149
Qaradawi, Yusuf al-, 44, 47
Qasmi, Obaidullah, 142, 143, 150

Qutb, Sayyid, 19, 25, 152
Racine, Jean-Luc, 129
Rahman, Fazlur, 123
Rahman, Sherry, 152
Ramadan, Said, 46
Ramadan, Tariq, 19, 20, 46, 137, 138
Razvi, Qasim, 84
Redfield, Robert, 226, 228
Reif, Ruth Renée, 50
Rice, Chris, 204
Richardson, James T., 169, 180
Rida, Rashid, 18, 20
Rippin, Andrew, 137, 138, 223
Robert, Dana, 133
Roberts, Bob, 217
Roberts, Bob, Jr., 216
Robinson, Mike, 104
Rodriguez, Jason, 42
Roggema, Barbara, 145
Rosner, Brian S., 208
Ross, Cathy, 120, 121, 131, 133
Ross, Kenneth R., 102
Rousselin, Mathieu, 172
Roy, Olivier, 13, 24, 25, 41
Ruano, Delfina Serrano, 146, 147
Rushdie, Salman, 139, 142, 148
Ryan, Patrick J., SJ, 232, 233
Saada, Tass, 214
Sabri, Amjad, 135
Sachedina, Abdulaziz, 157, 176
Saeed, Abdullah, 140, 141
Saeed, Hassan, 140, 141
Saigol, Rubina, 128
Saleh, Walid A., 145
Samaj, Arya, 96
Sani, Ahmed, 73
Sanneh, Lamin, 63, 64, 82, 103
Schenk, Arnfrid, 49
Scherman, Taylor C., 84
Schielke, Samuli, 232, 237, 239
Schimmel, Annemarie, 145, 146
Selwyn, Tom, 104
Shafi'i, Hasan Mahmud 'Abd Al-Latif al-, 124, 144
Shafik, Doria, 127
Shaheed, Fareeda, 127, 128, 129, 131
Shankar, Shobana, 69
Sharan, Abhishek, 93
Sha'rawi, Huda, 127

Sharif, Manal al-, 126
Sharkey, Heather J., 107
Shaw, Dan, 192
Shea, Nina, 135, 139, 152
Shihaa, Rose, 127
Shubin, Russel G., 192
Siddiqi, Mona, 179
Siddiqi, Muzzamil, 221
Sikand, Yoginder, 84, 87
Smith, Christine, 172
Smith, Diane, 216
Smith, Wilfred Cantwell, 238
Sonn, Tamara, 171, 172, 174, 229
Spiewak, Martin, 49
Spinoza, Baruch
Spivak, Gayatri Chakravorty, 113
Stacey, Vivienne, 227
Stephen, M., 102
Stetzer, Ed, 213, 216
Stott, John, 205
Stricker, Beth, 133
Strong, Cynthia A., 133
Sukarnoputri, Megawati, 186
Sunquist, Scott W., 158, 175, 176
Swartley, Keith E., 227
Swigart, Jer, 216
Ṭabarī, al-, 143
Taha, Mahmoud Mohamed, 22, 23, 151, 152
Tahhan, Bassam, 43
Talman, Harley, 196

Taseer, Salman, 135
Taylor, Anthony, 196
Thabit, Labibah, 127
Thapar, Romila, 93
Thomas, David, 142, 146
Thompson, LaNette W., 133
Thomson, Mike, 84
Tibi, Bassam, 45, 53
Tilak, Narayan Vaman, 102
Tohidi, Nayereh, 221
Topcu, Canan, 49
Travis, Anna, 200
Trump, Donald J., 177
Turki, Abdelmagid, 142, 144, 147
Turner, Bryan S., 169, 180
Umaru, Thaddeus Byimui, 70
Varisco, Daniel Martin, 229, 239
Varma, Bhagya Reddy, 88
Vaughan, Olufemi, 58, 60, 70, 71, 73
Vaugier-Chatterjee, Anne, 83
Verkuyl, Johannes, 82
Vishwanathan, Gauri, 93
Volf, Miroslav, 207
Voll, John O., 18, 171, 172, 174
Vroom, Hendrik, 93
Wadud, Amina, 122, 123, 124
Wagner, Mark S., 140, 142, 144, 147, 148, 149
Watson, David, 197

Watt, W. Montgomery, 143
Waugh, Earl H., 229
Wensinck, A. J., 144
Wheeler, Brannon, 100
Whiteman, Darrell, 192
Wiederhold, Lutz, 140, 141, 144
Wilbanks, Dana W., 177
Williams, Patrick, 113
Williams, Rowan, 125, 131, 178
Winter, Ralph D., 192
Witherington, Ben, III, 205, 210
Wood, Roy, 104
Woodberry, J. Dudley, 113, 133, 189, 192, 223, 227
Wray, Yvette, 133
Wright, Christopher J. H., 130
Yaḥsubī, ʿIyā al-, 136
Yong, Amos, 157, 175, 176, 177
Young, Iris Marion, 114
Zaman, Muhammad Qasim, 162, 169, 170
Zein, Abdul Hamid el-, 228, 229, 230, 239
Zeynelabidin, Emel, 50
Zia, Khaleda, 186
Zia-ul-Haq, Muhammad, 128, 172
Zine, Jasmin, 225
Zubrzycki, Genevieve, 92
Zwemer, Samuel M., 98, 155, 226, 227, 228

Subject Index

Abbasid caliphate, 159, 160
Abraham, 32, 102, 130, 157
  seed of, 32
Abrahamic Alliance, 177
Abrahamic religions, 60-62,
  64-66, 70, 75
activism, activists, 42, 54, 94,
  107, 109, 115, 126, 127-29, 131,
  167, 208-9
  Islamic, 159, 167
  religious, 105
  women, 116, 126-27, 130
advocacy, 180
Afghanistan, 90, 101, 156, 162,
  214
Africa, 16, 31, 137, 184, 193
  East, 190
  North, 40-41, 130, 190
  West, 59, 63-64, 66, 77-78,
    80-81, 160, 190
African Calvary Guards,
  88-89, 91, 93
African traditional religions
  (ATR), 60-64, 80
Afro-Indian, 88-89, 93, 106
ahl-al-kitāb, 85
Ahl-e Hadith, 85-87
  Ahl-e Hadith-Deoband,
    84, 108
Ahmadi, 170, 185
ʿAlawites, 23, 29
al-Azhar University, 165
Albania, 38, 40
Alevi, 167, 185
Algeria, 40, 55, 156
Al-Huda movement, 117
al-Qaeda, 24
al-Ṭā'if, 143
America, 14, 177, 210,
  North America, 48, 177
Amritsar, 98
Anglican church, 103
animism, 63, 200, 226, 228
apostasy, 139-40, 144, 147, 149,
  151, 156, 173

apostles, 191, 195, 199, 215
as-salaf as-salih, 19
Arab Spring, 20, 52, 157, 171-72,
  176
Arab world, 13, 26, 172, 190
Arabian Peninsula, 184
Asante, 62, 65-66
Asia, 16, 31, 137, 193
  Eastern South, 190
  South, 41, 82, 85, 88, 90,
    94-96, 100-102, 108,
    135-36, 147-49, 165, 184,
    187
  Southeast, 99, 184, 187
  Western South, 190
Association for the Protection
  of the Environment (APE),
  126
asylum seeker, 104
Athens, 102
Australia, 158
Baath party, 22
Babri Masjid, 93
Baddibu (kingdom of), 63
Baghdad, 160
Baha'is, 13, 18
Bangladesh, 140, 186
Barelwi, 85, 87, 149
basti, 94, 88-89, 91, 105, 106
Beatitudes, 107, 205
Beijing, 121
Beirut, 25
Berar, 83
Berean, 196
Bible translation, 198, 200
Birmingham, 53
birth rate, 39-40
blasphemy, 6, 135-37, 139-41,
  143, 146-50, 152-53, 156
Boko Haram, 25
Bosnia, 40, 45
Britain, 12, 42, 54, 68, 71, 88,
  158, 170, 179
British, 69, 72, 93
Buddhism, 13, 169, 200

Bulgaria, 38
C1-C6 Spectrum, 189-91, 200
Cairo, 126, 165, 232
caliph, caliphate, 26, 119,
  160-61, 173, 214
capitalism, 67, 74
Carpathians, 38
Catholicism, Roman Catholic
  Church, 27, 53, 106, 168, 178
  Catholics, 38, 53, 88-90,
    94, 105
Center for Race and Gender,
  177
Charlie Hebdo massacre, 52,
  139
child custody, 179-80
Chishti, Chishtiyya, 89, 90, 101
Christ-centered communities,
  189
Christendom, 15, 31
  post-Christendom world,
    30, 33-34
  pre-Christendom world, 30
Christian-Muslim relations,
  57-61, 70-71, 75, 78, 80-81,
  206, 217
Christianization, 68
Christology, 195
church, 29-31, 33, 35, 38, 78, 95,
  97, 100, 105-6, 108, 133, 136,
  154, 168, 175, 177, 189, 194-96,
  198, 200, 203, 206, 236, 241
  attendance, 39
  church-centric mission,
    100
  early, 196, 208
  fellowship, 189, 190, 200
  global, 30, 31, 154, 155
  suprareligious, 33
Church Mission Society, 103
Church Missionary Society, 69
civil rights movement, 107
civilization, 13-17, 31, 67
  clash of civilizations, 12,
    14, 17-18

cold war, 12, 14-16
colonialism, 58, 64-66, 70, 122,
  159, 169, 186, 195
  colonial period, 127, 163,
    167, 186, 191
  colonial state, 66-70, 79
Common Word dialogue, 207
compassion, 48, 126, 130, 132,
  208, 222
confession of faith, 137, 235,
  237
contextualization, 100, 113,
  123, 133, 200
Convention on the
  Elimination of All Forms of
  Discrimination Against
  Women (CEDAW), 122
conversion, convert, 61-62,
  64-65, 70, 79, 80, 96, 97, 98,
  103
Council on American-Islamic
  Relations (CAIR), 177
Counter Reformation, 27
Crusades, 195
Cyprus, 38
Dalit, 88
Damascus, 144
Danish cartoons, 139
dar al-da'wa, 47
dar al-harb, 47
dar al-Islam, 47
darbar, 89-92, 100, 102
  Jesu darbar, 102, 108
dawa, 86
debate, 85-87, 95-96, 107-8
  interfaith, 85, 95, 96
  interreligious, 87
  intrafaith, 95, 96
  performative, 94
  public, 96, 118
  theological, 227
democracy, 16, 22, 157, 166,
  171-73, 179
  democratization, 169
  liberal, 67
demographics, 16, 17, 39, 56
demon, 191, 226-27
  demonic oppression, 194
  demonization, 215
Deoband, Deobandi, 84-89,
  142, 149, 150
Denmark, 168
Denmark's Democratic

Muslims, 51
dialogue, 86, 130, 240
  interfaith, 234
  interreligious, 58, 176
Disciple Making Movement,
  197
Discovery Bible Study (DBS),
  197
diversity, 2-3, 5-6, 7, 8, 30, 37,
  55, 82, 84, 86, 107, 135-37, 139,
  147-54, 175, 183-84, 187-88,
  200, 215, 219, 220-21, 223,
  231, 240
  cultural, 158
  Muslim, 137, 138, 139
  pluralistic, 163
  religious, 65
dream, 131, 193-95, 197
Druze, 185
du'a' prayers, 117
economy, 174, 229, 239
Edinburgh University, 179
Edinburgh World Missionary
  Conference, 105
education, 40, 49, 58, 63, 66,
  107, 109, 114, 122, 129, 168,
  187, 237
Egypt, Egyptian, 20, 43, 47, 99,
  117, 118, 126, 127, 129, 157, 165,
  169, 170, 172, 232
emir, 73
England, 42, 53, 163, 168, 186
Enlightenment, 27, 42, 45, 48,
  194
Ennahda (Renaissance) party,
  173-74
Esther, 131
ethics, 60
  of mission, 81
  religious, 125
ethnicity, 15-16, 185, 188
  ethnic group, 63-64, 67, 69,
    71, 79, 176, 184, 191, 213
Euro-Communism, 45
Euro-Islam, 37, 45, 56
Europe, 24, 37, 38-40, 42,
  46-48, 53, 55, 163, 170, 177
European Union (EU), 38
Europeanization, 41
evangelical, 208, 212, 217
evangelism, 59, 79, 113, 175, 200
  Muslim, 38
exploitation, 114

extremism, extremist, 4, 11,
  29-30, 35-36, 38, 42, 45,
  46-47, 54, 203, 212-17
family, 36, 93, 108, 113, 130,
  177-79, 185, 192, 198, 201, 213,
  235
  structure, 40, 56
fatwa, 26, 139
feminism, feminist, 39, 50, 115,
  121-22, 124, 128-29
  Islamic, 121, 129
fertility rate, 39, 40
fiqh, 138, 140, 159, 163
folk Islam, 185, 226-27
followers of Jesus/Christians
  from Muslim background,
  155, 188, 191-92, 194, 199,
  200, 236
forgiveness, 132, 175, 207
France, 12, 158, 166, 179, 186
friendship, 18, 91, 98, 103-4,
  183, 216-17
fundamentalism, 19, 47, 213,
  223, 236
  Islamic, 44, 55
Gambia, 59, 63
  river, 62
gender, 5, 55, 115, 188
  attitudes, 40
  equality, 125-26
  inclusive, 115
  inequalities, 121
  roles, 56
Germany, 46, 48, 50, 158, 179
Ghana, 59, 62
Global Immersion Project,
  216
Global Trends and Fruitful
  Practices (GTFP)
  Consultation, 189-90, 200
globalization, 13, 42, 48, 187,
  191
good news, 33-35, 120, 126,
  130, 175, 199, 200
good Samaritan, 207, 208
gospel, 31-35, 102, 133, 153, 155,
  175-76, 187, 192, 194-96, 199,
  207-8, 210-11, 229
Greece, 169
Gujarat, 88
gurudwara, 105
hajj, 224, 225
halâl, 52

Hanafi, 85, 86, 147-49
harâm, 52
Hausa-Fulani, 67, 69
healing, 126, 146, 147, 185,
    193-95, 227
hijab, 168
Hinduism, Hindus, 13, 83-85,
    88, 90, 105-6, 170, 200
    Adi-Hindu, 89, 94
Hizb an-Nahda, 21
Holland, 186
homosexuality, 54
honor killing, 163, 180
hospitality, 91-92, 95, 103-4,
    108, 176, 183, 208, 217
hudud, 143, 162
Hyderabad, 82, 83, 84, 88, 89,
    91, 93, 94, 100
Id Muharram, 105
identity, 11, 17-18, 47-48, 54-55,
    83-85, 88, 92-93, 114, 119-20,
    127, 198-90, 221, 236, 241
    Christian, 190
    collective, 45
    cultural, 14-15, 38
    ethnonational, 69
    ethnoreligious, 69, 75
    identity marker, 234
    Muslim, 47, 128, 138, 219,
        235, 237
    religious, 32, 45, 93, 128,
        167, 200
    self-identification, 39, 122
    self-identity, 88, 93
    suprareligious, 33
Ifa divination cult, 62
ijmā^c, 27, 143
ijtihad, 87
imam, 56, 86-87, 178, 216
immigrant, 41, 48, 56, 88, 104,
    178, 192
immigration ban, 177
imperialism, 22
    British, 66
    cultural, 114, 128
India, Indian, 83-85, 88, 90-91,
    93, 94, 95, 97, 101, 106, 150,
    160, 165, 169-70
Indo/Malaysia, 190
Indonesia, 21, 48, 127, 156, 160,
    169, 184, 186-88, 217, 221
inductive Bible study (IBS),
    197, 199

injil, 99, 197-98
injustice, 114, 126, 210
International Interfaith
    Network, 217
Internet, 53, 187, 191, 193
Iran, 21, 90, 156, 167, 184
Iraq, 11, 23, 166, 177
    Iraqi constitution, 161
Ireland, 38, 168
Isa (Jesus), 194-95, 197
    Isa al-Masih (Jesus the
        Messiah), 196, 198
    Isa followers, 190
ISIS, 2-3, 11-13, 17-19, 23-28, 36,
    156, 183, 212-15, 231
Islamic jurisprudence, 27
Islamic State, 11, 21, 22, 27, 42,
    52, 159-62, 169, 173, 186
Islamism, 18-21, 23, 51
    post-Islamism, 19-23, 33
Islamist, 21, 23, 25, 54, 122, 137,
    169, 172, 173, 213, 223
    governments, 21
    groups, 21, 23
    ideologies, 12
Islamization, 22, 64
Islamophobia, 176-77, 180
Ismaili, 138
Israel, 216
Italians, 40
Jamaat-e-Islami, 165
Japan, 163, 212
Java, 183
Jerusalem, 199, 208
Jesus, 7, 30, 32, 33, 35, 95, 102-3,
    105-9, 120-21, 125-26, 137,
    152-54, 158, 175, 184-85,
    187-88, 192-96, 198-200, 204,
    205-12, 214, 217
    Christ, 34, 36, 203-5
Jews, 13, 54, 178-79, 197, 208-9
    Messianic, 200
    Orthodox, 178
jihad, 24, 26-27, 42, 63, 68, 151
    war, 52
jihadism, jihadi, 12, 19, 54
    groups, 18
    Salafism, 12-13, 19-20, 23,
        25
jinn, 185, 194
John the Baptist, 91
Judaism, 14, 33, 44, 145
jurisprudence, 27, 44, 151, 160

jurist, 140, 143, 146, 148-50,
    160-61, 163
justice, 21, 35, 80, 107, 122,
    124-26, 130-32, 161-62,
    175-77, 207
    social justice, 80, 107, 109,
        126, 130, 171, 176
Justice and Development
    Party (AKP), 21, 167
Kaaba, 224-25
Ka^cb ibn al-Ashraf, 142
kalām, 138
Kano, 92
Karachi, 135
Karama, 126
kerygma, 34
    kerygmatic suprareligious
        approach, 30
    kerygma model, 195
    kerygmatic missiology, 33,
        34, 35
Khārijites, 137
Khawāraj, 137
khichdi madhab, 86
Khidr, 100-102
khilāfa, 27
kingdom of God, 32-33, 79,
    125-26, 130, 132-33, 191, 196,
    205
kinship, 104, 119
Kombo (kingdom of), 63
kufr, 86
laïcité, 34
Latin America, 16, 31, 193
law, 74, 106, 126-29, 170
    common, 72-73
    customary, 169
    family, 159, 165, 180
    Islamic, 26, 71, 73, 131,
        138-41, 143, 148, 150-51,
        158, 160, 162-65, 167, 169,
        176, 178-79
    legal school, 169, 213
    religious, 170, 179
    school of, 149, 159, 160,
        163
Lebanon, 99, 127, 169
Leitkultur, 45
liberalism, 19, 42
    social, 54
Libya, 157, 174
literacy, 40, 114, 129
logos, 101

London, 42, 54, 173
madrasa, 187
maghāzī, 142, 145
Maghreb, 40, 57
Mahdi, 22
Majlis-e-Ittehadul-
  Muslimeen (MIM), 83-84,
  88, 94
Maldives, 141
Mālikī, 149
manusmrit, 88
marginality, 114, 131
marginalization, 5, 28, 114-15,
  125, 129-30, 132, 166
Mary, 131
maslaks, 82, 84-86, 94
mawla, 91
Mecca, 143, 151, 224
media, 40, 42, 53, 107, 135, 183,
  192-93, 223
  social, 187
  Western, 139
Medina, 151, 173
Melchizedek, 101, 102
Messiah, 120, 155, 196, 200,
  204, 211
Middle East, 53, 122, 184, 186,
  190, 203
migrant, 40-41, 45, 56, 104
  communities, 13, 56
migration, 39, 41, 203
  labor, 66
  mass, 41
  patterns, 40
minority, 28, 52, 88, 108, 167,
  170
  Christian, 95
  communities, 55
  minoritization, 29
miracle, 146, 193-95, 197, 227
missio Dei, 32, 59, 77, 80, 175
missio Spiritus, 175
missiology, 33-35, 59, 78-81,
  113, 115, 126, 132-33, 176, 236
  contextual, 132-33
  gender-nuanced, 120
  managerial, 133
  of rights and human
    dignity, 125
  Trinitarian, 175
mission, 2-3, 5-7, 11-12, 30-31,
  33-34, 59-61, 64, 66, 69, 71,
  75, 79-81, 95, 98, 109, 113, 121,

125, 126, 131-32, 134, 192, 226,
  237
  Christian, 58, 76, 100, 108,
    115, 125, 130, 132-33
  field, 31, 69, 70, 81
  of God, 81, 203 (see also
    missio Dei)
  history, 130
  mission practitioner, 98,
    220, 224, 229
  organization, 241
  practice, 113, 131, 220, 227,
    230
  strategies, 95, 113, 131, 133
missiological framework, 196,
  227
missional approach, 191
  missional perspectives, 7,
    14, 29
  missional vision, 17, 30
missionary, 6, 31, 59, 62,
  69-70, 80, 95, 97, 99, 103,
  109, 130, 133, 191, 227
modernity, 17, 138, 152, 167, 224
  Islamic Modernism, 51, 54
  modernist, 137, 149, 150,
    169, 213
  modernization, 41
monotheism, 64
Montreal, 92
Morocco, 20-21, 40-41, 48, 55,
  136, 186, 221
Moses, 32, 100-101, 141, 197
mosque, 24, 39, 44, 46, 55-56,
  78, 105, 115-16, 177-78, 227,
  235
mosque movement, 115, 117
Mosul, 11
movement, 189-91
  insider, 198-99, 240
  Jesus, 196
Mughal Empire, 160
Muhammad, 16, 20, 51, 116,
  119, 127, 139-48, 150, 152,
  153-55, 157, 159, 170, 194, 197,
  231
multiculturalism, 56, 178, 180
munazara, 82, 84, 85, 87
Munich, 46
Murji'ite, 137
Muslim Brotherhood, 19,
  21-22, 25, 46-47, 53, 56, 165,
  167, 172

Muslim-Christian relations,
  58, 59, 70, 73, 80, 177
Muslim Women's Network
  UK, 180
Mu'tazila, 137
mystic, 89
nahḍah, 53
Naomi, 131
na't, 135
nation building, 107, 109
nationalism, 18, 88, 127
nationalization, 168
nation-state, 76, 160, 163,
  165-66
Netherlands, 42, 43
New Delhi, 143
Nicodemus, 32
Nigeria, 59-62, 66-71, 74, 76,
  77-80, 92, 177
Nineveh, 143
Nobel Peace Prize, 174
Organization of Islamic
  Cooperation (OIC), 156
Orthodox Church, 169, 224
Ottoman Empire, 12, 160, 164,
  166, 186
Oyo empire, 65
pacifism, 63
Pakistan, 22, 41, 83, 85, 88, 113,
  117, 126-28, 135, 140, 147, 149,
  153, 158, 162-63, 169-71, 186,
  214
Pakistan's People Party (PPP),
  171
panchama, 88
Paul, 102, 195-96, 204-5
peace, 2, 15, 26, 89, 93, 103,
  203-6, 211-12, 216-17
  peacemaker, 96, 107,
    204-6, 208, 216-17
  peacemaking, 7, 94-95,
    103, 105-8, 203-6, 210-13,
    216-17
Peace Catalyst International,
  177, 203, 217
Pentecost, 157, 175-77
Pentecostalism, 76-77, 79, 224
people group, 184, 193
persecution, 62-63, 177, 203,
  206
Persian World, 190
pesantren system, 187
Peter, 33, 196, 208

phenomenology, 234
piety, 24
  movement, 115-20
pilgrimage, 224-25, 238
pluralism, 6, 58-59, 156-58, 163
  cultural, 177
  legal, 6, 164, 169, 180
  religious, 34
Poland, 168
polemics, 103, 146
political Islam, 21, 128, 159,
  165, 169, 173-75, 231
polygamy, 180
popular Islam, 185, 226-28
Portugal, 163
postcolonial period, 6, 15, 70,
  74, 159, 163, 167
postcolonial state, 70, 75,
  78-79, 122, 173
post-Islamism, 19-23
poverty, 24, 171, 206
power encounter, 227
primitive accumulation, 74-75
procession, 89-90, 92, 94-95,
  105-6, 108
proselytization, 68
Protestantism, 27, 168
public theology, 78
Punjab, 135, 136
Qadiani, 150
qawwal, 91, 135
qiṣaṣ al-anbiya (stories of the
  prophets), 138
Quraysh, 143
racism, 24, 206, 210
radicalism, 46, 56
radicalization, 54
Rahab, 131
Ramadan, 39, 135, 232, 235
Rawalpindi, 135
razakar, 83
reconciliation, 59, 78-79, 155,
  204, 206-7, 216
redemptive analogy, 175
reformers, 17-18, 20, 27, 42, 45,
  88, 159
  Islamic, 44
  women, 122
reformist, 50
  Islam, 53
  movements, 51
refugees, 1-2, 4, 104, 157, 177,
  212, 217

righteousness, 126, 130, 144
rights, 153
  cultural, 170
  gender, 125
  human, 116, 121, 125-26,
    129-31, 156-57, 170,
    173-74, 176, 180, 215
  religious, 171
  women's, 54, 123, 129, 168,
    179
royal court scene, 94-95,
  100-101, 103, 108
Royal Niger Company, 66
Russia, 12, 38, 163, 169, 186
Ruth, 131
sabbath, 32, 208
Safavid Empire, 160
saint, 41, 101-2, 108
  Islamic, 90
  Sufi, 89, 95
salaf, 146
Salafi, 18, 20, 88
  ideologies, 12
  Political Literalist
    Salafism, 20
  Salafi Hizb an-Nour, 21
  Salafi-Literalism, 20
  Salafi-Reformism, 20, 47,
    138
Salafism, Salafist, 12, 17, 18, 19,
  41, 174, 179
ṣalāt, 220
Samaria, 199
Samaritan woman, 32, 120, 131,
  188, 208
satellite television, 40, 53
Saudi Arabia, 22, 50, 55, 126,
  156, 162, 187
secret believer, 95-96, 98-100
secularism, 18, 34, 45, 53, 166
  secularist, 20, 174, 213
  secularization, 40, 115, 125
Senegal, 169
Sermon on the Mount, 206
servanthood, 121, 132
Shāfiʿī, 148, 149
sharḥ al-ḥadīth, 138
shariʾa, 21, 26-27, 51, 71-74, 76,
  147, 150-51, 156, 158-64, 167,
  169, 170, 172-75, 177-78
  council, 180
  court, 73, 179
  law, 127, 128, 165

Shiʾa, Shiʾite, 11, 18, 170, 185,
  213, 220
  Shiʾa-Sunni split, 137
shrine, 41, 105, 149
Sikh, 170
silent majority, 3, 11, 13, 28-30
Simon the Pharisee, 208
sira, 139, 142-45
  sirat an-nabī, 138
siyasa sharʿiyya, 160
social action, 77
social change, 127, 167
social media, 13, 220
social transformation, 59, 75,
  79, 80
Sokoto caliphate, 68, 73
Soninkes, 63
Soviet Union, 14
Spain, 163
Spirit, 32, 101-2, 176, 177, 200
  Holy Spirit, 33, 34, 76, 104,
    158, 175-76, 193, 198-99
  Spirit of Jesus, 105
Sri Lanka, 169
state formation, 57, 59-61,
  65-67, 69-70, 76, 78-81
statistics, 39, 56
Sudan, 22, 162
Sufism, Sufi, 20, 82, 89, 101-2,
  137, 183, 185, 213, 228
  Sufi order, 90, 100
  Sufi Urs, 105
sunna, 117, 137, 141-43, 145-46,
  148, 150, 159, 231
Sunni, Sunnism, 11, 29, 87,
  137-38, 147, 149, 170, 185-86,
  213, 220
suprareligious approach,
  30-35
Switzerland, 46
Sykes-Picot Agreement, 12
Syria, Syrian, 11, 21-23, 28, 46,
  117, 126, 156, 157, 166, 177
Syrophoenician woman, 125,
  131
tafsīr (commentary on the
  Qurʾan), 115, 123, 138
tajwid, 116
takfir, 19
Taliban, 156, 183
Tangier, 226
tanzīl, 23
Tanzimat, 164

taqiyya, 47
taqlid, 51, 86-87
ta'rīkh, 142
taṣliya, 145, 154
Taurat, 197-98
tawḥīd, 97, 123, 221
Teheran, 226
televangelist, 53
terrorism, 18, 24, 42, 52, 54,
  206, 212-13, 216
    terror attack, 156
    terror organization, 176
    terrorist, 51, 212, 213, 214
theocracy, 173
theologizing, 199
theology, 79, 132, 135, 169
    of agency, 121
    indigenous, 199
    missiological, 79
    of mission, 75, 78, 81, 120
    of rights and human
      dignity, 125
    of subjectivity, 121
Torah, 99, 197
traditionalist, 137, 213

Trinity, 99, 195
Tunisia, 20-21, 40, 136, 157-58,
  167, 169, 172-73, 175
Turkestan, 190
Turkey, 21, 55, 156, 158, 166-67,
  185-86
ulama, 73, 146, 160-65, 169
ummah, 24-25, 27, 97, 99, 114,
  117, 121, 123, 157
United Kingdom (UK), 163,
  178-79
United Nations (UN), 121, 129,
  157, 171, 186
United States (US), 22, 136,
  158, 163, 168, 170, 177-79, 214,
  216-17
United States Institute of
  Peace, 173
unreached people group, 119
urbanization, 41
veil, 185, 219
violence, 114, 116, 123, 125-26,
  213, 240
Wahhabi, 41
West Bank, 216

Westernization, 48
witness, 104-5, 191, 194-96, 207
    proximate, 191-92
Women Living Under Muslim
  Law (WLUML), 126
Women's Action Forum
  (WAF), 126
wonder, 193, 195
World War I, 11
World War II, 157, 164, 178,
  186, 212
worldview, 183, 187, 192, 198
Yazidi, 11, 13
Yemen, 126, 127, 129
Yeshua (Jesus), 200
Yoruba, 61-62, 65, 66, 71
    Yorubaland, 61
Yugoslavia, 38
Zabur, 197, 198
Zacchaeus, 208
zakāt, 73
Zamfara, 73
Zealot, 205

MISSIOLOGICAL ENGAGEMENTS

Series Editors: Scott W. Sunquist,
Amos Yong, and John R. Franke

Missiological Engagements: Church, Theology, and Culture in Global Contexts charts interdisciplinary and innovative trajectories in the history, theology, and practice of Christian mission at the beginning of the third millennium.

Among its guiding questions are the following: What are the major opportunities and challenges for Christian mission in the twenty-first century? How does the missionary impulse of the gospel reframe theology and hermeneutics within a global and intercultural context? What kind of missiological thinking ought to be retrieved and reappropriated for a dynamic global Christianity? What innovations in the theology and practice of mission are needed for a renewed and revitalized Christian witness in a postmodern, postcolonial, postsecular, and post-Christian world?

Books in the series, both monographs and edited collections, will feature contributions by leading thinkers representing evangelical, Protestant, Roman Catholic, and Orthodox traditions, who work within or across the range of biblical, historical, theological, and social-scientific disciplines. Authors and editors will include the full spectrum from younger and emerging researchers to established and renowned scholars, from the Euro-American West and the Majority World, whose missiological scholarship will bridge church, academy, and society.

Missiological Engagements reflects cutting-edge trends, research, and innovations in the field that will be of relevance to theorists and practitioners in churches, academic domains, mission organizations, and NGOs, among other arenas.

Finding the Textbook You Need

The IVP Academic Textbook Selector
is an online tool for instantly finding the IVP books
suitable for over 250 courses across 24 disciplines.

ivpress.com/academic